TOP 50 TANKS

Martin Dougherty

CHARTWELL
BOOKS

This edition published in 2017 by Chartwell Books, an imprint of The Quarto Group,
142 West 36th Street, 4th Floor, New York, NY 10018, USA
T (212) 779-4972 F (212) 779-6058 www.QuartoKnows.com

10 9 8 7 6 5 4 3 2 1

ISBN: 978-0-7858-3563-9

Project Editor: Michael Spilling
Design: Colin Fielder
Picture Research: Terry Forshaw

Printed in China

PICTURE CREDITS:
Alamy: 12 (Yuya Shino/Reuters), 28 (Rolf Richardson), 43 (Colin C. Hill), 60 (Jia Yuchen/Xinhua)
Art-Tech: 15, 16, 29, 39, 44–52 all, 63, 64, 71–73 all, 79–91 all, 95–99 all, 104 bottom, 111–113 all, 119, 121, 127, 129, 132–137 all, 141–147 all, 152, 153, 160, 165, 167, 169–172 all, 177 bottom, 179, 180, 187–197 all
BAE Systems: 183, 184
Cody Images: 40, 53, 65, 92, 107, 114, 117, 149, 176
Nik Cornish/STAVKA: 69, 131, 151
Dreamstime: 75 (Jukgrit Chaiwised), 101 (14Locl2), 105 (Stephen Gates), 109 (Rafael Ben Ari), 128 (Mikhail Starodubov), 164 (14Locl2), 168 (Imran Ahmed), 177 top (Oknebulog), 204 (Zabii)
Getty Images: 23 & 25 (Jung Yeon-Je/AFP), 31 & 32 (Raveendran/AFP), 33 (Hindustan Times), 35 & 37 (Greg Baker/AFP)
Vitaly Kuzmin: 59, 61
Photoshot: 62 (UPPA)
Ukrainian State Archive: 4, 203
U.S. Department of Defense: 5, 7, 8, 19, 21, 93, 116, 123–125 all, 139, 154–157 all, 198, 200 both

All Artworks Art-Tech except for the following:
Alcaniz Fresnos, S.A.: 14/15, 39, 41 both, 55, 70/71, 83, 89, 115 bottom, 126, 129 both, 134, 135, 144, 146, 147, 155, 158/159, 166, 168, 186, 187, 188, 190–197
Amber Books: 24, 58/59, 6, 130/131, 137, 139, 161 both
Vincent Bourguignon: 57 top
Oliver Missing: 57 bottom, 66/67, 68, 69, 93, 119, 133 both, 148, 150, 151, 153, 181, 202, 204, 205
Tank Encyclopedia: 10/11, 22/23, 30/31, 34/35

CONTENTS

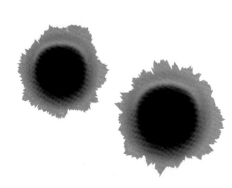

Introduction

Counting from 50 down to the greatest at number 1, this book rates the 50 best tanks in history. Each tank is selected based on what made it superior to other vehicles of the same period.

'What is the best tank of all time?' is not an easy question to answer. True, a cutting-edge modern main battle tank could blast any number of World War I tanks right off their tracks, but that is hardly a fair comparison. Instead, we must consider what a given design achieved, what it might have achieved if it had had the opportunity, and how good it was compared to its contemporaries. Each design featured in these pages has been considered in terms of its potency, potential, longevity and achievement, and must be taken on its merits relative to its contemporaries.

During the earliest appearance of 'landships' in World War I there were no armoured opponents to fight, and the tank was very much an infantry support platform or mobile artillery emplacement. Tank-versus-tank battles were very rare until World War II, prompting a move from a system of 'light', 'cruiser' and 'heavy' tanks – similar to the way warships were rated – to the creation of an all-round battle tank that could take on anything on the battlefield.

FIRST MODERN TANK

Therefore, the tank arguably assumed its modern form at some point during World War II. There are two primary candidates for the first 'modern' tank – the T-34 and the PzKpfw V Panther – but a case can be made for several others both before and after these designs appeared. The World War II era is also important because it was the harsh crucible in which the characteristics of a successful tank design were established. Since then, advancing technology has produced some interesting new possibilities, but the core requirements have not changed much.

The qualities needed in an armoured fighting vehicle are right there in its name. It must have a high level of combat capability and be able to deliver this capability wherever it is needed, while protecting its crew and its critical systems. This gives us the three key characteristics of an armoured fighting vehicle: protection, firepower and mobility.

Some designs emphasize one of these factors to the detriment of the others, and this is not always a bad thing. A lightly protected but fast tank armed with a small gun can do good work on the battlefield in a reconnaissance or screening role, whereas a heavier vehicle might not be at all suitable. Similarly, very heavily armoured but slow 'breakthrough tanks' have proven deadly under the right conditions – jamming an oversized gun into a very lightly protected hull can create a potent tank-killer, for example. One factor to consider when rating one tank against another is how good it was at fulfilling its particular role.

However, very specialized vehicles tend to perform badly outside their own niche. In the fluid conditions of

Whitewashed T-34/76 Model 1941 tanks move along a snow-covered road near Kharkov on the Eastern Front, January 1942. The T-34 proved to be Soviet Russia's most effective tank of World War II, and had an impact on types that followed it, such as the German Panzer V Panther.

US Army M1A1 Abrams main battle tanks from the 1st Armored Division pose for a photo under the 'Hands of Victory' monument in Ceremony Square, Baghdad, Iraq, following the capture of the city in 2003. The Abrams has proved one of the most effective main battle tanks of the 21st century.

the armoured battlefield, it is likely that a specialist vehicle will be forced to fight under conditions it simply was not designed for. Thus, all-round capability, or the ability to handle unexpected situations, is another asset to be considered.

IMPACT

It is also necessary to take into account the impact of the vehicle. Some tanks never really had the chance to show what they could do, or underperformed due to difficult circumstances, yet were still a powerful influence on later designs. Others were excellent but appeared at a time when there were several other good tanks in service and thus did not stand out as much as they perhaps deserved. There are also a few that can be considered bold experiments, pushing the boundaries of what could be achieved. Although these designs generally fell short of expectations, they still might have contributed to the development of armoured fighting vehicles in the long run.

And thus we arrive at the question we should perhaps be asking. Not 'What is the best tank of all time?' but 'Which tanks changed the world of armoured combat – and indeed the world as we know it – to the greatest degree?' Some were a vehicle born from an innovation in technology or tactics. Some were exactly the balance of mobility, firepower and protection that the marketplace needed at a certain time, and became an enormous success despite quite modest capabilities. And some, of course, earned their place in history by destroying all opposition.

M551 Sheridan

The M551 Sheridan was developed in the 1960s to provide US forces with an air-transportable light armoured fighting vehicle. Its gun/missile system was innovative but proved less than satisfactory in practice, and with very light armour the Sheridan was vulnerable to a wide variety of weapons.

LONG-RANGE ACCURACY

The Shillelagh missile was intended to engage armoured targets out to 3km (2 miles) and was also used on the unpopular M60A2 variant.

GUN/MISSILE SYSTEM

The Shillelagh missile/152mm (5.9in) gun system was a failure, but more recent gun-launched missiles have proven effective.

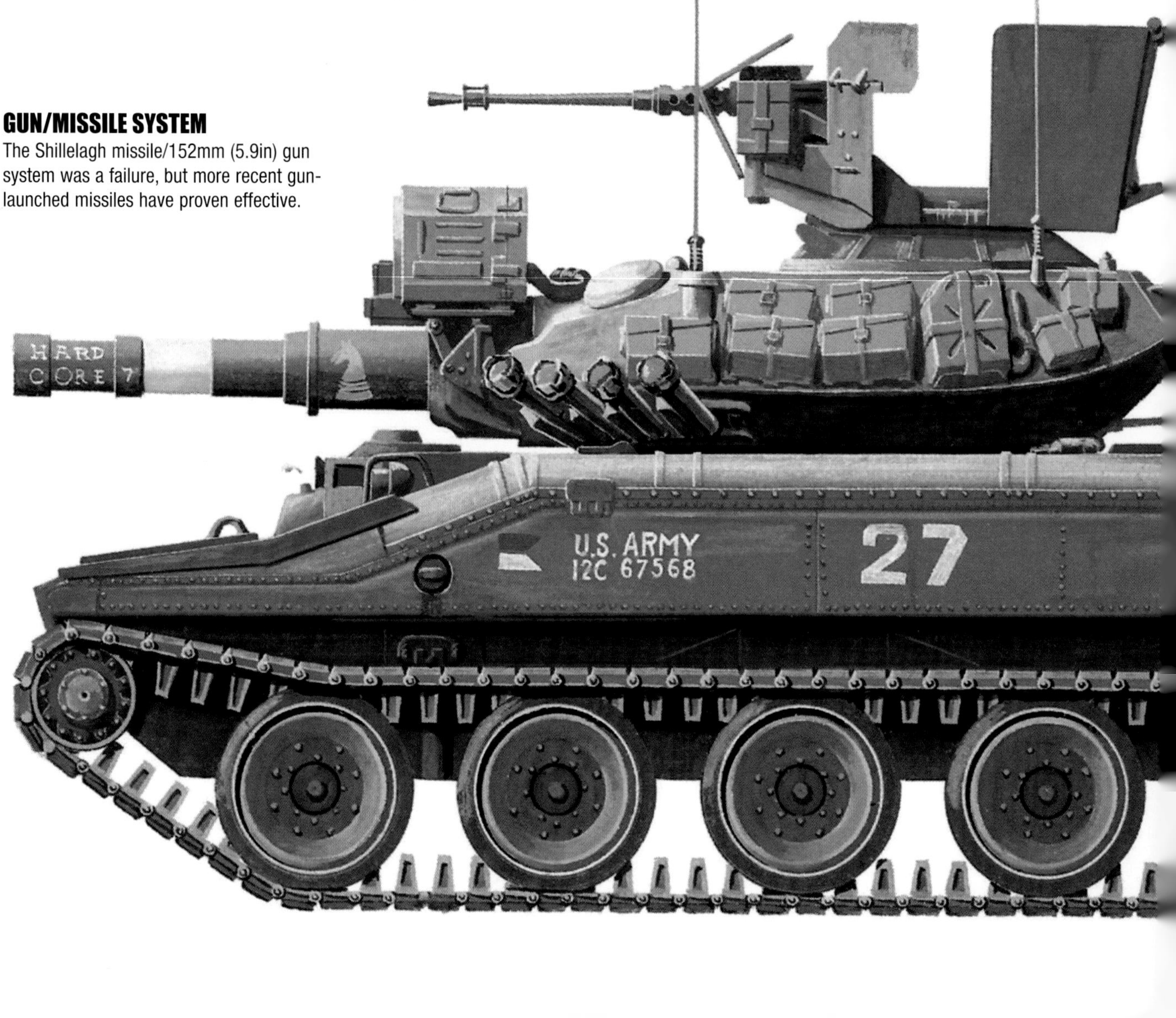

ARMOURED RECONNAISSANCE/AIRBORNE ASSAULT VEHICLE

The M551 Sheridan had to meet a very challenging set of requirements. It needed to be armed with a weapon suitable for infantry support and capable of engaging enemy tanks, mounted on an amphibious hull that was light enough to be rapidly transported by air. Naturally, this meant that heavy armour was out of the question, and mounting a full-sized tank gun on such a light vehicle was problematic.

The end result of the development process was designated an 'Armoured Reconnaissance/Airborne Assault Vehicle' rather than a light tank. With a body largely of aluminium and a steel turret, the Sheridan was light enough to be carried by helicopter and could be airdropped into almost any location. In theory this made it a potentially very useful platform, providing tank support in areas that would normally be inaccessible.

The US 82nd Airborne Division retained its M551s longer than most units, mainly for lack of a suitable replacement. Here, a Sheridan tank from the 82nd Airborne takes part in training in Central America.

LIGHT WEIGHT
The Sheridan was easily air-transportable, making it an asset to rapid-response units or those operating where conventional armour could not.

SPECIFICATIONS (M551 SHERIDAN)

Dimensions: Length: 6.3m (20ft 8in), Height: 2.95m (9ft 8in), Width: 2.82m (9ft 3in)

Weight: 14.1 tonnes (15.6 tons)

Engine/powerplant: Detroit 6V-53T 6-cylinder diesel engine

Speed: 72km/h (44.7mph)

Armament: 152mm (5.9in) rifled gun/missile system, Co-axial: 7.62mm (0.3in) machine gun, Turret top: 12.7mm (0.5in) machine gun

Crew: 4

TROUBLESOME GUN/MISSILE SYSTEM

The solution to the armament problem was an innovative 152mm (5.9in) gun/missile system. High-explosive shells were available for general support work or against lighter targets, and could also successfully engage some tanks. However, the gun was found to be inaccurate and its recoil put too much strain on the Sheridan's structure. The shells also posed an explosion risk if the vehicle's very thin armour was penetrated.

For armoured targets at longer ranges, the Shillelagh missile system was to provide accurate firepower using

an infrared link. The missile was manually guided by the gunner, who had to keep his sights on the target during the missile's short flight time. Development of the missile took longer than expected, and it proved troublesome in service. To prevent the missile being spun by the gun's rifling, it had a 'key' that passed along a slot in the gun barrel. This caused weaknesses that resulted in rapid deterioration of the barrel when firing conventional ammunition. In the event, the missile component was very rarely used.

SHERIDAN IN SERVICE

The M551 first saw action in Vietnam. No missiles were yet available, but this was not a major drawback in a war that featured very few enemy tanks. The mobility of the lightweight Sheridan was very beneficial, and its large-calibre gun was effective as an infantry support weapon. However, Sheridans were very vulnerable to mines and rocket-propelled grenades and their aluminium components burned fiercely.

An M551 Sheridan light tank disguised as opposing forces takes time out at a nearby trail during their rotation at the Joint Readiness Training Center. The Sheridan was widely used to represent OPFORS (opposing forces) in exercises, with cosmetic modifications to represent enemy tanks.

MISSILES

No more than six Shillelagh missiles have ever been fired in anger by the M551 Sheridan.

MOBILITY

The M551 Sheridan is amphibious, requiring about two minutes of preparation, and can be carried by a Sea Stallion helicopter.

The Sheridan had only been in service for ten years when it began to be phased out. However, the failure of a project intended to create a possible replacement required that some units retain their M551s into the 1990s. During the invasion of Panama in 1989–90, the air mobility of the Sheridan proved useful, with some examples being airdropped and others delivered by helicopter. The last combat operations took place in 1991 during the Gulf War and were mostly confined to armoured reconnaissance, although a handful of Shillelagh missiles were launched – the only live use of this weapon system. The Sheridan was withdrawn from service in the 1990s, with a few examples retained until around 2003 or so for use as OPFORS vehicles in training.

TURRET
The gunner, loader and commander are housed in the turret, with the driver at the front of the hull.

Type 10

49

The Japanese Type 10 main battle tank was designed for flexibility and strategic mobility. Its modular design enables it to be reconfigured to meet current strategic needs or to reduce its weight for transportation. It reflects the changing combat environment of the modern world.

CHANGING REQUIREMENTS

Tanks of the World War II and Cold War eras were expected to take part in large-scale tank-versus-tank battles, and were optimized for the ability to fight and survive against other tanks. An increase in weight in order to carry heavier protection and guns capable of penetrating the armour of other vehicles was inevitable. Mobility could be maintained by using more powerful engines as technology advanced, but an increase in weight and size had other implications. Transportation of tanks, and their ability to use roads and bridges, becomes ever more difficult as weight increases.

The threats faced by tanks have changed over the years. The increasing proliferation of infantry-launched weapons, improvised devices and portable guided missile systems have imposed new protection requirements, and

ARMAMENT

Armament is fairly conventional, with a 120mm (4.7in) main gun and 7.62mm (0.3in) co-axial machine gun, plus a 12.7mm (0.5in) machine gun on the turret roof.

AUTOLOADER

The 120mm (4.7in) smoothbore gun is fed by an autoloader in the rear of the turret, reducing crew requirements.

ARMOUR

Armour is modular, enabling the tank to be stripped down for transport or up-armoured to deal with major threats.

The Type 10 is an advanced and ambitious design specifically tailored to Japan's requirements. So far no export sales have been achieved.

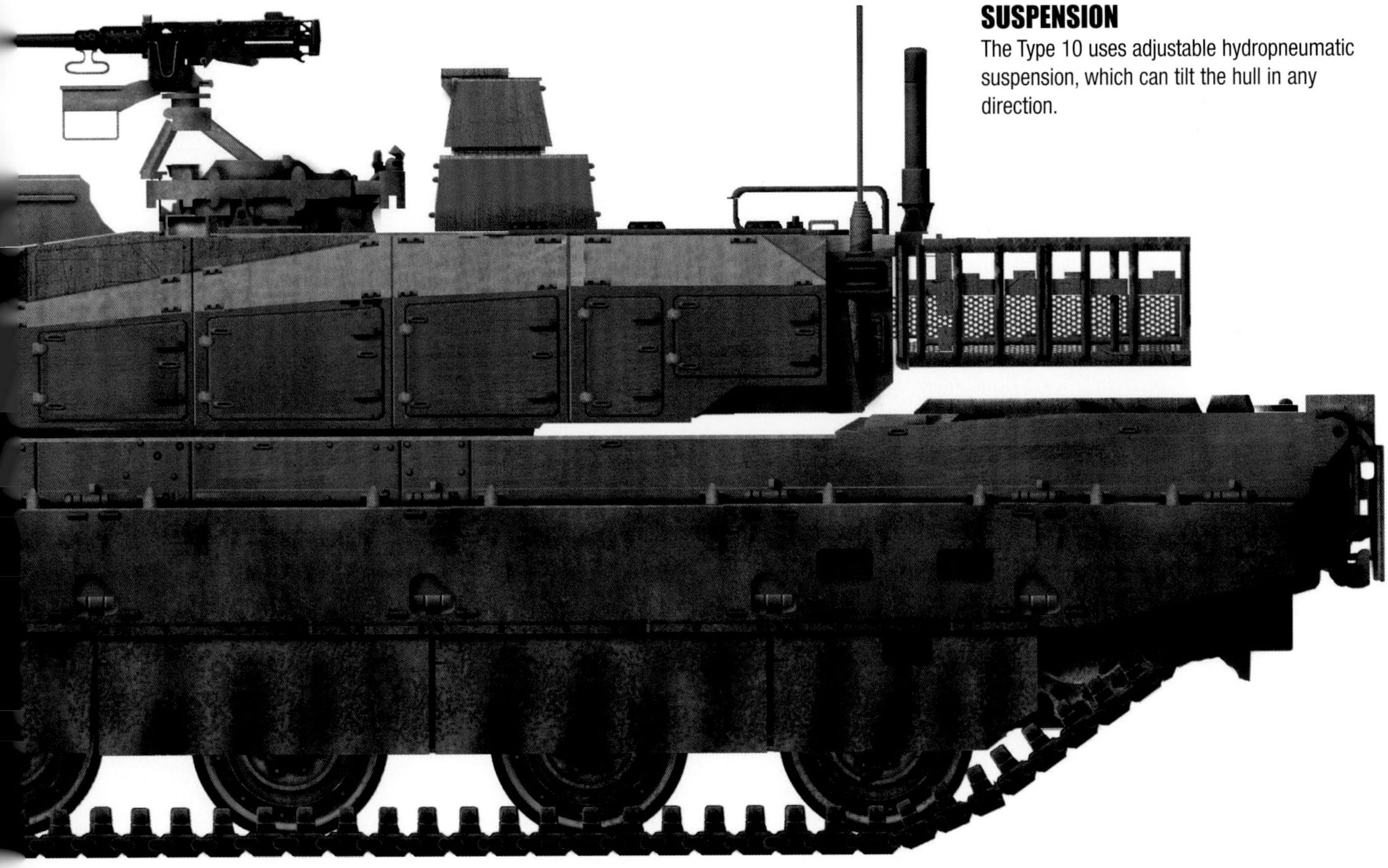

SUSPENSION

The Type 10 uses adjustable hydropneumatic suspension, which can tilt the hull in any direction.

Advanced information sharing allows the Type 10 to receive targeting information from other sources, engaging targets to which it has no direct line of sight.

in the meantime the chances of taking fire from another tank's gun have been reduced. Huge numbers of tanks are in service worldwide, but many are obsolescent and armed with what is now second-rate weaponry. It is possible to achieve a good level of protection against most threats for much less weight than that required to provide armour against top-end penetrators, and in any case more advanced vehicles can often 'break the kill chain' by eliminating threats before the enemy can get into effective range.

ADVANCED MODULAR DESIGN

The Type 10 weighs significantly less than an Abrams or a Challenger, which is an important consideration for a nation made up of a great many islands. Its 120mm (4.7in) gun is capable of endangering any known tank, and is directed by advanced electronics. It is fed by an autoloader, enabling the crew to be reduced to three.

Designed with flexibility in mind, the Type 10 is designed for an environment where a tank might face multiple and varied threats, many of them of an asymmetric nature. Its armour is optimized for defence against the shaped-charge warheads of rocket-propelled grenades. Armour modules can be added or removed, lightening the tank for transportation or increasing its protection for heavy combat. An active protection system detects laser rangefinders or designators, allowing smoke grenades to be launched to break the lock.

The Type 10 uses a hydropneumatic suspension that allows the tank's height to be altered either as a whole or in order to position the vehicle. Applications include dealing with rough ground and obtaining extra elevation or depression on the gun as well as the ability to hide behind an obstruction or climb over one. Top speed is just as high in reverse as when going forwards courtesy of the continuously variable transmission.

The Type 10's battle-management system allows constant information sharing between the tanks of a force, and can integrate with infantry systems to ensure close cooperation. Data from sensors aboard the tank is augmented by information coming in from elsewhere, sometimes allowing commanders to effectively see around corners and over hills.

SPECIFICATIONS (TYPE 10)

Dimensions: Length: 9.485m (31ft 1.5in), Height: 2.3m (7ft 6.5in), Width: 3.24m (10ft 7.5in)

Weight: 43.5 tonnes (48 tons)

Engine/powerplant: V8 diesel engine

Speed: 70km/h (43.5mph)

Armament: Main gun: 120mm (4.7in) L44 smoothbore gun, Co-axial: 7.62mm (0.3in) machine gun, Turret top: 12.7mm (0.5in) machine gun

Crew: 3

TYPE 90
The Type 10's predecessor was the Type 90, which also featured an autoloader and hydropneumatic suspension.

WEIGHT PROBLEMS
The Type 90 was too heavy for many of Japan's roads and bridges, limiting where it could be deployed.

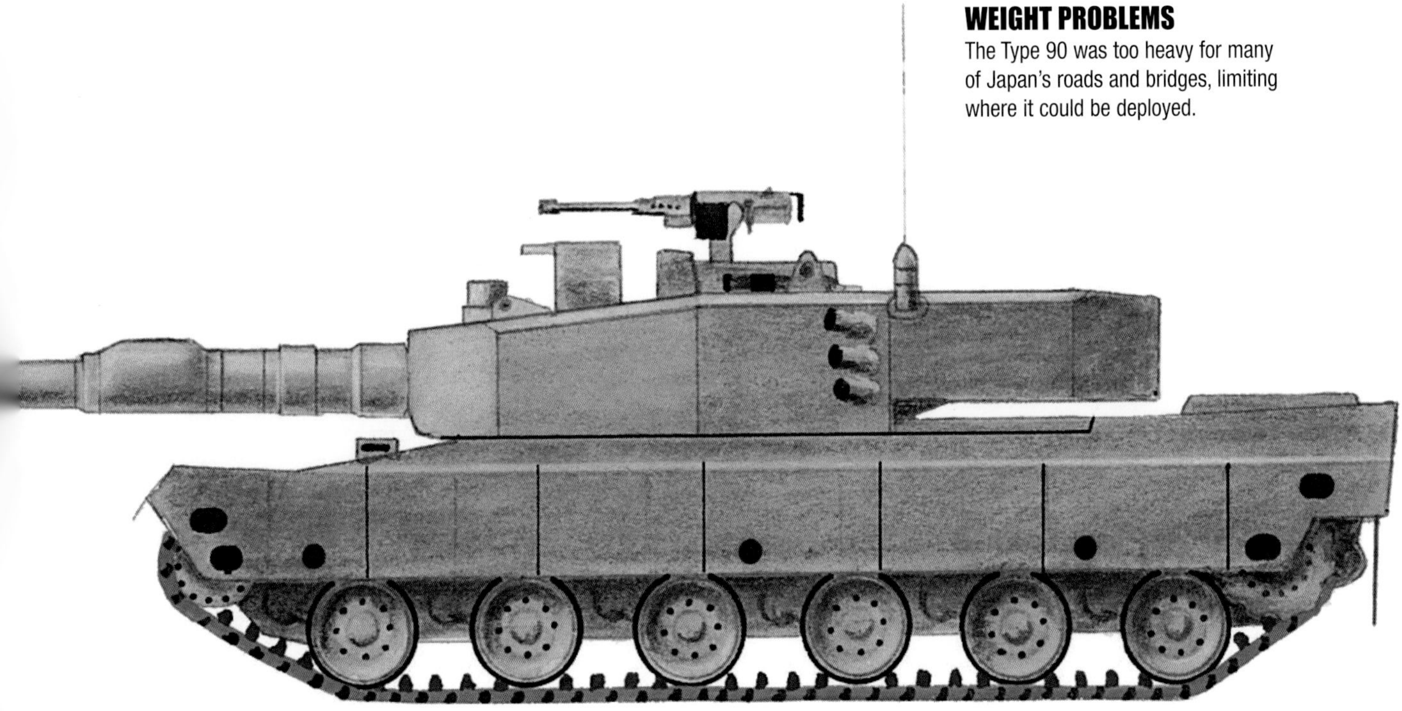

AMX-30

Initial attempts to create a post-war main battle tank for the French military focused on cooperation with Germany on the 'Europanzer' project. However, France eventually withdrew and instead developed its own design. The resulting AMX-30 was very lightly armoured, a defect only partially remedied by the upgraded B2 version.

SPEED IS ARMOUR

At the time the AMX-30 was being designed, there were many who felt that the days of heavily armoured tanks were over. Advances in anti-tank weaponry meant that giving a vehicle sufficient protection to defeat most threats would weigh it down unacceptably. Lighter, smaller tanks might be able to avoid being hit by moving fast and choosing positions carefully. The almost unarmoured AMX-13 light tank took this concept to an extreme, and while the AMX-30 looked a lot more conventional it was still very lightly armoured.

Intended to replace US-supplied tanks then in service, the AMX-30 was built around a 105mm (4.1in) gun, initially with a conventional co-axial armament. This was later replaced with a 20mm (0.78in) cannon. Attempts to create an oscillating turret like that of the AMX-13 failed, resulting in a conventional design. This went into service with the designation AMB-30B.

EXPORTS AND UPGRADES

The AMX-30 did not find much favour on the export market, though a handful of nations adopted it. The contemporary Leopard 1 was considered lightly protected by most observers but still carried more armour than the AMX-30. It was much more widely purchased, a factor that may not be unconnected.

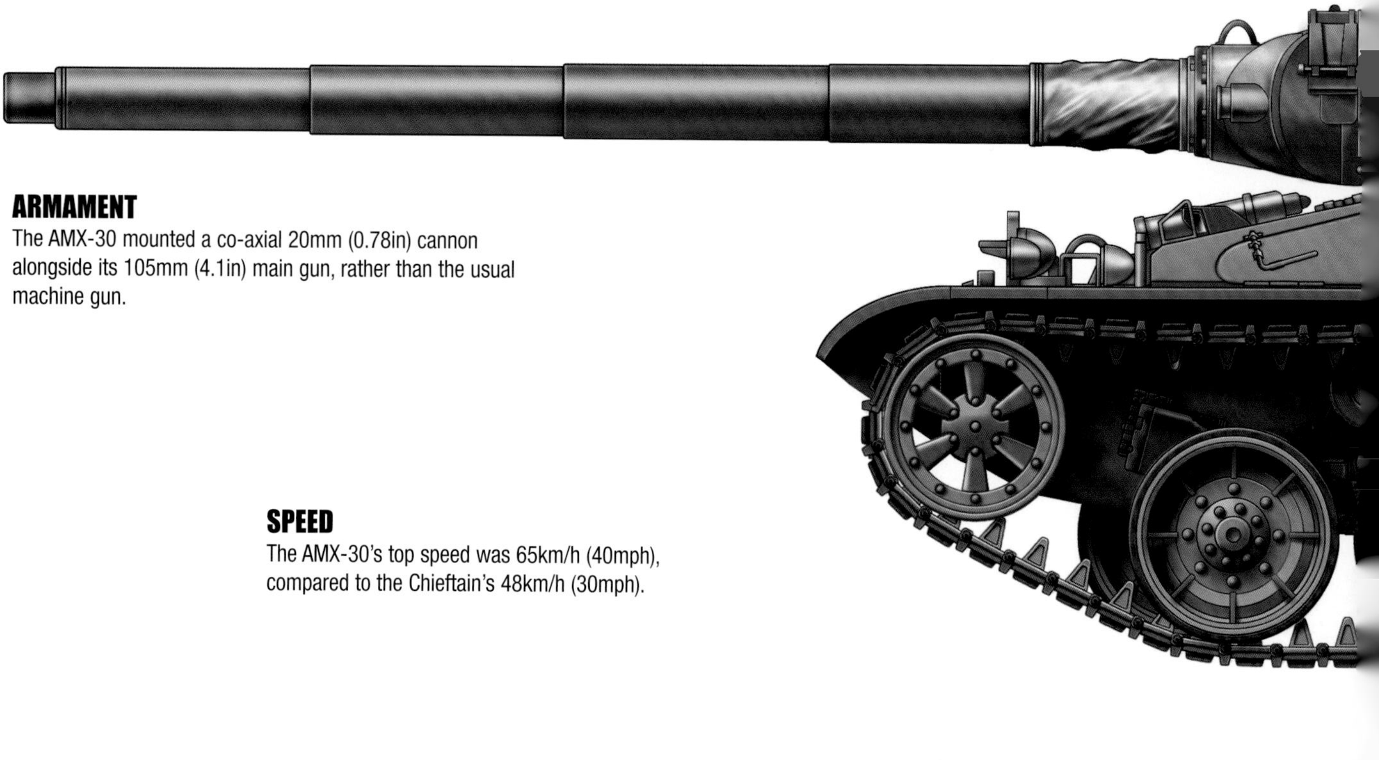

ARMAMENT

The AMX-30 mounted a co-axial 20mm (0.78in) cannon alongside its 105mm (4.1in) main gun, rather than the usual machine gun.

SPEED

The AMX-30's top speed was 65km/h (40mph), compared to the Chieftain's 48km/h (30mph).

SPECIFICATIONS (AMX-30)

Dimensions: Length: 8.48m (31ft 1in), Height: 2.29m (7ft 6in), Width: 3.1m (10ft 2in)

Weight: 32.13 tonnes (35.43 tons)

Engine/powerplant: Hispano-Suiza HS110 multifuel engine

Speed: 65km/h (40.4mph)

Armament: Main gun: 105mm (4.1in) F1 gun, Co-axial: 20mm (0.78in) Hispano-Suiza automatic cannon, Turret top: 7.62mm (0.3in) machine gun

Crew: 4

The AMX-30 can ford water 1–2m (4–6 ft) deep with little or no preparation. With deep-wading gear in place it can handle water obstacles up to 4m (14ft) deep.

TRANSMISSION TROUBLES

Early-model AMX-30s were difficult to drive due to a complex and intolerant gearbox.

Well-sloped hull and turret surfaces made the most of the armour they were given, but this was very light for a main battle tank.

Upgraded AMX-30s began to appear in the 1970s, with the AMX-30B2 entering service in the 1980s. In addition to the usual electronics upgrades, the new version also received an improved transmission and a more powerful engine. An additional armour kit was fitted to some vehicles and was made available for others if required.

Variant vehicles included a range of engineering equipment – bridgelayers, mine-clearance vehicles, bulldozers and general engineering vehicles – as well as the Roland anti-aircraft platform. The erector-launcher vehicle for the PLUTON tactical missile system is also based on the AMX-30 chassis.

IN SERVICE

The AMX-30 saw action in the 1991 Gulf War, initially in the hands of an export customer. Qatari AMX-30s performed well against Iraqi armour, delivering a solid kill/loss ratio against a force of T-55s. Once the Coalition build-up was complete and offensive operations began, French AMX-30s were given a task suited to their capabilities. While more heavily armoured British and US tanks engaged the main enemy force, the AMX-30s operated in support of light reconnaissance vehicles on the flank. Specialist vehicles including mine-clearance tanks operated with this force, which was successful in meeting its objectives despite encountering resistance.

The AMX-30 has been replaced in French service by the Leclerc, but some examples remain active elsewhere. The thinking behind its rather extreme design concept has never really been put to the test, but it is notable that the more heavily protected Leopard was considerably up-armoured in the course of its career. In the current environment, where tanks are increasingly forced to operate in urban areas or exposed to attack with improvised explosive devices, the high mobility intended to protect the AMX-30 against other tanks may not be relevant, resulting in excessive vulnerability to common threats.

French AMX-30s performed well during the 1991 Gulf War, supporting lighter vehicles during a rapid advance on the Coalition left flank.

ANTI-HELICOPTER CAPABILITY

The co-axial 20mm (0.78in) cannon provided a counter to the tank-hunting attack helicopter – a major threat on the Cold War battlefield.

LIGHT ARMOUR

The AMX-30's frontal armour was just 50mm (2in) thick, less than half that of the contemporary British Chieftain.

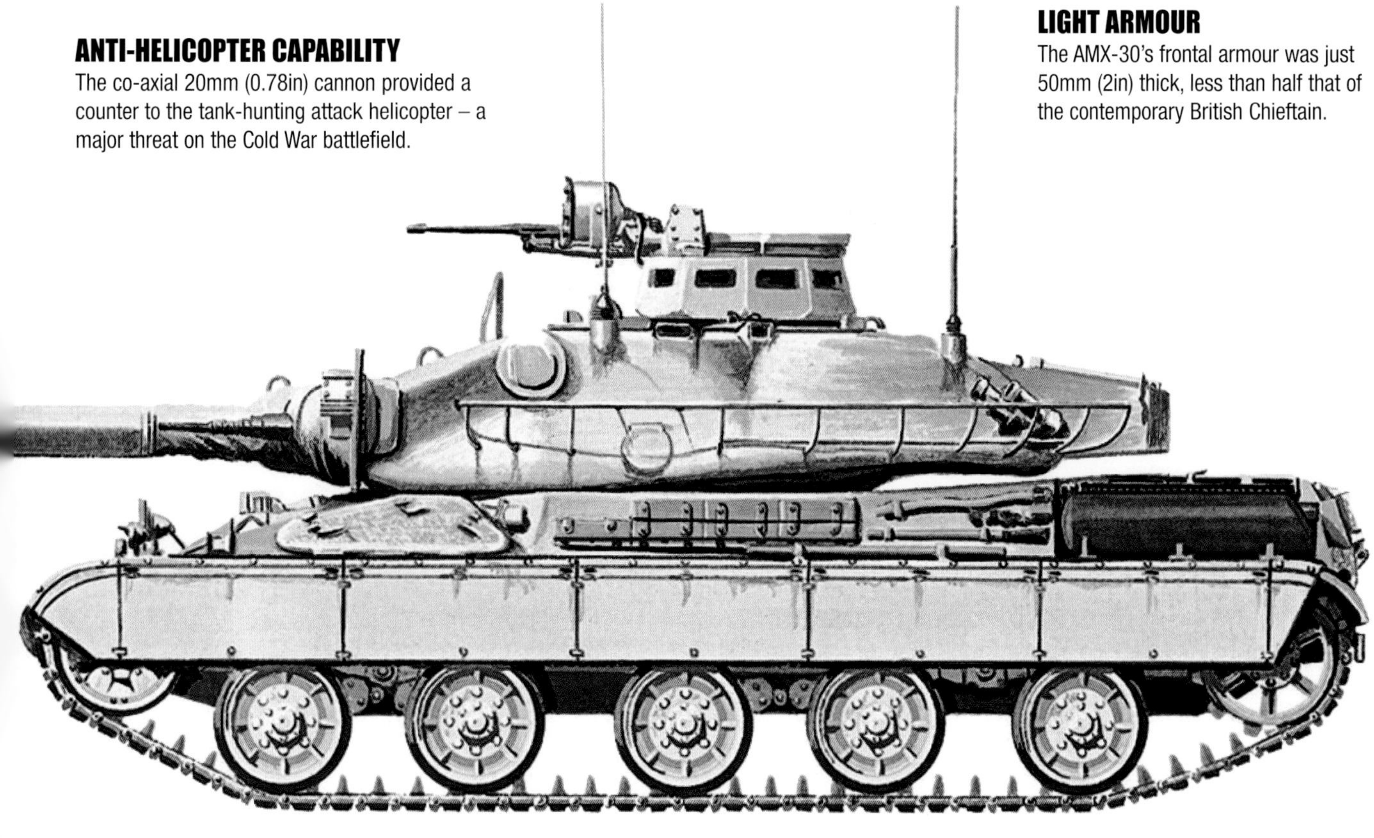

T-62

The T-62 had its origins in attempts to upgun the Soviet T-54/55 to deal with the new generation of Western tanks. A bigger gun required a larger turret ring and thus an enlarged hull. By the time the process was complete, the T-62 was essentially a new design, although visibly a member of the same family as its predecessor.

COUNTERING THE M60

The T-54/55, with its 100mm (3.9in) gun, was capable of taking on any post-war Western tank with a reasonable expectation of success. New warheads for the 100mm (3.9in) weapon enabled it to remain effective against most targets. However, upon examining an M60 Patton delivered by a defecting Iranian officer, Soviet experts determined that the new generation of tanks would require a more potent gun. They decided on a long 115mm (4.5in) gun capable of firing an Armour-Piercing Fin-Stabilized Discarding-Sabot (APFSDS) round. This was the world's first smoothbore tank gun.

To carry this weapon, the T-62 hull was largely based on the T-54/55, with a low silhouette and the typically Soviet mushroom-shaped turret. Like most Soviet tanks, the T-62 was given the capability to generate its own smokescreen by injecting oil into the exhaust, and a snorkel to facilitate deep wading. With the same engine as the T-54/55 and a greater weight, performance was somewhat reduced.

A LIMITED SUCCESS

In addition to arming the Soviet military and its Warsaw Pact allies, the T-62 was widely exported and was built in several countries. More than 20,000 were produced, but the T-62 never fully supplanted the T-54/55 in Soviet service. This was in part due to the sheer numbers of tanks required by the Red Army, but other factors may have been at play too.

The T-62 had a number of issues that reduced its performance. The gun's autoloader/ejector system used the recoil of the weapon and was notorious for trying to feed pieces of the gunner into the breech. Combined with a very cramped turret this made operating the gun a hazardous

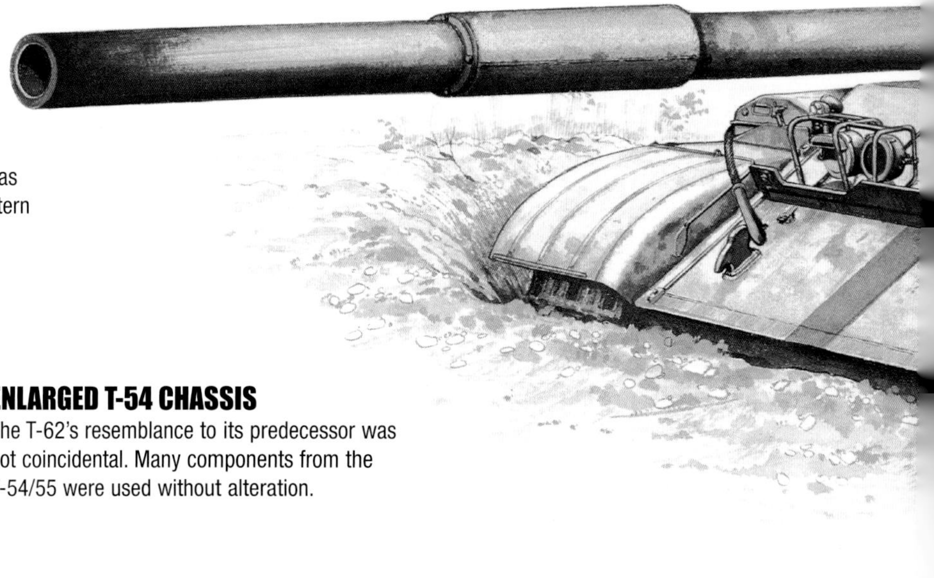

MAIN GUN
The innovative 115mm (4.5in) smoothbore gun was designed to penetrate the new generation of Western tanks emerging in the 1960s.

ENLARGED T-54 CHASSIS
The T-62's resemblance to its predecessor was not coincidental. Many components from the T-54/55 were used without alteration.

Like many Soviet tanks, the T-62 had the capability to create a smokescreen by injecting oil into its exhaust system.

TURRET
One limitation of the T-62 design was its slow turret traverse, which proved a serious liability in fluid situations.

CREW
The driver sat in the hull, with gunner, loader and commander jammed into a very cramped turret.

business. The ejection system did not always work as planned – instead of being flung outside, shell casings sometimes bounced around inside the turret. The gun, although powerful, was limited in other ways too. Turret traverse was slow and elevation limited. Combined with poor accuracy, this greatly reduced the effectiveness of the weapon.

T-62 IN SERVICE

Despite its limitations, the T-62 was widely exported and was built in North Korea for a time. It saw action in Russian hands in the Sino–Soviet conflict and the invasion of Afghanistan, and remained in service after the fall of the Soviet Union. Modernized T-62s were used in the conflicts in Chechnya and Georgia. The T-62 was extensively used by the Iraqi army during the Iran–Iraq war. A programme of upgrades and modernization packages greatly reduced the problems associated with the T-62 design, with the result that they performed well against Western-supplied Iranian tanks.

The T-62 fared less well against the Israelis in the 1973 Yom Kippur War. Captured Syrian T-62s were given a Western gun and engine, and they served for several years before being placed in reserve. Large numbers of T-62s were in service with the Iraqi army during the 1991 and 2003 conflicts. Greatly outmatched by more modern Western designs, they did not fare well. Despite this, several thousand T-62s remain in service worldwide, and upgrade programmes are still on offer. A civilian firefighting version is also available.

SPECIFICATIONS (T-62)

Dimensions: Length: 6.63m (21ft 9in), Height: 2.39m (7ft 10in), Width: 3.3m (10ft 10in)

Weight: 35.7 tonnes (39.4 tons)

Engine/powerplant: V55 12-cylinder diesel engine

Speed: 40km/h (31.1mph)

Armament: Main gun: 115mm (4.5in) Rapira smoothbore gun, Co-axial: 7.62mm (0.3in) machine gun, Turret top: 12.7mm (0.5in) machine gun

Crew: 4

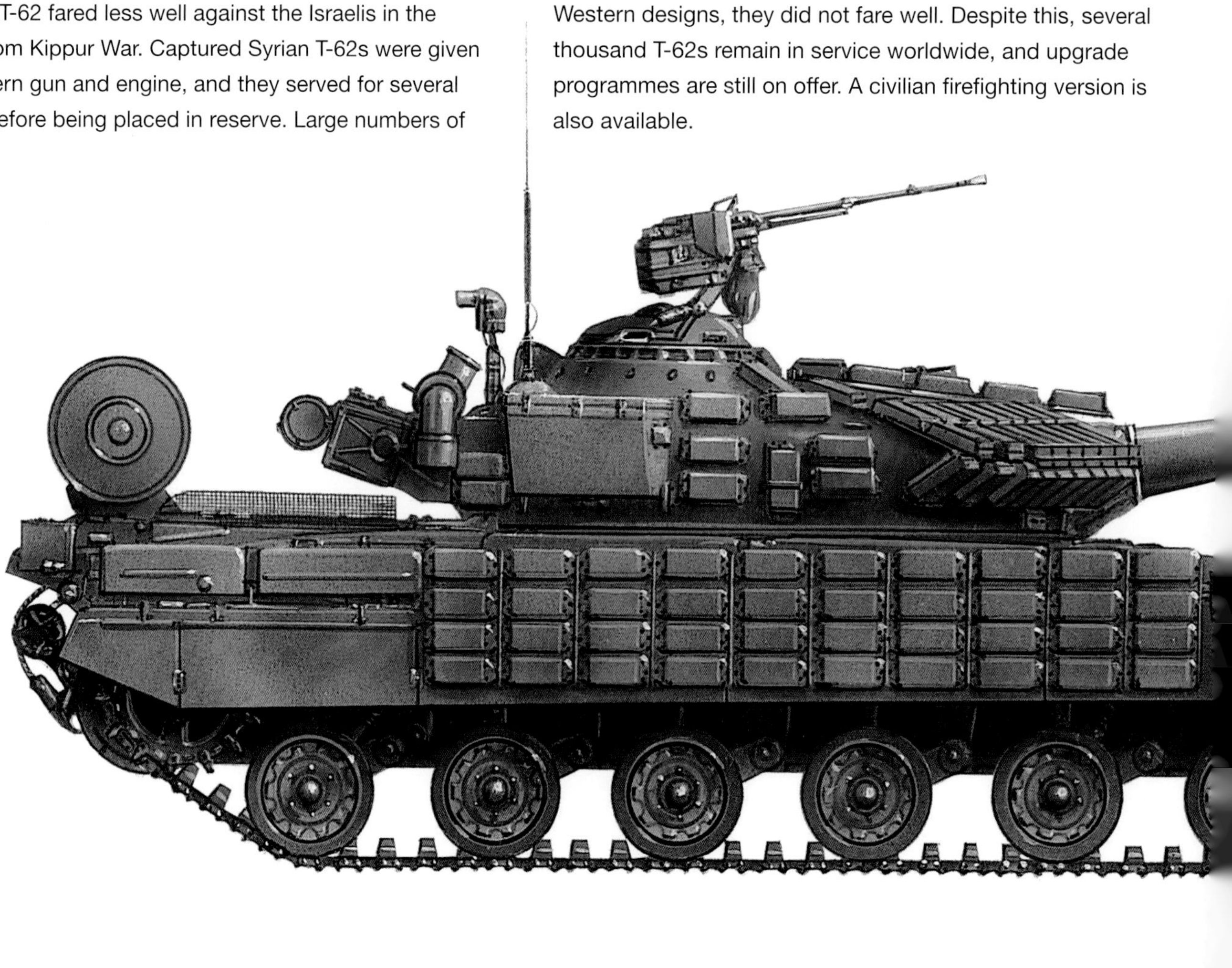

A view of a Soviet T-62 battle tank on display at the Warrior Preparation Centre, Germany. The T-62 used a different armour configuration to its predecessor, increasing protection in critical areas but offering lighter protection elsewhere.

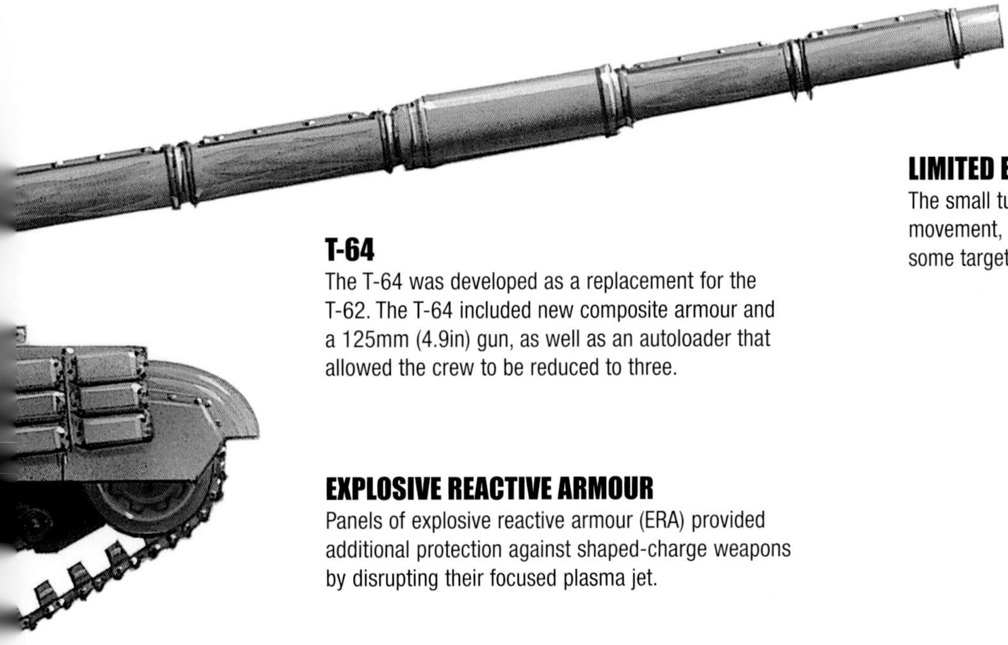

LIMITED ELEVATION AND DEPRESSION

The small turret limited the gun's range of movement, making it impossible to engage some targets on sloping ground.

T-64

The T-64 was developed as a replacement for the T-62. The T-64 included new composite armour and a 125mm (4.9in) gun, as well as an autoloader that allowed the crew to be reduced to three.

EXPLOSIVE REACTIVE ARMOUR

Panels of explosive reactive armour (ERA) provided additional protection against shaped-charge weapons by disrupting their focused plasma jet.

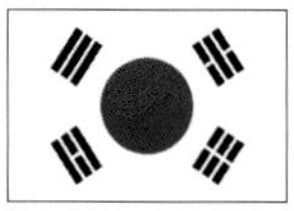

K2 Black Panther

The armed standoff between North and South Korea is in many ways a microcosm of the Cold War. South Korean military equipment is intended to provide a qualitative superiority over the more numerous North Korean forces. The K2 Black Panther exploits rapid information exchange to create such an advantage.

AMERICAN INFLUENCES

At the end of the Korean Conflict in 1953, South Korea was left with stocks of US equipment including M4 Shermans and M48 Pattons. The latter were upgraded over time, but it was obvious that a new tank was needed to counter T-62 variants in North Korean service. South Korea explored a number of options, including buying the M60 and the Leopard 1, but ultimately decided upon developing an indigenous main battle tank.

Influenced by the project that would eventually produce the M1 Abrams, South Korean designers produced a tank that was visually similar to the M1, but smaller and lighter. It was built around the proven 105mm (4.1in) gun, backed up by advanced electronics, and incorporated panoramic

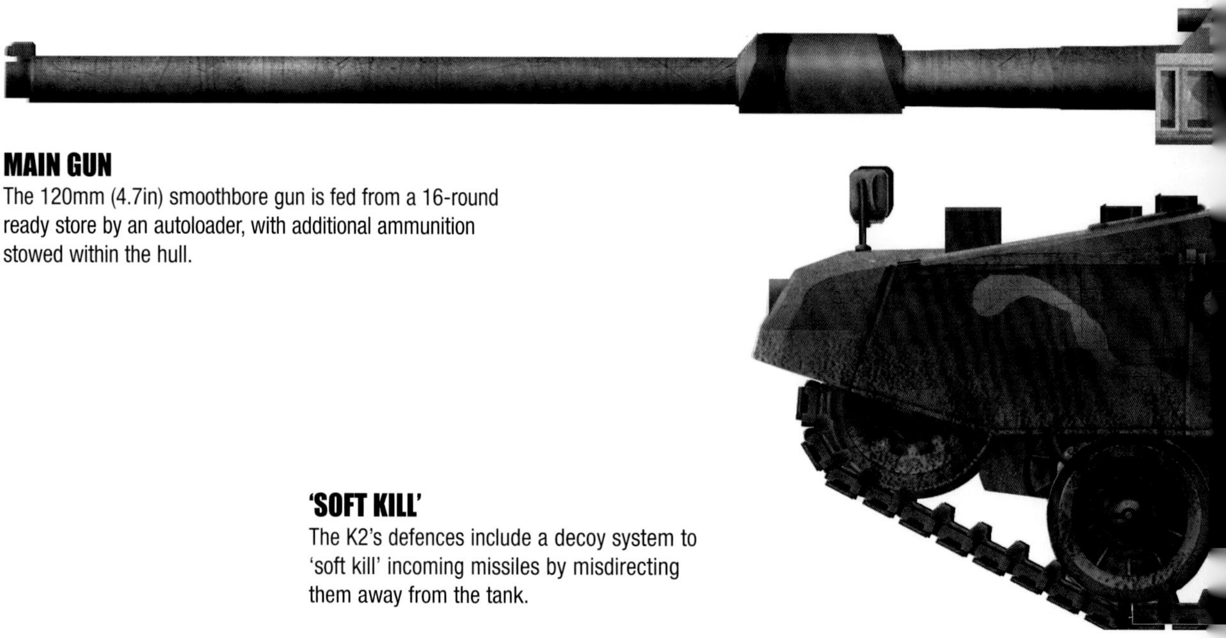

MAIN GUN

The 120mm (4.7in) smoothbore gun is fed from a 16-round ready store by an autoloader, with additional ammunition stowed within the hull.

'SOFT KILL'

The K2's defences include a decoy system to 'soft kill' incoming missiles by misdirecting them away from the tank.

SPECIFICATIONS (K2 BLACK PANTHER)

Dimensions: Length: 10.8m (32ft 10in), Height: 2.4m (7ft 10.5in), Width: 3.6m (11ft 10in)

Weight: 49.8 tonnes (55 tons)

Engine/powerplant: MT 833 diesel engine

Speed: 70km/h (43mph)

Armament: Main gun: 120mm (4.7in) smoothbore gun, Co-axial: 7.62mm (0.3in) machine gun, Turret top: 12.7mm (0.5in) machine gun

Crew: 3

An indigenous design enabled South Korea to dispense with complex component supply agreements and to offer its new tank for export sales.

CREW

Use of an autoloader enables the K2 Black Panther to operate with a crew of three: driver, gunner and commander.

SOPHISTICATED ARMOUR

The K2's armour consists of a steel base layer overlaid with modular composite blocks. Reactive armour may also be fitted.

sights for better situational awareness. The K1 was upgraded during its service life, gaining extra protection at the expense of mobility. The K1A2 version incorporated experience gained during the development of its successor, the K2 Black Panther, which in some ways allowed it to act as a testbed.

K2 BLACK PANTHER

The K2 has superior mobility over the preceding K1, with a larger gun capable of firing advanced ammunition. This includes a top-attack munition designed to target the weakest parts of a tank's protection. Tank armour is generally sloped to increase effective thickness against direct fire impacts, and presents a more or less flat plane against attacks from above. The top-attack munition is fired above the target, deploying a parachute to slow it as it approaches. Thus, rather than striking in a fairly flat trajectory against the armour, the projectile falls steeply from above. This munition has the added advantages that it can be lobbed over an intervening obstacle or fired indirectly from cover or concealment.

The K2's suspension can be adjusted to create greater ground clearance when needed or to counteract sloped or uneven ground. It can also be used to angle the hull up or down, creating greater depression or elevation of the main gun. Its deep-wading kit allows water over 4m (13ft) deep to be crossed without the assistance of engineering vehicles.

WARFARE IN THE INFORMATION AGE

In addition to advanced information sharing and battle-management systems, the K2 has a very sophisticated target identification, tracking and engagement capability. It

SUSPENSION SYSTEM
The K2's advanced suspension system can be used to increase the elevation of the main gun by lowering the rear of the tank and raising the front.

AMMUNITION
The main gun normally fires tungsten-cored penetrator rounds or high-explosive anti-tank ammunition for 'softer' targets.

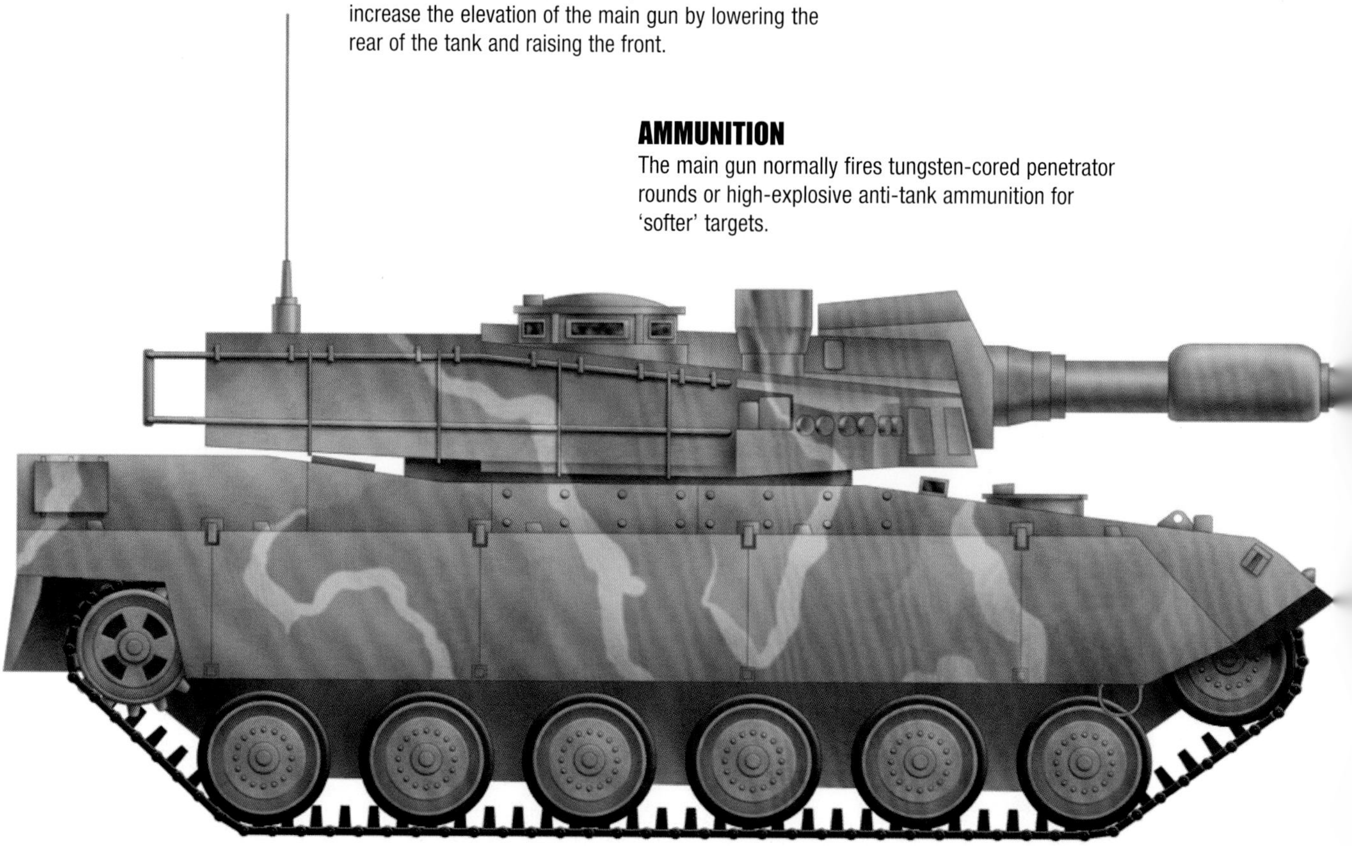

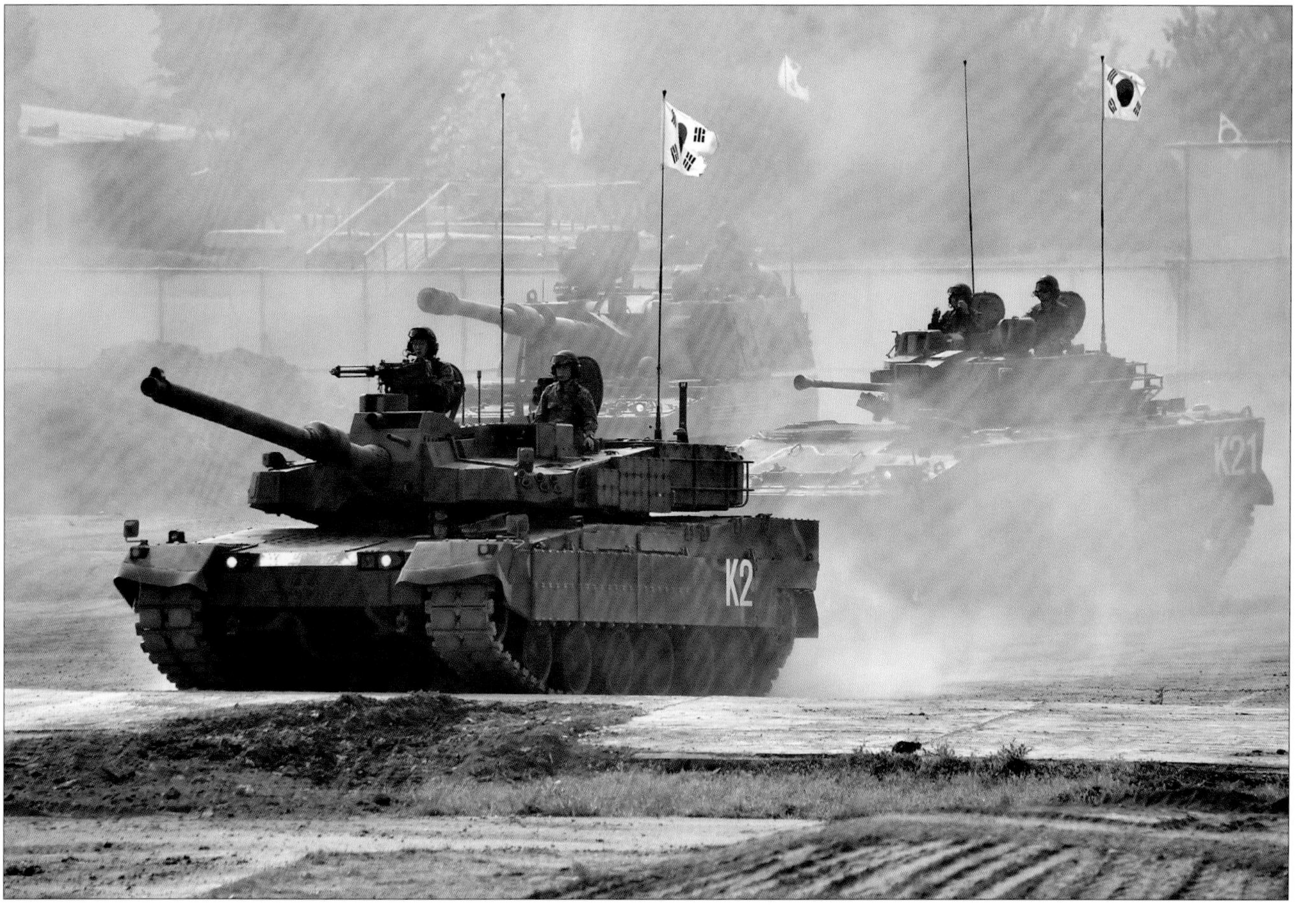

A planned enhancement will permit the tank to scan the terrain ahead for obstacles and pre-adjust the position of its suspension to compensate.

ADVANCED AMMO

A special high-trajectory top-attack munition is available, with a range of up to 8km (5 miles).

has a crew of three – commander, gunner and driver – and is capable of functioning without one or even two of them. Automated targeting systems enable the gun to engage targets without direct gunner interaction. Instead, the driver or commander can indicate to the tank's computer system what is to be fired upon, and leave the details to the machine. The tank will also automatically detect and track potential targets without engaging.

Like other new main battle tanks, the K2 can also detect and counter incoming anti-tank weapons. Laser designators can be screened with smoke, while missiles can be 'soft-killed' by decoys or 'hard-killed' by interception. These defensive actions can be carried out automatically by the tank's systems, reacting faster than a human crewmember would be able to.

AMX-13

With its unusual oscillating turret, the French AMX-13 was upgraded several times and achieved notable export success. No European design has been produced in such numbers, with almost 8000 built for the domestic and export market. However, the AMX-13 is considered by some to be 'only just' a tank, having more in common with a tank destroyer.

INNOVATIVE LIGHT TANK

In urgent need of effective armoured forces at the beginning of the Cold War, France explored many options. The AMX-13 was technically innovative but in other ways quite conventional. It was influenced by the light tank destroyers fielded by many nations, mounting a tank-calibre gun on a lightly armoured chassis. However, unlike most tank destroyers, the AMX-13 was given a fully rotating turret.

The initial armament chosen for the new light tank was a 75mm (2.9in) gun, which at that time was an effective weapon against most tanks. Fitting such a gun would normally require a large turret, but pushing up the weight and size of the vehicle was undesirable. The problem was ingeniously solved with an oscillating turret. Rather than the gun being elevated and depressed inside a rotating turret, instead the top half of the turret was elevated with the gun fixed within it. The lower half rotated as normal. Use of an autoloader eliminated one crew position and all the associated equipment.

The AMX-13 presented a small target to enemy fire, which was perhaps just as well. It was vulnerable to machine-gun fire in most areas, with only the frontal arc protected against cannon ammunition. Good mobility and high speed offset this to some degree, and additional armour sheets could be applied, but overall the AMX-13 was very lightly protected.

EVOLVING DESIGN

A more powerful gun was an obvious requirement, and in the mid-1960s the AMX-13 was given a 90mm (3.5in) weapon. Upgrades also included wire-guided anti-tank missiles and enhanced armour protection. A version with a 105mm (4.1in) gun appeared in the 1980s and was an

AUTOLOADER
The autoloader consisted of two revolver-type magazines, each containing six ready rounds for the main gun.

LIGHTLY ARMOURED
Frontal armour was about 40mm (1.5in) thick, with as little as 15mm (0.59in) on the rear hull.

SPECIFICATIONS (AMX-13)

Dimensions: Length: 4.88m (16ft), Height: 2.3m (7ft 6.5in), Width: 2.51m (8ft 3in)

Weight: 13.4 tonnes (14.8 tons)

Engine/powerplant: 8-cylinder petrol engine

Speed: 60km/h (37.3mph)

Armament: 75mm (2.9in) SA50 gun, Additional: 2 x 7.62mm (0.3in) machine guns

Crew: 3

OSCILLATING TURRET

The oscillating turret design allowed the AMX-13 to mount a powerful gun for such a small vehicle.

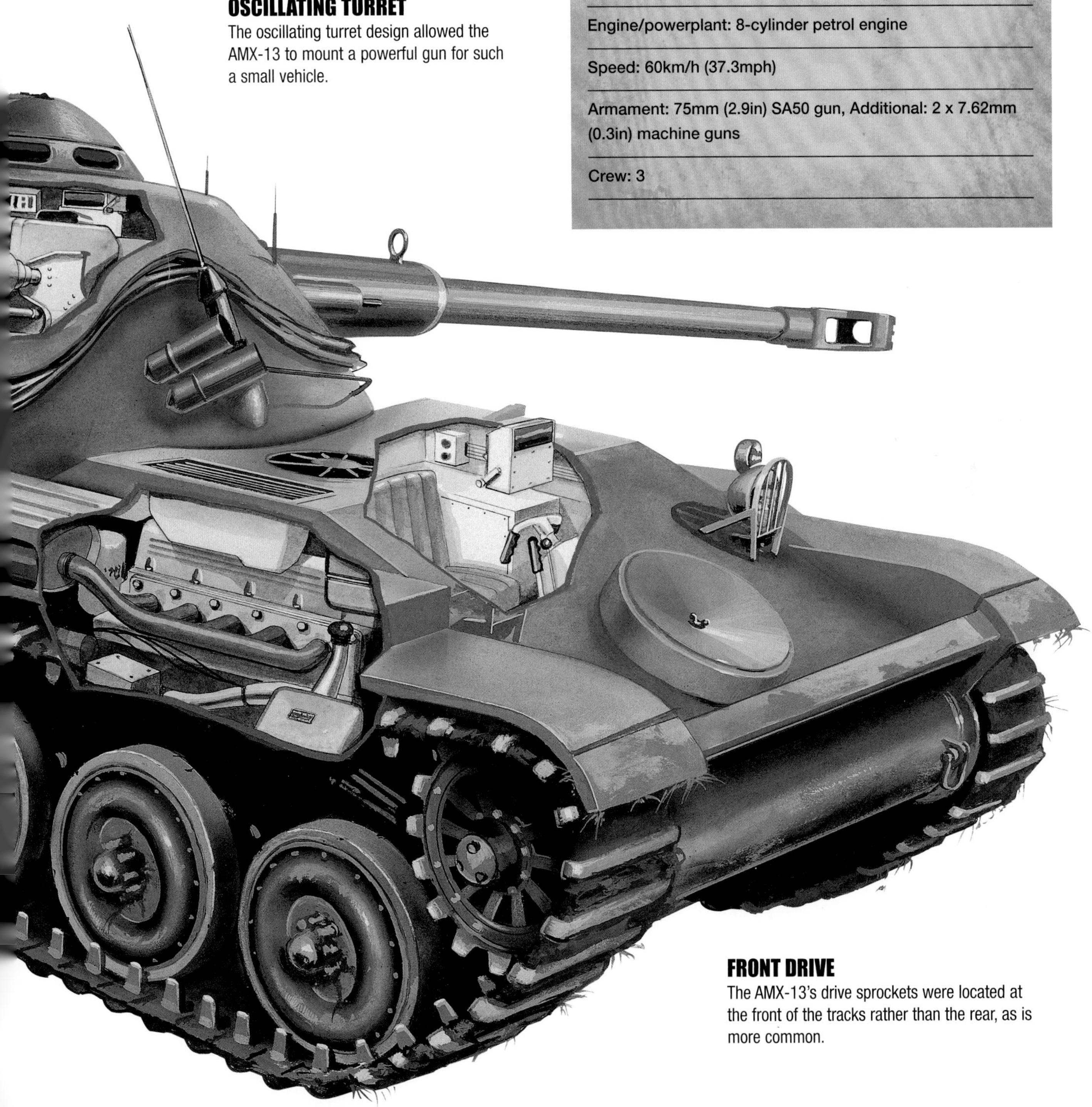

FRONT DRIVE

The AMX-13's drive sprockets were located at the front of the tracks rather than the rear, as is more common.

The AMX-13 enabled its users to field a large number of guns capable of destroying a main battle tank at a relatively low cost.

export success. The chassis, which had demonstrated its good performance, was used as the basis for a self-propelled anti-aircraft system armed with two 40mm (1.5in) cannon. This vehicle was designated AMX-13 DCA.

The oscillating turret design was clever but suffered from technical issues, perhaps explaining why it was not adopted more widely. A number of experiments did take place, including the development of an oscillating turret for a main battle tank, but no heavy version was successful. The design did prove workable for lighter weapons, however.

IN SERVICE

The French military took around 3000 AMX-13s, intending to use them in an armoured reconnaissance and advance-to-contact role, engaging the enemy until heavier supports arrived. Attempting to operate in the open against tanks would have been suicidal, so tank-destroyer tactics were to be used, firing from ambush and then retiring at speed. With no major war during their career, French AMX-13s were used in various smaller-scale conflicts where they did not encounter tanks.

Israeli AMX-13s were reasonably effective against T-55s and other tanks in the 1956, 1967 and 1973 wars, while those used by India fared badly against Pakistani M48s. Small numbers have also taken part in minor conflicts in Africa.

Among the largest export customers were Singapore and Indonesia, with various upgrade packages keeping their fleets from becoming obsolete. Several South American nations also purchased quantities, with many still in service.

EBR ARMOURED CAR

The oscillating turret was also used on the EBR armoured car, which saw action in various minor conflicts.

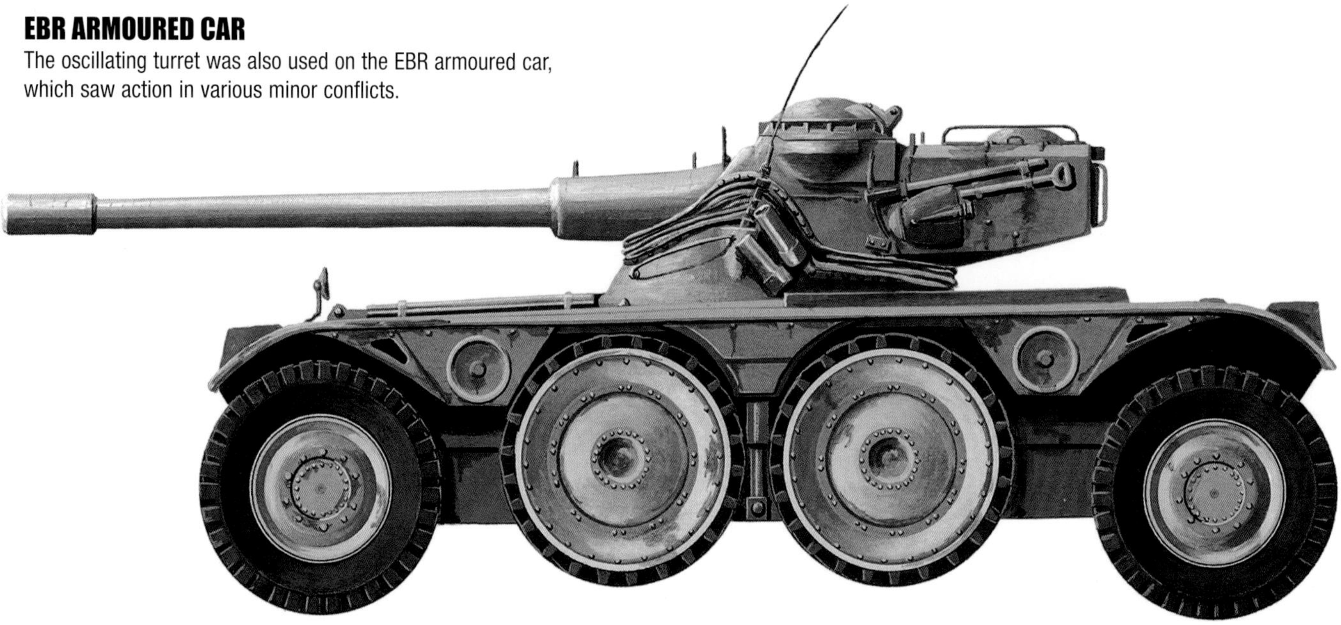

With such flimsy armour, camouflage and ambush tactics were essential to the survivability of an AMX-13 force, as was the ability to make a speedy withdrawal.

AMX-13

Many observers would define the AMX-13 as a tank destroyer, but it was always intended for light-tank roles such as screening and reconnaissance.

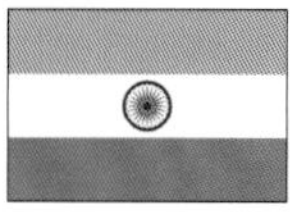

Arjun

Development of the Arjun main battle tank was heavily influenced by the German Leopard 2. The original Arjun was not a great success, but was the basis for the greatly superior Mk2 version. It is armed with a 120mm (4.7in) gun that, unusually for such a weapon, is rifled.

AN INDIGENOUS TANK FOR INDIA

India's military forces are unusual in that even during the Cold War they operated a mix of Western and Soviet equipment. British-built Centurions were supplanted by the Vijayanta, a licence-built version of the Vickers Mk 1, with a locally manufactured version of the T-72 named Ajeya also in service from the early 1970s onwards.

Plans to develop an indigenous tank, eventually to be designated 'Arjun', progressed more slowly than had been hoped, leading to the selection of the Russian T-90 as an interim measure. In Indian service, the T-90 was designated 'Bhishma'. Some T-90s were imported whole, some as components for local assembly, and a licence was obtained to produce more in Indian factories.

RIFLED GUN

The Arjun's 120mm (4.7in) gun is rifled, giving accuracy advantages over equivalent smoothbores at longer ranges.

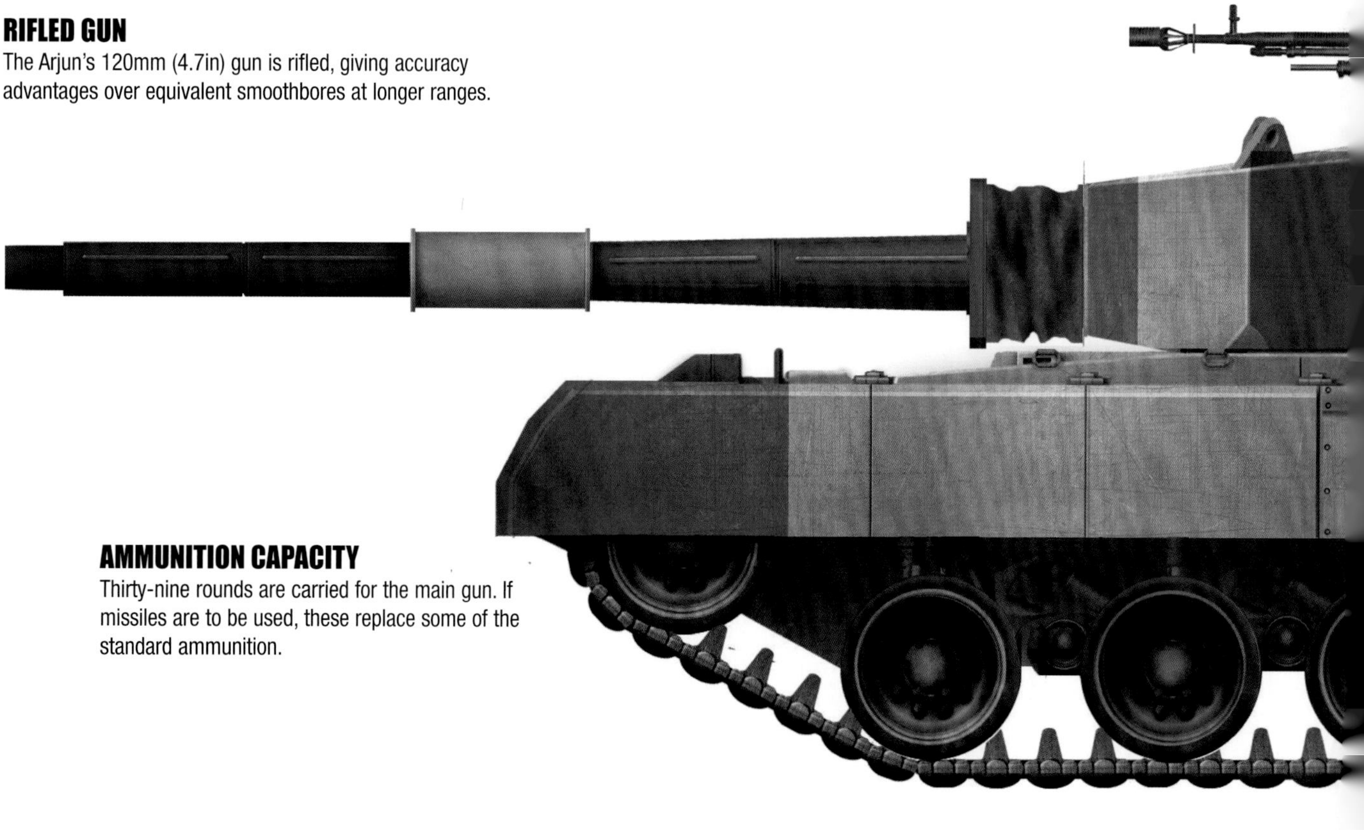

AMMUNITION CAPACITY

Thirty-nine rounds are carried for the main gun. If missiles are to be used, these replace some of the standard ammunition.

A column of Arjun tanks on parade. The Arjun's crew layout is conventional, with the driver in the hull and the commander, gunner and loader in the turret.

REMOTE CONTROLLED WEAPON STATION

The turret-top 12.7mm (0.5in) machine gun can be controlled from within the tank, permitting infantry defence from a position of safety.

BLOW-OUT PANELS

Ammunition storage in the turret has blow-out panels, which will vent an explosion to protect the crew.

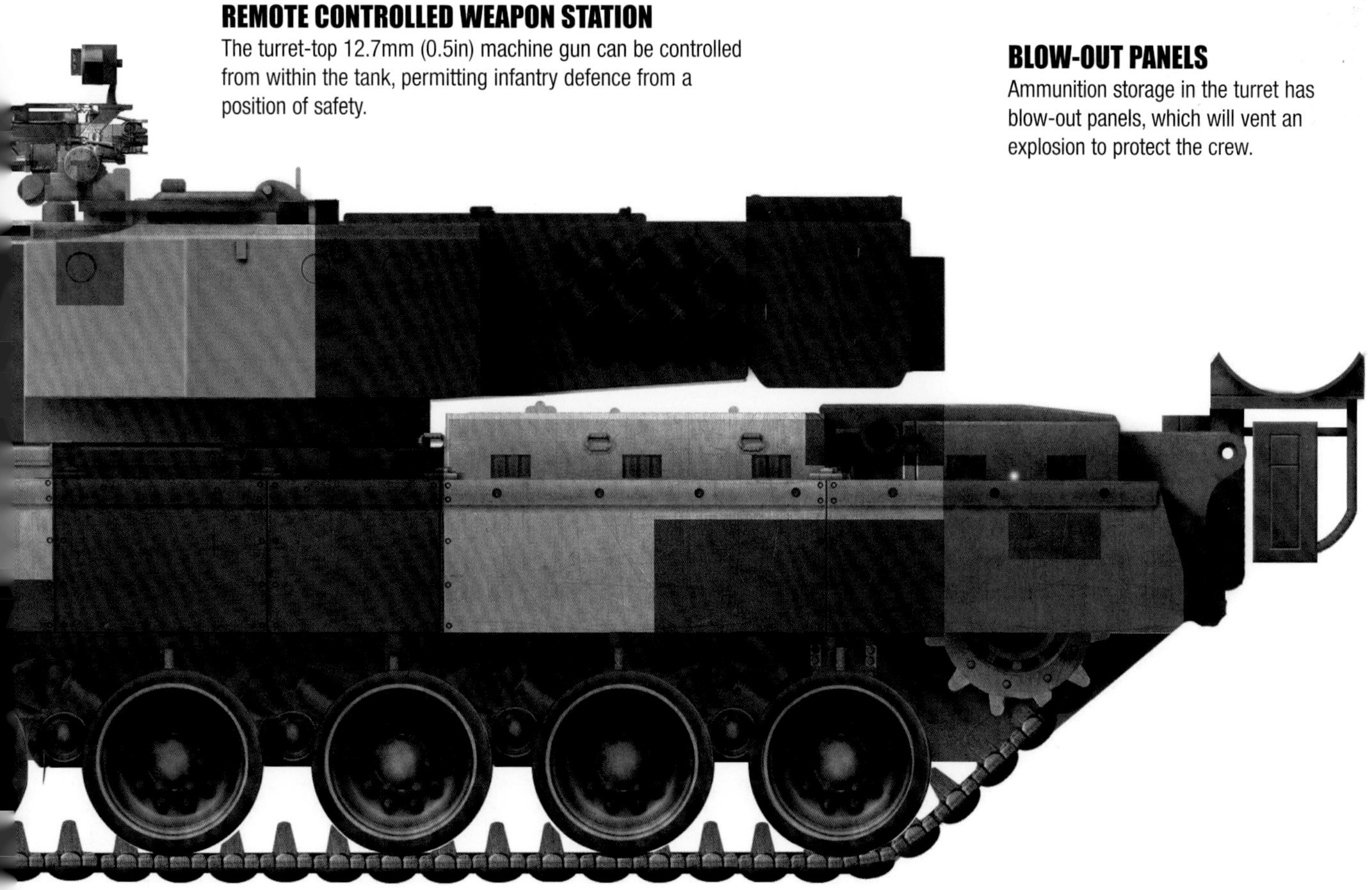

The adoption of the T-90 Bhishma jeopardized the Arjun project, as the Bhishma proved satisfactory in service. However, competitive trials between the T-90 Bhishma and the Arjun demonstrated the Arjun's superior mobility. It was decided that the T-90 variant would replace the ageing Ajeya fleet but that Arjun would still be produced.

ARJUN MK2

The original Arjun was only produced in small numbers, but these formed the basis for a more advanced version designated Arjun Mk2. This was armed with the same gun – a fully stabilized 120mm (4.7in) rifled weapon capable of firing conventional projectiles or LAHAT (Laser Homing Attack) missiles. Effective against tanks, helicopters or

SPECIFICATIONS (ARJUN MBT)

Dimensions: Length: 10.64 (34ft 11in), Height: 2.32 (7ft 7in), Width: 3.86m (12ft 8in)
Weight: 53 tonnes (58.5 tons) (Mk2: 61.6 tonnes/68 tons)
Engine/powerplant: MTU MB 838 Ka 501 diesel engine
Speed: 72km/h (44.7mph)
Armament: Main gun: 120mm (4.7in) rifled gun, Co-axial: 7.62mm (0.3in) machine gun, Turret top: 12.7mm (0.5in) machine gun
Crew: 4

The Arjun's resemblance to the Leopard – especially its turret – is largely due to German assistance in its development process.

An Arjun tank stands outside Parliament House in New Delhi, India.

point targets such as enemy strongpoints in an urban area, missiles of this sort give tanks a precision strike capability. The only other user of a rifled 120mm (4.7in) gun is Britain; other nations prefer smoothbores.

It has been reported that the original Arjun's gunnery was less accurate than had been hoped for, but this was remedied on the Mk2. Computerized target identification and engagement systems are complemented by panoramic sights and an integrated battle-management system for real-time information sharing. The Arjun Mk2 is protected by composite armour that can be augmented with explosive reactive armour (ERA) panels. Additional protection in the form of an Urban Survival Kit is available. A remotely controlled machine-gun mount provides protection from infantry attack. Fall-off of crew efficiency over time is reduced by attention to ergonomics and crew comfort, which results in lowered fatigue and a subsequent improvement in long-term capability.

The Arjun Mk2 has been criticized for being overweight – it requires specialist rail transport and cannot be carried by the Indian military's IL-76 aircraft. These problems can be remedied by creating or purchasing suitable transportation, but this adds to the cost of operating a fleet of Arjun main battle tanks. Cross-country performance is actually better than the lighter T-72-derived Ajeya due to improved suspension and lower ground pressure.

Various upgrades have been proposed for the Arjun, including more powerful engines and a different gun-launched missile system. The Arjun and Arjun Mk2 chassis have also been the basis of experimental projects including self-propelled artillery and engineering vehicles.

Type 99

Chinese tank design during the Cold War era was heavily influenced by Soviet designs – indeed, several Chinese tanks were direct copies of Russian ones. More recently, Chinese tanks have developed a character of their own, with features seen on some Western tanks alongside obvious Russian concepts.

CHANGING INFLUENCES

Early Chinese tank design was heavily influenced by Russian thinking – not surprisingly, since Russian advisors worked with Chinese designers until relations between the two powers broke down in the 1960s. Early Chinese designs drew heavily on the Russian T-54/55 and its successors. However, improved relations with the West gave access to new ideas and Western technology, and while second-generation Chinese main battle tanks such as the Type 80 still showed very strong Russian influences they could no longer be considered direct equivalents of Russian tanks.

The Type 90-II appeared in 1991, and while its basic design was still heavily influenced by the Russian T-72, it had some typically Western features as well. Further development created the Type 98 and then Type 99 (also designated ZTZ99), which incorporated lessons learned from the 1991 Gulf War. Later upgrades included

AUTOLOADER
The Type 99's 125mm (4.9in) smoothbore main gun is fed by a carousel-type autoloader.

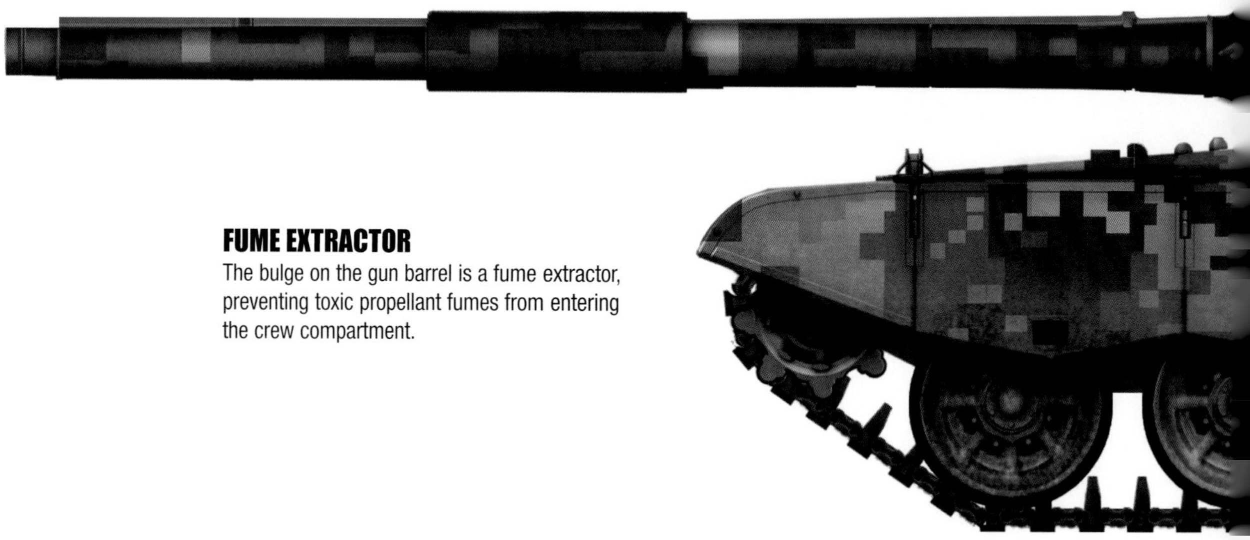

FUME EXTRACTOR
The bulge on the gun barrel is a fume extractor, preventing toxic propellant fumes from entering the crew compartment.

Type 99 tanks take part in a military parade in China. The Type 99 can launch guided missiles from its main gun. Four missiles are reportedly carried by each tank.

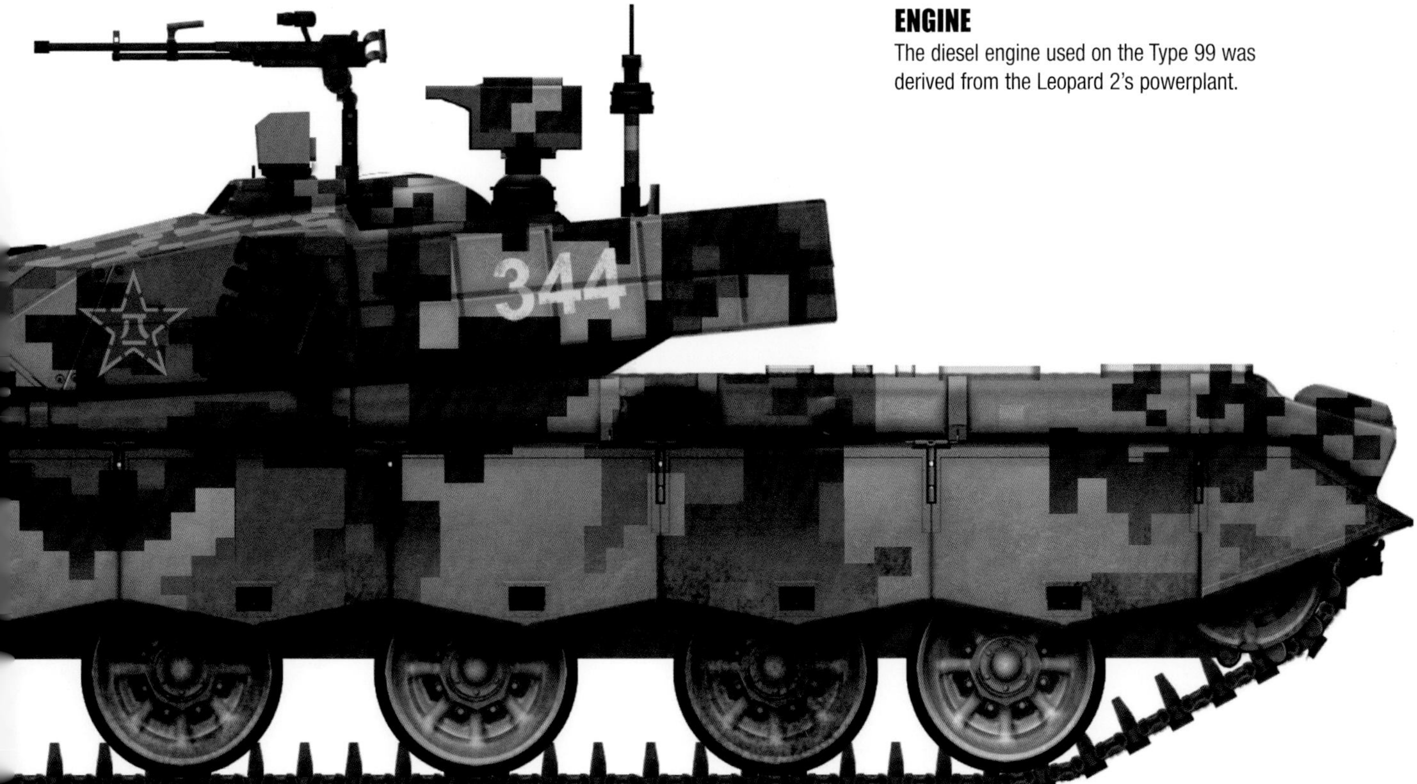

ENGINE
The diesel engine used on the Type 99 was derived from the Leopard 2's powerplant.

improved electronics and the addition of explosive reactive armour (ERA).

NEW TANKS FOR THE NEW CENTURY

The Type 99 hull design is very similar to the T-72, although it is a metre longer. The rounded cast turret of early designs has been replaced by a more Western design incorporating composite armour. As with other modern tank designs, armour is modular and designed to be replaced when damaged or if improved armour becomes available.

Western guns were adopted for use on the Type 80 and its derivatives, such as the Type 85. At the time, a 105mm (4.1in) gun was standard, with the new generation of MBTs using ammunition manufactured under licence to NATO specifications. However, the Type 99 uses a 125mm (4.9in) smoothbore gun compatible with Russian and former Warsaw Pact ammunition. The gun can also launch anti-tank guided missiles, currently using a licence-built version of the Russian 9K119 Refleks missile.

The Type 99 is powered by a turbocharged diesel engine derived from the Leopard 2's powerplant. Its advanced electronics include a fire control system that can function in hunter-killer mode, identifying and engaging targets automatically. An autoloader reduces the crew requirement to three.

The Type 99 makes extensive use of laser technology. Protection is enhanced by an active laser system, designed

SPECIFICATIONS (TYPE 99)

Dimensions: Length: 11m (36ft), Height: 2m (6ft 6in), Width: 3.4m (11ft 2in)

Weight: 48.9 tonnes (54 tons)

Engine/powerplant: Turbocharged diesel engine

Speed: 65km/h (40.6mph)

Armament: Main gun: 125mm (4.9in) smoothbore gun, Co-axial: 7.62mm (0.3in) machine gun, Commander's cupola: 12.7mm (0.5in) machine gun

Crew: 3

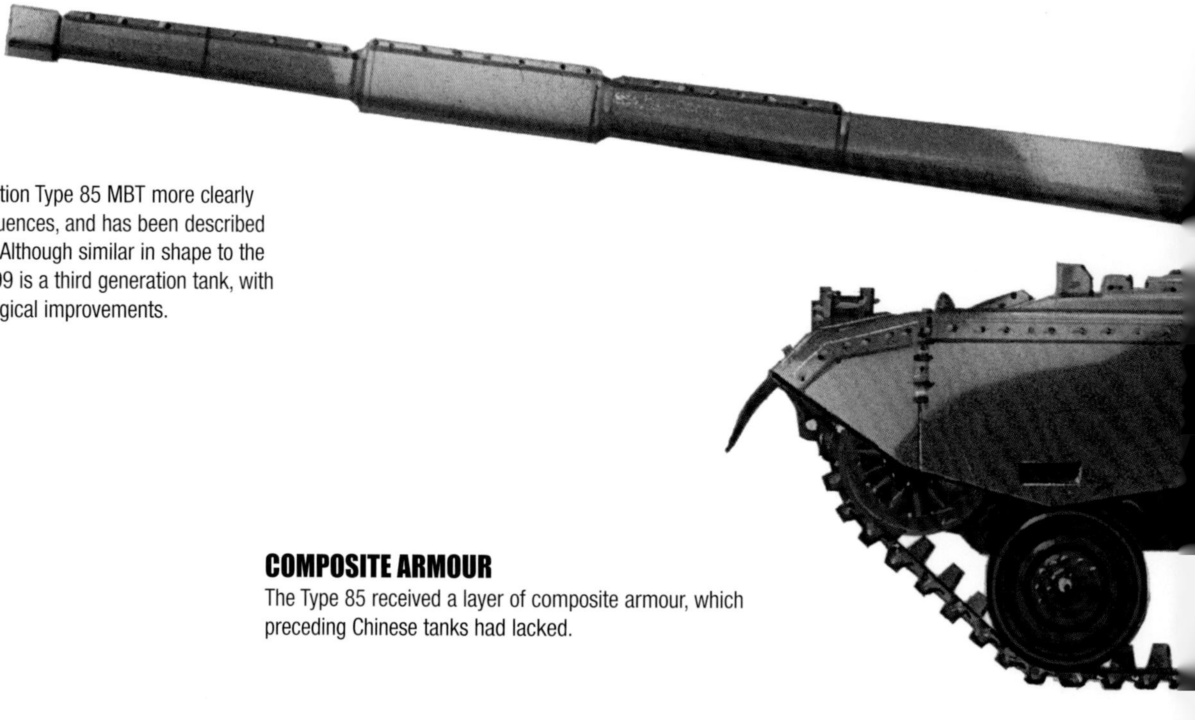

TYPE 85
The second generation Type 85 MBT more clearly shows Russian influences, and has been described as a Chinese T-72. Although similar in shape to the Type 85, the Type 99 is a third generation tank, with numerous technological improvements.

COMPOSITE ARMOUR
The Type 85 received a layer of composite armour, which preceding Chinese tanks had lacked.

In general appearance, the Type 99's hull looks very Russian, whereas the turret clearly shows Western influences.

to disrupt infrared or laser targeting, and there is a secure laser communications system. So long as tanks are within line of sight of one another they can communicate with virtually no chance of interception – a distinct asset in today's battlespace, where electronic warfare is prevalent. The same system also provides an identification-friend-or-foe capability.

EXPORTS

The Type 90-II was offered for export under the designation MBT 2000, and was taken up by Pakistan under the name Al-Khalid. Similarly, a downgraded version of the Type 99 was created specifically for the export market. Like many export versions of high-end systems, this tank has a reduced price due to the deletion of some of its advanced features. It has achieved some international success, and as the parent Type 99 is further developed a new export variant may well appear. As yet, the design has not been tested in combat. If and when that happens, sales of derivative models will be affected according to its performance.

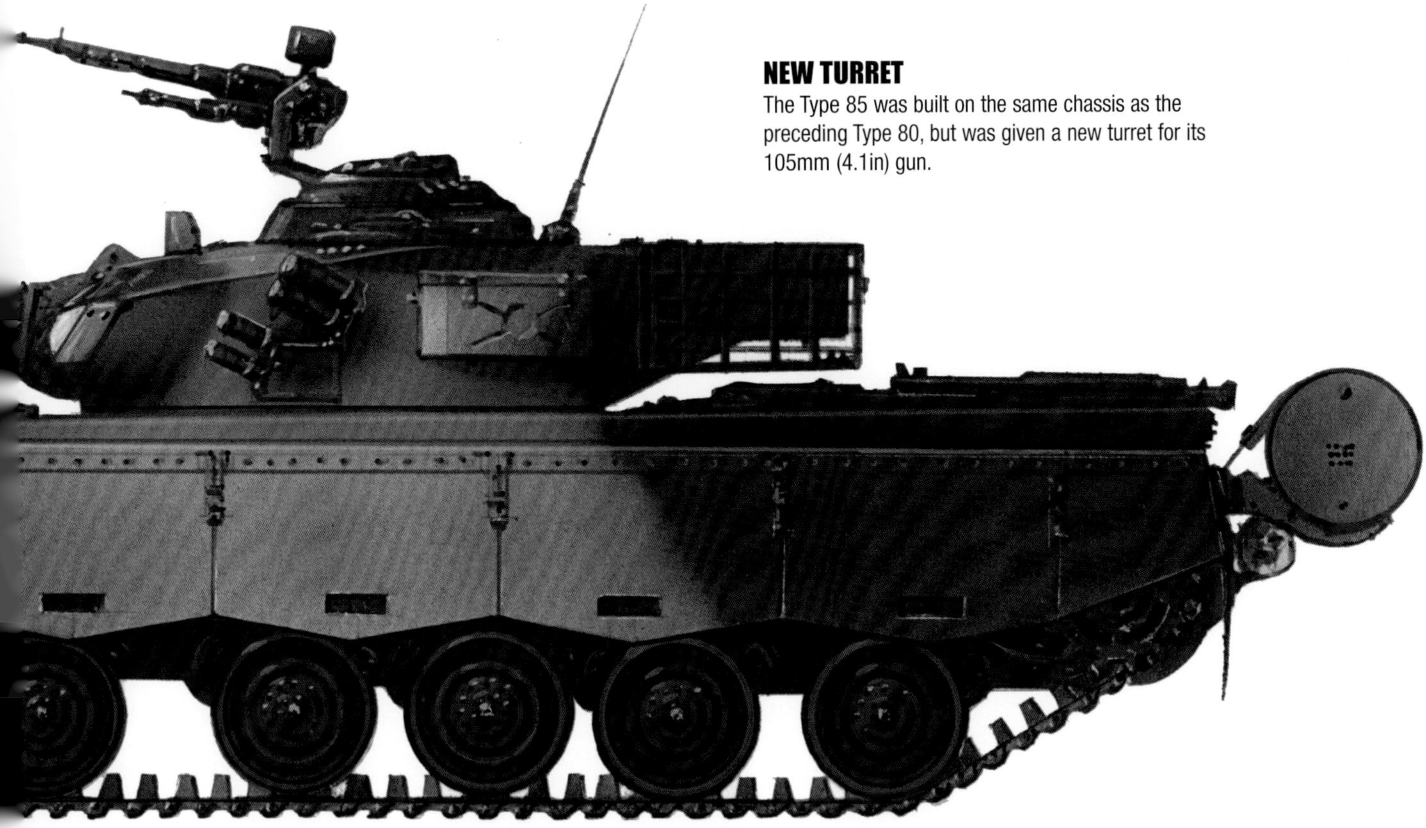

NEW TURRET

The Type 85 was built on the same chassis as the preceding Type 80, but was given a new turret for its 105mm (4.1in) gun.

M24 Chaffee

Powerfully armed for a light tank, the M24 Chaffee entered service late in World War II and was widely exported afterwards. Its rugged and reliable chassis was used as the basis for several other armoured vehicles, including self-propelled guns and mobile anti-aircraft platforms.

A LIGHT TANK WITH A BIG GUN

The M3 Stuart performed sterling service during World War II, but it was soon obvious that a more powerful light tank would be required. Development began on a project intended to create a light tank armed with a 75mm (2.9in) gun. The design became increasingly overweight to the point that it was redefined as a medium tank, and one with insufficient engine power at that. A much better medium tank was already available in the form of the M4 Sherman, so the project was cancelled.

The M24 was a wholly new design, although it incorporated lessons learned in the previous effort. Its sloped armour and a generally modern appearance reflected the experience gained during World War II, as did its capabilities. While not up to the task of battling medium and heavy tanks, the M24 could tackle most targets with its 75mm (2.9in) gun.

There were plans for the M24 to form the basis of a family of combat vehicles including engineering tanks, self-propelled guns and ant-aircraft platforms. Not all of the variants were successful, but the M41 Howitzer Motor carriage, mounting a 155mm (6.1in) artillery piece, and the M19 Multiple Gun Motor Carriage both proved effective. The latter was an anti-aircraft system but was also found to be useful for direct-fire support.

The problem of fitting a relatively large gun in a light tank was solved with some clever engineering, and a lightweight weapon originally designed for the B-25 Mitchell bomber was used. The M24 could carry a crew of five, but often the assistant driver also acted as loader for the main gun, reducing manpower requirements without greatly reducing efficiency. The prototype lived up to expectations and production rapidly began.

DOZER BLADE

Provision was made to fit a dozer blade when necessary, enabling the M24 to create its own firing positions.

MAIN GUN

A lightweight 75mm (2.9in) gun with a short recoil distance was required to fit in the M24's small turret.

CHASSIS

It was intended that the M24 chassis would be the basis for a family of combat vehicles, greatly reducing maintenance costs.

The M24 saw action in Southeast Asia in both French and South Vietnamese hands. Its light weight was an asset in the mountainous and jungle terrain of the region.

SPECIFICATIONS (M24 CHAFFEE)

Dimensions: Length: 5.49m (18ft), Height: 2.46m (8ft 1in), Width: 2.95m (9ft 8in)

Weight: 16.3 tonnes (18 tons)

Engine/powerplant: Two Cadillac 44T24 V8 petrol engines

Speed: 55km/h (34mph)

Armament: Main gun: 75mm (2.9in) gun, Co-axial: 7.62mm (0.3in) machine gun, Commander's cupola: 12.7mm (0.5in) machine gun, Additional 7.62mm (0.3in) machine gun in hull

Crew: 5

ARMOUR

Weight restrictions required that the M24's thickest armour was only 38mm (1.5in), with some areas virtually unprotected.

M24 IN SERVICE

The M24 saw action in the last months of World War II, with the first examples arriving just in time to become involved in the German Ardennes Offensive of December1944–January 1945. Some reached British units before the end of the war, and while none saw action in the Pacific Theatre, the Chaffee was deployed to Japan as part of the occupying forces.

At the outbreak of the Korean Conflict, the M24 was rushed into action against North Korean forces. Although never intended to serve as a battle tank, its 75mm (2.9in) gun performed well during the difficult early stages of the conflict. Similarly, M24s in French service were effective during their wars in Indochina. A small force was parachuted into the surrounded perimeter at Dien Bien Phu; although the position was eventually overrun, the M24s were valuable in prolonging the defence.

A simple and reliable light tank with a credible armament, the M24 was popular on the export market. Many nations received ex-US vehicles once the Chaffee was withdrawn from US service. In some cases, the M24 remained operational into the 1980s or even the 1990s.

Much of the military equipment used by the post-war French army was of US origin. M24s were nicknamed 'Bison' in French service.

CO-AXIAL WEAPON

The co-axial machine gun, mounted in the main gun mantlet, and the bow gun were both 7.62mm (0.3in) weapons. The 12.7mm (0.5in) machine gun on the turret top provided a measure of air defence.

BOW MACHINE GUN

The M24 was one of the last US tank designs to mount a bow machine gun. This was manned by the assistant driver.

Stridsvagn 103 ('S Tank')

Developed to suit the needs of its native Sweden, the S Tank was highly unusual in that it lacked a turret – one of the defining characteristics of a tank. Its operators called it a tank rather than a tank destroyer, and used it as a tank – so a tank it was.

REPLACING THE CENTURION

Although determinedly neutral, Sweden needed to find a replacement for the Centurion MBTs then serving in its armed forces. Rather than buy a foreign tank, it was decided to develop an indigenous design specifically for defensive combat within Sweden. A tank without a turret offered some real advantages, notably a very low profile, resulting in a vehicle that was hard to spot or target, with incoming fire likely to strike its extremely sloped armour.

On the other hand, a turret offered the ability to engage targets in any direction far more quickly than a vehicle that had to turn to face a threat, which might also require leaving cover. Elevation and depression of the gun was also a problem that had to be addressed. The solution was to create a vehicle with variable suspension, allowing the whole tank to be angled up or down as needed in a precise and rapid manner. This concept was tested in the prototype stage and found to work, with full production beginning in 1965.

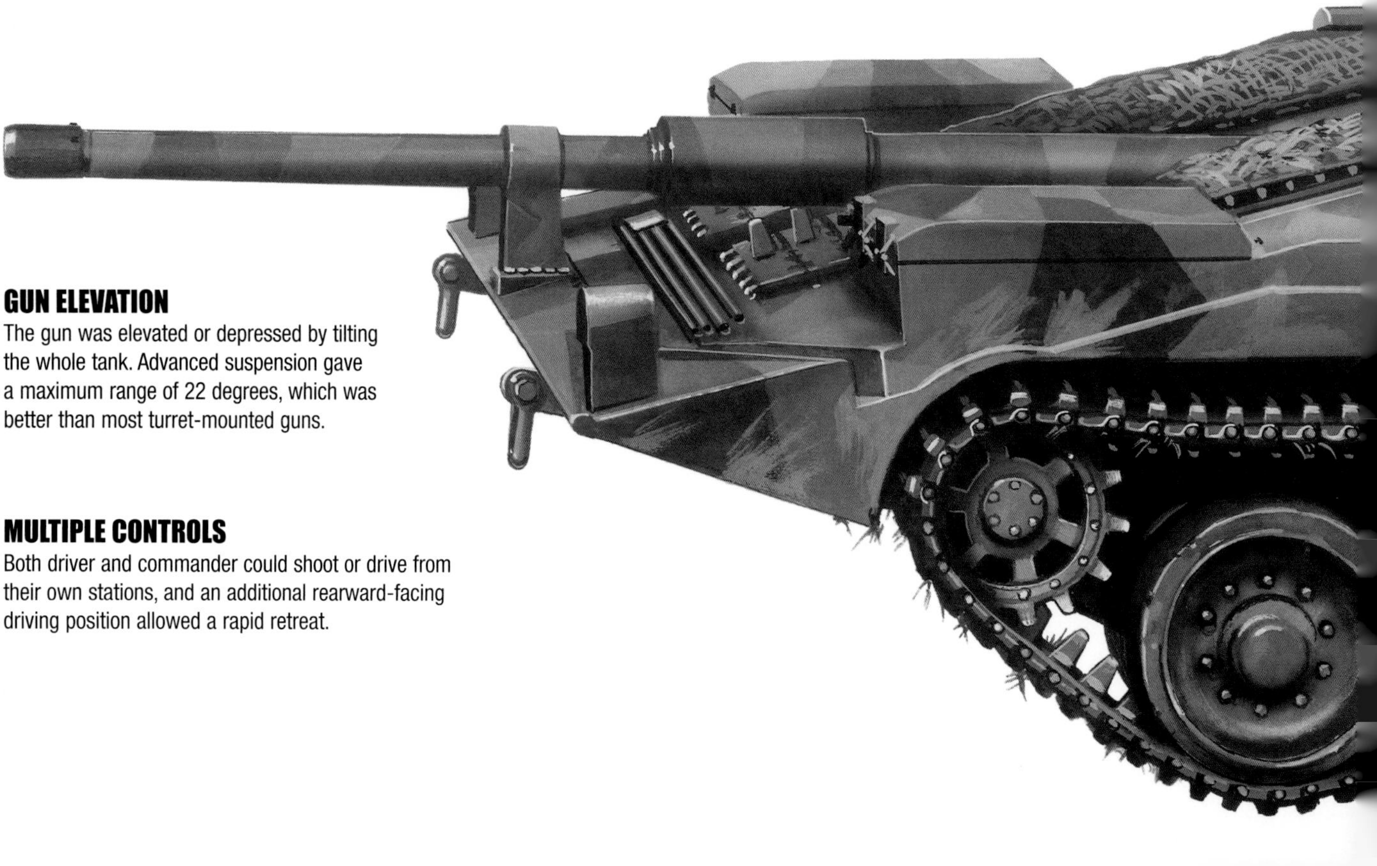

GUN ELEVATION

The gun was elevated or depressed by tilting the whole tank. Advanced suspension gave a maximum range of 22 degrees, which was better than most turret-mounted guns.

MULTIPLE CONTROLS

Both driver and commander could shoot or drive from their own stations, and an additional rearward-facing driving position allowed a rapid retreat.

SPECIFICATIONS (STRIDSVAGN 103)

Dimensions: Length: 8.42m (27ft 7.5in), Height: 2.50m (8ft 2.5in), Width: 3.62m (11ft 10.5in)

Weight: 35.3 tonnes (39 tons)

Engine/powerplant: Diesel engine plus Boeing GT502 gas turbine or Caterpillar 553 gas turbine

Speed: 50km/h (31.1mph)

Armament: Main gun: 105mm (4.1in) gun, Co-axial: 2 x 7.62mm (0.3in) machine guns, Commander's cupola: 12.7mm (0.5in) machine gun

Crew: 3

'Slat' armour could be fitted to the front of the S Tank to defeat shaped-charge weapons. This was a closely guarded secret during the Cold War.

LOW PROFILE

Mounting the main gun directly on the hull gave the S Tank a very low silhouette and ensured that any hit arrived at a very acute angle.

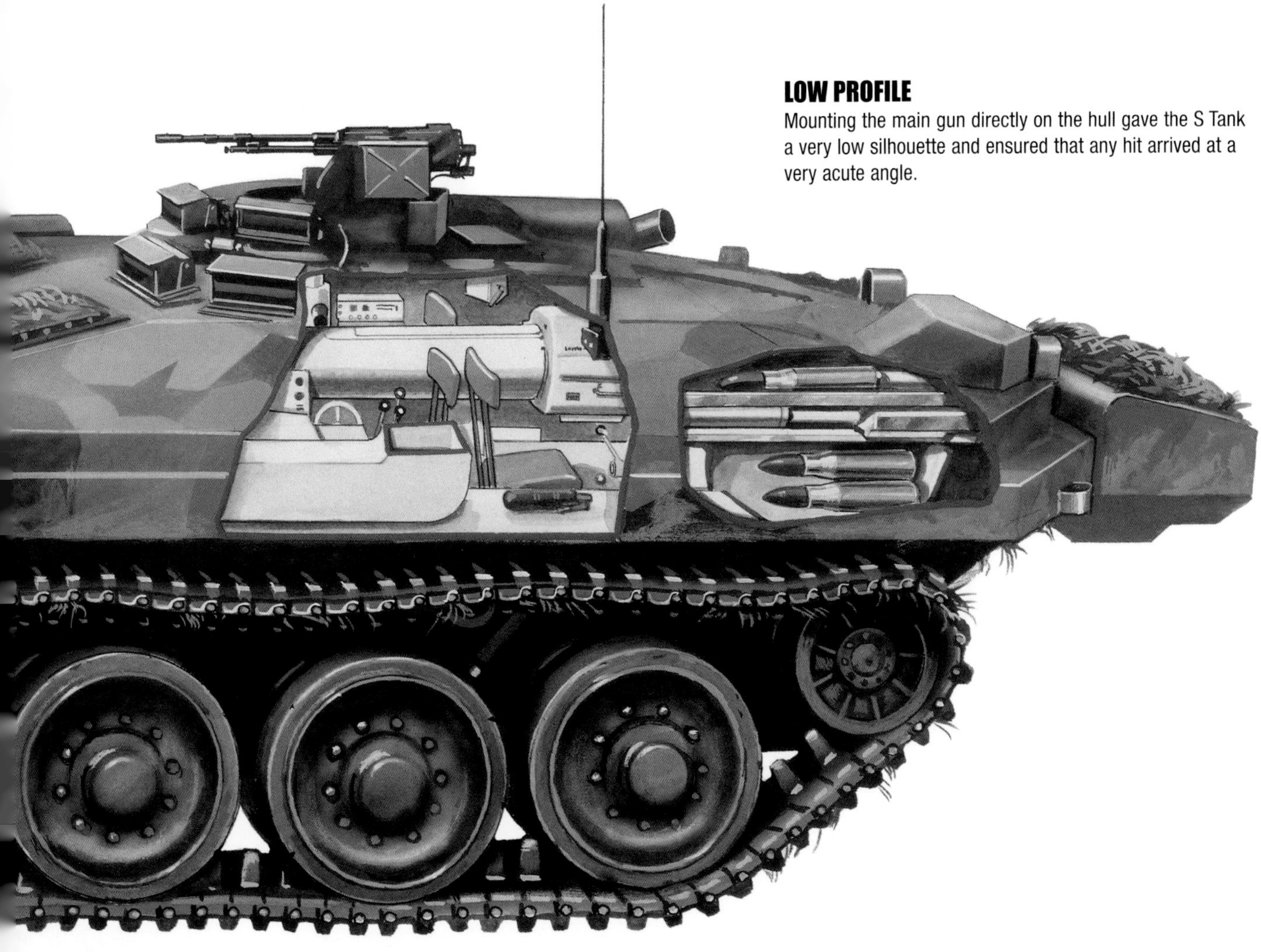

The S Tank was well suited to its intended role, but would be severely hampered in a conventional gun tank mode. Training reflected these advantages and limitations.

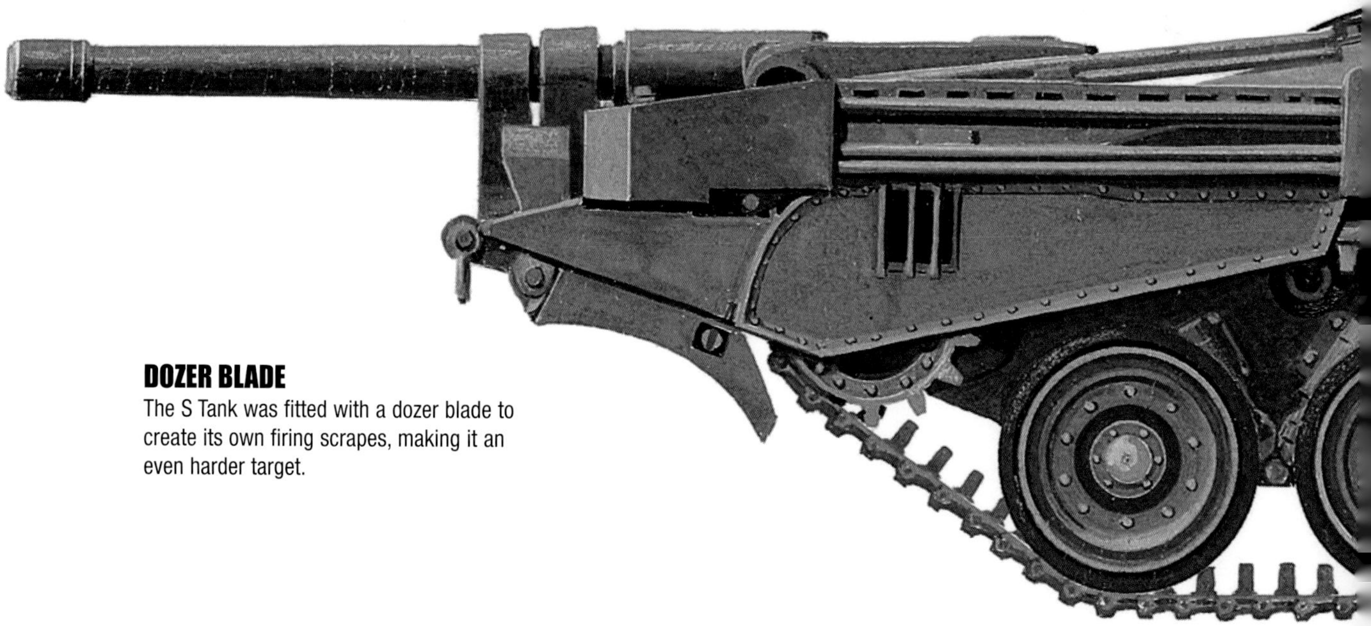

DOZER BLADE

The S Tank was fitted with a dozer blade to create its own firing scrapes, making it an even harder target.

TANK DESTROYER TACTICS

Sweden's political stance was such that its forces never expected to fight a war outside home territory. The most likely – and frightening – major war scenario was attempted annexation by the Soviet Union. While it was unlikely that Sweden could fight off an invasion alone, its forces could make the cost too high to be acceptable or delay the invading force until another solution presented itself.

To this end, the S Tank was designed for survivability in a tank destroyer role. Equipped with a dozer blade at the front, it was able to prepare its own firing scrapes, shooting from a hull-down position screened and protected by an earth bank with very little of the tank showing over the top. Once the position was compromised, a rapid retreat would be made in reverse, with the radio operator taking over driving using his own rear-facing controls. Turning around would take time and expose the more vulnerable sides of the tank to enemy fire, necessitating an early retreat or else running grave risks. By optimizing the tank to run in reverse, its heaviest armour could thus be presented to the advancing enemy at all times.

AMPHIBIOUS CAPABILITY

The S Tank could be prepared for a water crossing in under half an hour, using a flotation screen.

ALL-TERRAIN OPERATIONS

The S Tank's home landscape included marshy and mountainous regions, forests and open farmland. It was designed from the outset to operate equally well in all such terrain.

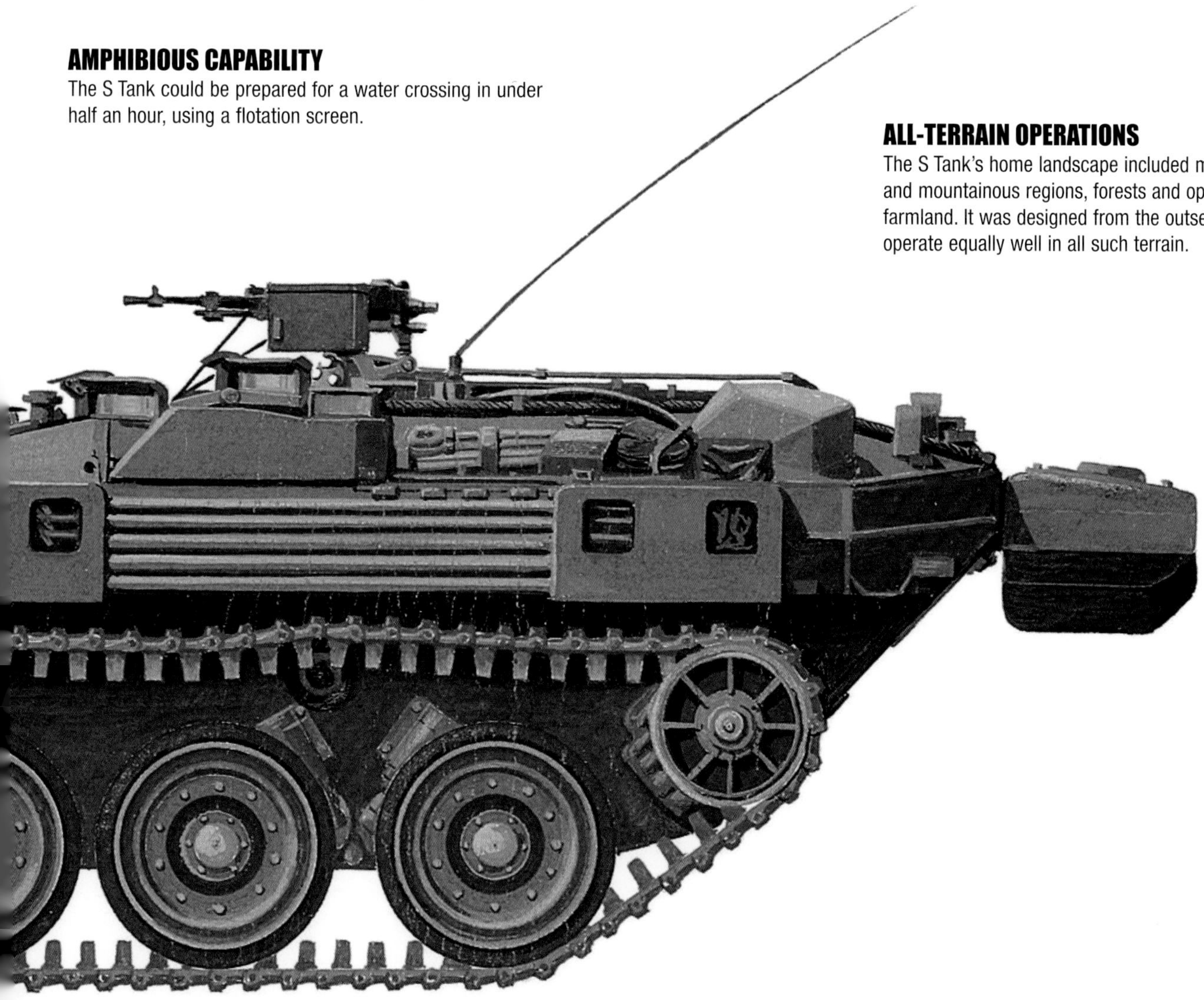

NOVEL DESIGN, PROVEN COMPONENTS

Although the S Tank's design was unusual, with both the driver and commander able to drive and fire the main gun, the gun itself was the well-proven 105mm (4.1in) currently arming many NATO tanks. At the time, this gun could penetrate any known Soviet tank – and those of any other nation – and was supplemented by two co-axial machine guns in fixed mounts. An additional machine gun was mounted on the commander's cupola for anti-aircraft and infantry defence work.

The S Tank's powerplant was also unusual. A conventional diesel engine provided sufficient power to drive under normal conditions and to aim the tank's weapon. When necessary, this was supplemented by a turbine to increase tactical speed. The original turbine was not powerful enough, so an uprated engine was fitted on the Strv-103 B model. Another round of upgrades added improved fire control, creating the S-103 C, but the S Tank was retired from service in the early 1990s before being tested in combat.

Leclerc

The French-built Leclerc main battle tank, although much better protected than the preceding AMX-30, is still the most lightly armoured of all Western MBTs. Whether this was a good design choice remains to be seen, as the Leclerc has not to date seen action against other tanks.

DEVELOPMENT BEYOND AMX-30

The AMX-30 was followed by a project designated AMX-32, which featured improved armour and a choice of 105mm (4.1in) or 120mm (4.7in) main guns. Developed for the export marketplace, AMX-32 was not successful there but the project did influence the AMX-30B variant. The following AMX-40 was equally unsuccessful in the tough export market of the 1980s.

The project leading to the Leclerc MBT benefited from the development work done on these designs. Mobility was still emphasized, but not to the extreme seen on the AMX-30. Composite armour, first trialled on the AMX-32, was incorporated into its design along with other forms of protection. Rather than the huge slabs of Chobham armour used by the Abrams and Challenger, the Leclerc's armour is in modular blocks. This facilitates removal of

A Leclerc in front of the Arc de Triomphe, Paris. The Leclerc's 52-calibre gun gives a higher muzzle velocity than most similar weapons.

SPECIFICATIONS (LECLERC)

Dimensions: Length: 9.87m (32ft 4.5in), Height: 2.53m (8ft 3.5in), Width: 3.71m (12ft 2in)

Weight: 49.9 tonnes (55.1 tons)

Engine/powerplant: SACM V8X-1500 diesel engine

Speed: 72km/h (44.7mph)

Armament: Main gun: 120mm (4.7in) smoothbore gun, Co-axial: 7.62mm (0.3in) machine gun, Turret top: 12.7mm (0.5in) machine gun

Crew: 3

MAIN GUN

The 120mm (4.7in) GIAT gun uses ammunition that is compatible with NATO rounds. The turret was designed especially to accommodate this main gun.

ARMOUR

The hull and turret are welded steel. Their basic armour thickness is increased with modular armour containing Kevlar and ceramics, along with tungsten and titanium.

A Leclerc tank goes through its paces in a desert landscape. With its 120mm (4.7in) gun and advanced fire-control electronics, the Leclerc is a quantum leap ahead of the AMX-30 main battle tank that it replaced.

CREW

The Leclerc had a crew of just three: driver, gunner and commander.

damaged sections or replacement by improved armour. Developed in the 1980s, the Leclerc also benefited from emerging 'stealth' technologies. The tank's radar signature was reduced by using a small, two-man turret – made possible by the use of an autoloader – and by radar-absorbent coatings. Like many modern tanks, the Leclerc has a laser warning system, which indicates when a rangefinder or designator is aimed at the tank. Smoke grenades or a rapid repositioning can be used to break the laser lock. Launch tubes for 80mm (3.1in) grenades can deliver smoke, infrared decoys or anti-personnel grenades to deter infantry attack.

The main gun is a 120mm (4.7in) smoothbore with a slightly longer barrel than is common on Western MBTs. This contrasts with the tank's overall small size, giving the impression of a much bigger gun. Experiments have been carried out with a larger calibre weapon, although gun calibres have tended to remain much the same in recent years. Instead, lethality is increased by advanced ammunition and targeting systems.

UPGRADES AND VARIANTS

The Leclerc went into French service in 1992. A 'tropicalized' version was bought by the UAE, entering service there in 1995. Production took place in several batches, each incorporating improvements on the last. These include modified armour and the elimination of mechanical defects. In 2006 an urban warfare kit appeared, consisting of composite armour side skirts and additional protection from both rocket-propelled grenades and incendiary devices. A remote-controlled machine gun allows the crew to engage personnel targets from behind armour. In recent years, information sharing and handling has become increasingly important to military operations. The Leclerc is fitted with an advanced battlefield-management system, giving the tank commander access to a wide range of information, presented graphically as customizable maps. The result is an enhanced ability to cooperate with other forces including infantry, air support and artillery.

Armoured recovery and armoured engineering vehicle versions of the Leclerc also exist. The engineering vehicle can be outfitted for mine clearance or can employ a variety of tools in modular mountings. Other prospective variants include a heavy reconnaissance vehicle and export variants for a number of potential customers. However, few overseas orders have materialized. This is due at least in part to the Leclerc's very high price tag.

TURRET
The turret is is a two-man design, the crew's loader being replaced by an autoloader.

DRIVER
The Leclerc's driver sits forward in the hull to the left. The commander and gunner are seated in the turret to the left and right.

The Leclerc has served in Lebanon and Kosovo in operations in support of peace, but has never been involved in a major war.

M3 Lee/Grant

39

The M3 medium tank was an interim measure intended to get a 75mm (2.9in) gun onto the battlefield as quickly as possible. Despite an inefficient armament layout, the M3 was effective in combat. Its 75mm (2.9in) hull-mounted gun was especially useful against static positions in an infantry support role.

BIGGER GUNS NEEDED

At the outbreak of World War II, the US military lacked an effective medium tank. The M2 was so disappointing that it was used only in a training role. By 1940, work was underway that would produce the M4 Sherman, but there were many problems to be overcome before production could begin. Among these was the creation of a rotating turret capable of taking the 75mm (2.9in) gun deemed necessary to engage well-armoured German tanks.

Those guns were urgently needed by both the USA and Britain, so the M3 was conceived as a temporary measure. Drawing on the M2 design, it was to mount a 37mm (1.4in) gun in a rotating turret, with the 75mm (2.9in) gun in a hull sponson. Although this limited the weapon's arc of fire and could be a liability in a fluid engagement, it was a much simpler arrangement than placing the gun in a turret, enabling the M3 to go into production very quickly.

TURRET
The small turret of the M3 was only able to accommodate a 37mm (1.4in) gun.

MAIN GUN
The main 75mm (2.9in) gun was mounted on a sponson in the hull.

SPECIFICATIONS (M3 GRANT)

Dimensions: Length: 5.64m (18ft 6in), Height: 3.12m (10ft 3in), Width: 2.72m (8ft 11in)

Weight: 24.2 tonnes (26.7 tons)

Engine/powerplant: Continental R-975-EC2 petrol engine

Speed: 42km/h (26mph)

Armament: Hull-mounted: 75mm (2.9in) M2 or M3 gun, Turret-mounted: 37mm (1.4in) M5 or M6 anti-tank gun, Additional: 2–4 x 7.62mm (0.3in) M1919 machine guns

Crew: 6

BALANCE

The main turret was offset to the left, shifting the weight for balance with the installation of the 75mm (2.9in) gun in the hull.

SUSPENSION

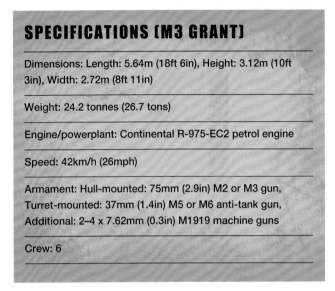

The vertical volute suspension was used in many American models, including the more famous Sherman tank.

39

The resemblance between the M3 Lee/Grant and M4 Sherman was not coincidental. The general hull design and many components were common to both tanks.

LEE AND GRANT

The British practice of naming US tanks after Civil War generals was eventually adopted by the US as well. In the meantime, the standard M3 was named 'Lee' and the version supplied to Britain under lend-lease as 'Grant'. The primary difference was a larger turret to accommodate radio equipment, allowing the radioman to also load the 37mm (1.4in) gun and thereby reducing crew size. The two can be told apart most easily by the lack of a commander's cupola on the Grant.

Several developed versions of the Lee and Grant emerged, and the project also proved useful in hastening the arrival of the M4 Sherman. The M3 was the basis for the Canadian Ram cruiser tank, which had obvious visual similarities to the M3 and M4. Other derivative vehicles included the Priest and Sexton self-propelled guns. Numerous variants were also created, ranging from command tanks and personnel carriers to engineering and mine-clearance platforms. The hull was also used for the Canal Defence Light vehicle.

WARTIME SERVICE

British M3s were the first to see action, and generally performed well. Despite being vulnerable to flanking fire due to their slow speed and high profile, M3s inflicted serious losses on Rommel's Afrika Korps. The M3's armour proved effective against most weapons, and the 75mm (2.9in) gun could deal with targets previously invulnerable to Allied tank armament. The 37mm (1.4in) gun was still useful, especially from the flanks or against lighter targets.

US M3s initially fared less well than their British equivalents, largely due to the inexperience of their crews. Losses of M4 Shermans at the Battle of Kasserine Pass in Tunisia in February 1943 were made good by returning the M3 to service with some units. As these tanks were lost or broke down they were gradually replaced by new-build M4s. Smaller numbers were deployed to the Pacific, where their main gun was useful in engaging enemy strongpoints.

The M3 was also supplied to Russia, where it suffered heavy losses before being withdrawn from the main combat sectors. Facing obsolete tanks in secondary theatres, the M3 did better but was not well regarded by the Soviets.

A British Lee/Grant makes progress in the North African desert, 1942. The M3's 75mm (2.9in) gun was effective against most tanks and strongpoints, but its limited arc of fire was a liability in fast-moving desert warfare.

ARMOUR
The M3 had up to 76mm (3in) of armour on the sides of the hull and turret.

LEND-LEASE TANK
More than 4200 M3 tanks were shipped to the British and Soviet armies by the Americans during World War II.

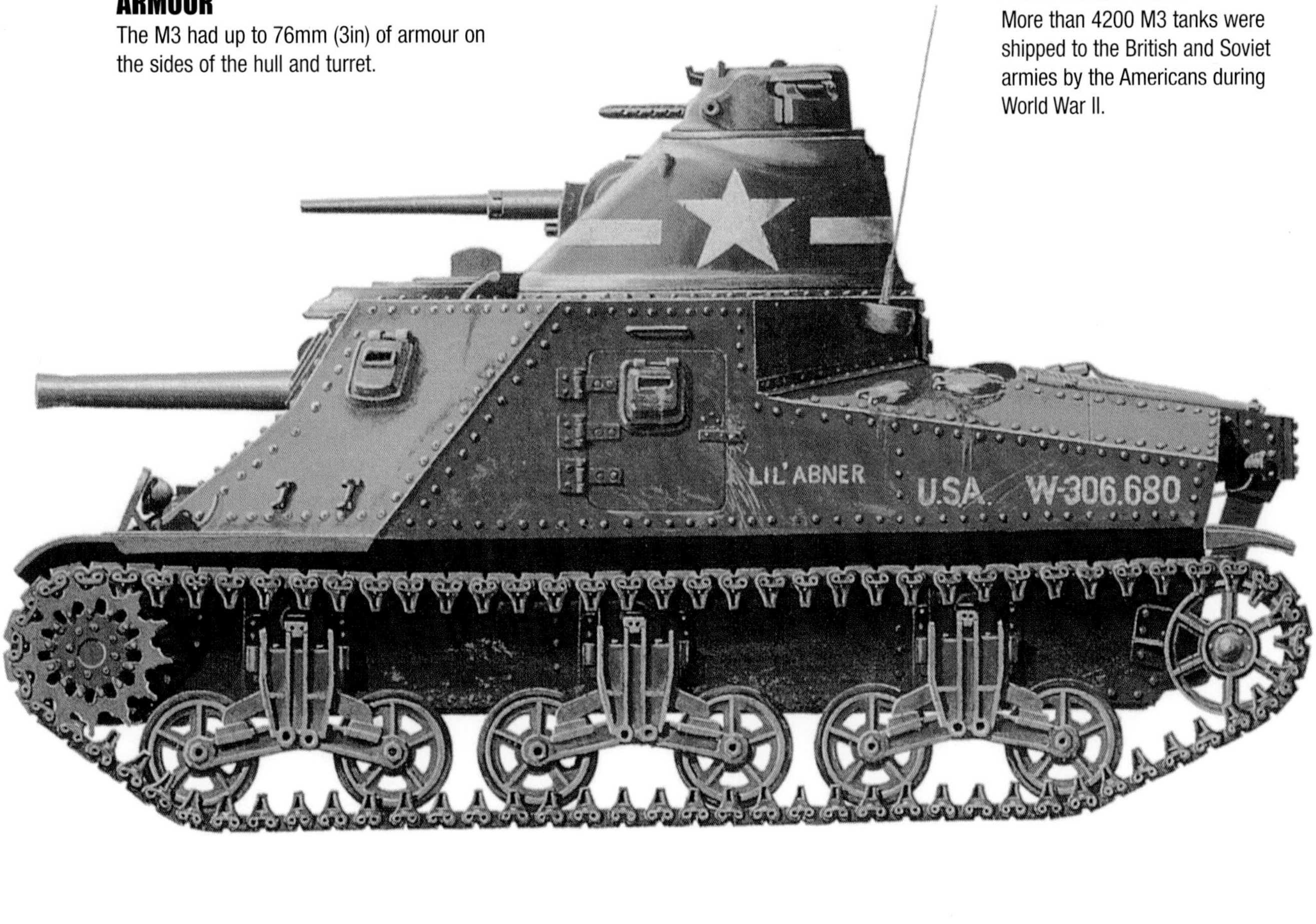

Vickers 6-ton Light Tank

The Vickers 6-ton, or Mark E, was a hugely influential design that was widely copied worldwide. Inexpensive, reliable and simple to operate, it offered a good balance of firepower, mobility and protection on the battlefields of the day. The Soviet T-26 and Polish 7TP were both derived from the Vickers 6-ton.

BIGGER AND BETTER TANKETTE

During the inter-war years, 'tankettes' were the subject of much experimentation. As the name suggests, these were essentially a very small armoured vehicle mounting a machine gun. Armoured against small-arms fire, tankettes might be useful for reconnaissance or as mobile fire support platforms. However, their advantages did not offset their vulnerability and the concept was short-lived.

The Vickers 6-ton tank had much in common with these vehicles, especially the involvement of Carden and Lloyd in its development, but was considered a true – if very small – tank due to its possession of a rotating turret. In fact, the Type A variant of the 6-ton was equipped with two small turrets, enabling it to deliver machine gun fire in two directions at once.

Multi-turret tanks were not a success, however, and the Type B reverted to a more conventional single two-man turret. This initially carried a 47mm (1.8in) gun, but this was later replaced by a high-velocity 37mm (1.4in) gun. A co-axial machine gun was also mounted. This so-called 'duplex

SPECIFICATIONS (VICKERS 6-TON TYPE E)

Dimensions: Length: 4.57m (15ft), Height: 2.08m (6ft 10in), Width: 2.42m (7ft 11in)

Weight: 6.3 tonnes (7 tons)

Engine/powerplant: Armstrong-Siddeley 4-cylinder petrol engine

Speed: 32km/h (20mph)

Armament: Type A: 2 x 7.7mm (0.3in) machine guns, Type B: 47mm (1.8in) gun with co-axial 7.7mm (0.3in) machine gun

Crew: 3

POLISH 7TP LIGHT TANK

Based on the Vickers Mk E, the 7TP was fitted with a Saurer diesel engine and thicker armour. It was armed with two 7.92mm (0.3in) machine guns.

Vickers 6-ton tanks of the Type A design. The twin turret configuration was inefficient but reasonably effective in an infantry support role.

In its day, the 'duplex mounting', with both a machine gun and a main gun in the same turret, was ground-breaking, but it quickly became standard on all tanks.

mounting' set the pattern for tank armament thereafter, eliminating the need for mixed units of 'male' and 'female' tanks to deal with different targets.

COMMERCIAL SUCCESS AND OVERSEAS SERVICE

The Vickers 6-ton was offered to the British Army, which did not adopt it. It was widely exported, however, with many clients taking quantities of both the Type A and Type B variants. Some users modified their tanks to fit locally produced armament. Others produced derived versions that eventually acquired an identity of their own. Among these were the Russian T-26 and Polish 7TP.

The Vickers 6-ton tank saw action in the early 1930s during the Chaco War between Bolivia and Paraguay. Although not well handled, the tanks proved useful in a fire support role, but were not quite impervious to small-arms fire. Rifle bullets failing to penetrate the armour might still injure crewmembers due to spallation.

Vickers 6-ton tanks in Siamese (Thai) service were successful against French FT17s, but those used by China were less effective against the Japanese army during the Sino–Japanese War. On some occasions, original 6-ton tanks fought against derived versions, such as during the Winter War of 1939–40. Finnish 6-ton tanks were fitted with a locally made 37mm (1.4in) weapon, whereas the Russian T-26 had been developed from the 6-ton into what was essentially a new design.

The T-26 was produced in vast numbers and was the main Russian tank at the time of the German invasion in 1941. By then it was outmatched by heavier and better-protected tanks, and suffered enormous losses. Similarly, the Polish 7TP was outmatched against German tanks, but still gave a good account of itself. Many were lost for lack of fuel rather than to enemy action.

At the outbreak of World War II, a number of 6-ton tanks were under construction or awaiting delivery to overseas clients. These were co-opted by the British Army as training vehicles.

VICKERS MK A

The Vickers Mk A was thinly armoured, with just 19–25mm (0.75–1in).

MACHINE GUN

The Vickers Mk A was fitted with two individual turrets, each mounting a Vickers-brand 7.7mm (0.3in) machine gun.

SOVIET T-26 LIGHT TANK

The Soviets modified the basic design with a new turret and their own high-velocity, long-barrel anti-tank 45mm (1.7in) gun.

SOVIET PRODUCTION

The Soviets produced more than 12,000 T-26 light tanks during the 1930s, and the model was still the mainstay of the Red Army's armoured forces when the Germans invaded in 1941.

T-14 Armata

Currently entering Russian service, the T-14 Armata incorporates a host of advanced features and has been hailed as the first of a new generation of main battle tanks. Whether it lives up to its reputation remains to be seen; other tanks have been lauded as world-beaters at their first appearance.

LEGACY EQUIPMENT

Russia struggled through economic and political upheaval after the end of the Cold War, with little money for advanced military systems. This was in some ways offset by the vast amount of military equipment already in service. This situation tends to occur at the end of a large-scale war, and usually results in a period of making do with the legacy equipment followed by an urgent need to implement new systems. Whereas a power will normally upgrade or replace its military equipment on an ongoing basis, the phenomenon of block obsolescence can make the process of catching up very expensive.

Russian tank design did not halt entirely after the fall of the Soviet Union. Upgraded versions of the T-72 appeared, along with more advanced T-80 and T-90 main battle tanks. The T-80, along with other tanks of a similar

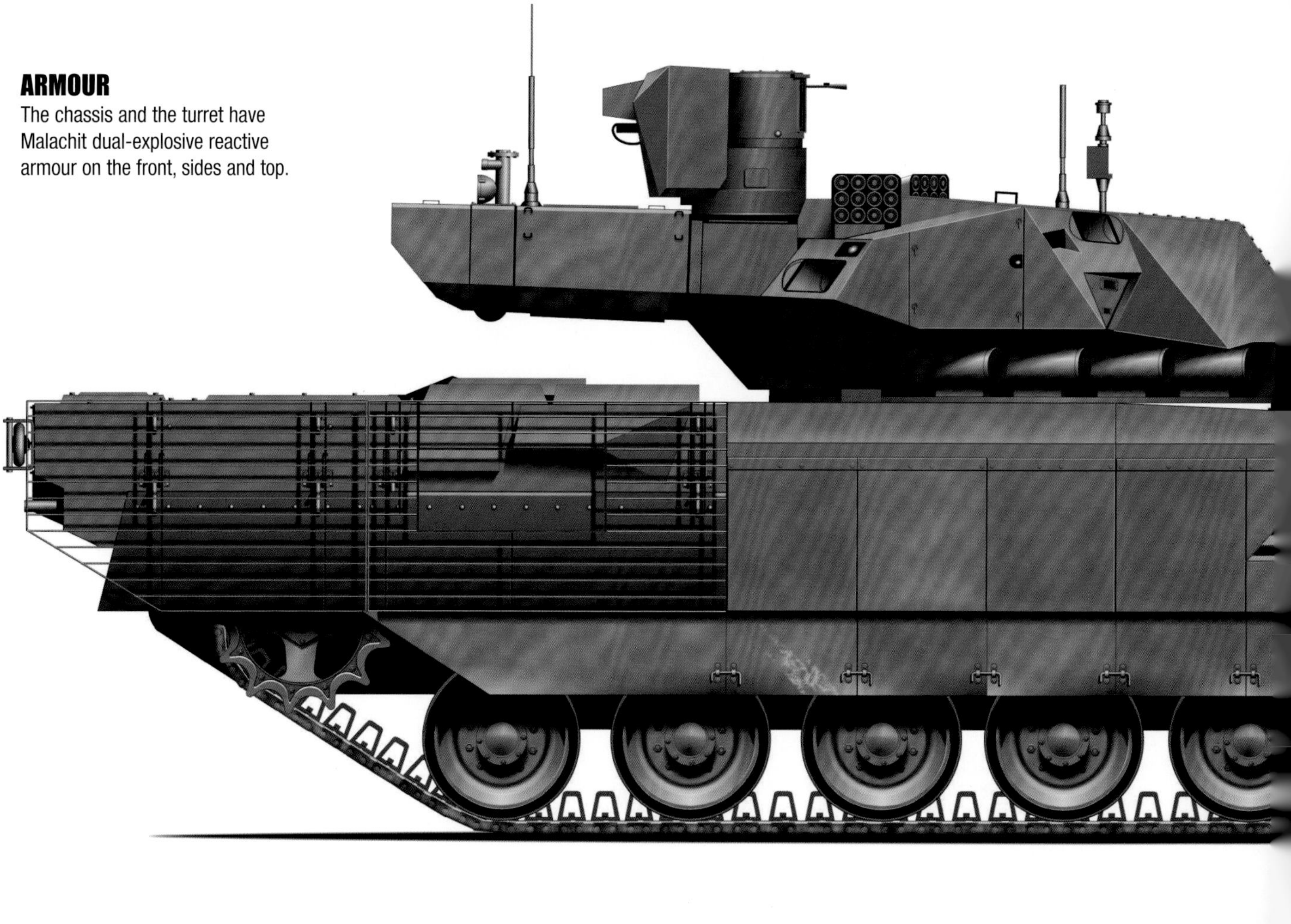

ARMOUR

The chassis and the turret have Malachit dual-explosive reactive armour on the front, sides and top.

SPECIFICATIONS (T-14 ARMATA)

Dimensions: Not known

Weight: 43.5 tonnes (48 tons)

Engine/powerplant: A-85-3A turbocharged diesel engine

Speed: 90km/h (55.9mph)

Armament: Main gun: 2A82-1M 125mm (4.9in) smoothbore gun; other or additional armament possible, Remote-controlled weapon station: 7.62mm (0.3in) or 12.7mm (0.5in) machine gun

Crew: 3

The T-14 is an advanced and impressive design, but one that has yet to prove itself in combat against other armoured forces.

MAIN GUN

The main armament of the T-14 is the 2A82-1M 125mm (4.9in) smoothbore cannon.

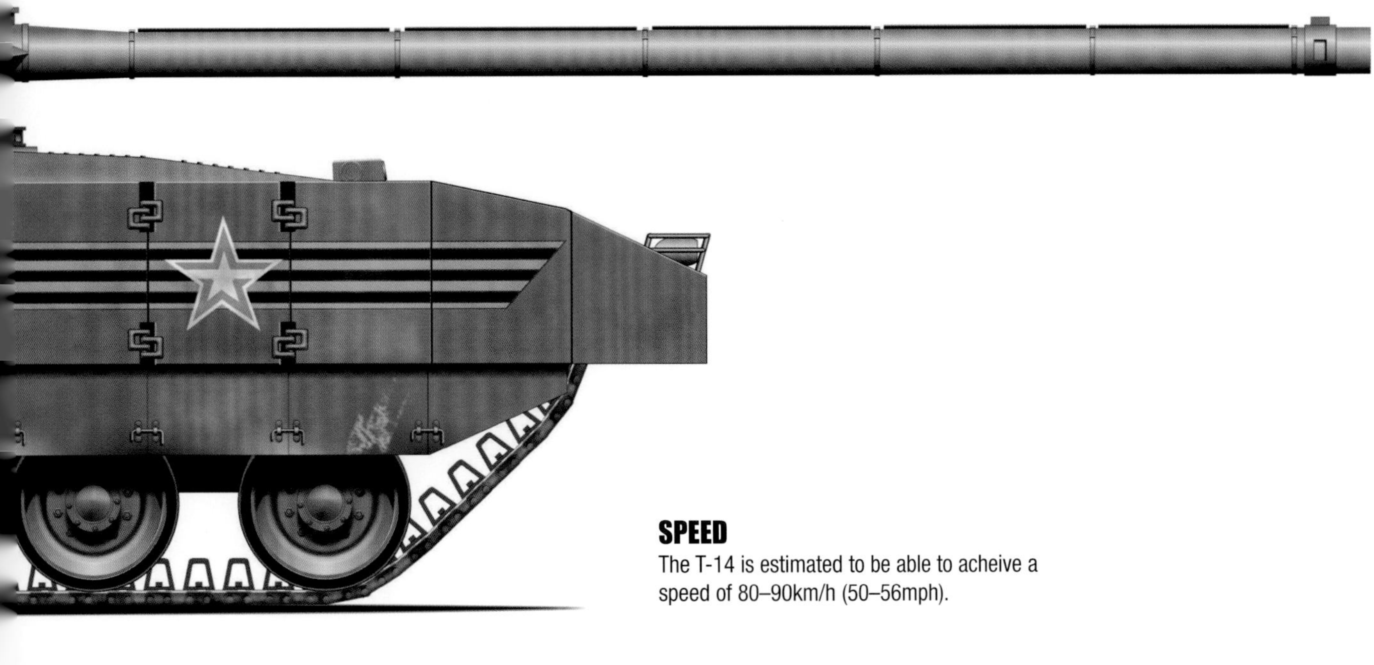

SPEED

The T-14 is estimated to be able to acheive a speed of 80–90km/h (50–56mph).

vintage, adopted a turbine powerplant instead of the more conventional diesel or multifuel engine. No new tank designs appeared for some years, although there were attempts; upgrade programmes were also implemented.

MODULAR DESIGN

The T-14 Armata, officially presented to the world in 2015, is constructed on a modular basis. The crew of three is contained in an armoured capsule in the frontal section of the tank, with the engine in a separate compartment at the rear. Between them is the turret mechanism. The turret is unmanned but supports a range of advanced electronics equipment. It contains a 125mm (4.9in) smoothbore gun capable of firing conventional ammunition or guided missiles, and an autoloader that serves the gun. It has been suggested that a 152mm (5.9in) gun could be fitted instead, or perhaps other weapons.

Protection incorporates advanced versions of traditional concepts, such as a low silhouette and good mobility, and advanced armour tailored to the likely threats a tank faces in the modern battlespace. Reactive armour is used on the frontal areas to disrupt shaped-charge weapons, whereas the rear sections feature bar armour intended to counter the lighter warheads of rocket-propelled grenades. An active protection system is also incorporated, and Russian designers claim it is capable of successfully defending the tank against even high-velocity kinetic penetrators. Interception of relatively slow-moving and fragile missiles and grenades has been possible for many years, but while a shower of fragments from an intercepting weapon might 'hard kill' a missile, it is unlikely to do much damage to a depleted uranium penetrator, even if it can make the intercept in time. In theory, it might be possible to destabilize the projectile sufficiently that the tank's armour will defeat its reduced ability to penetrate. It remains to be seen whether the system will be effective in combat.

The modular design is well suited to the creation of a whole family of vehicles on the same chassis. An advanced Infantry Fighting Vehicle is a likely prospect, along with a variety of specialist platforms created as the need arises. This may go some way towards offsetting the expense of creating an advanced piece of hardware by spreading the development costs between a large number of gun tanks and other vehicles.

The T-14 Armata has well-sloped armour with few external features to act as a shell trap. This gives it a clean and futuristic look.

The T-14 Armata gives its crew enhanced protection by housing them in the hull. A disabling hit to the turret might leave the entire crew unharmed.

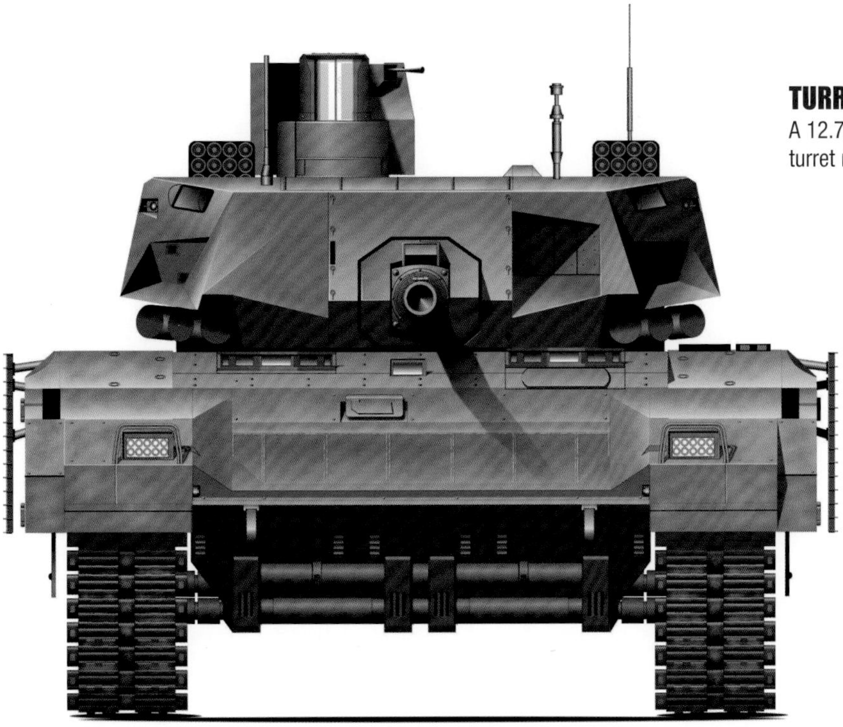

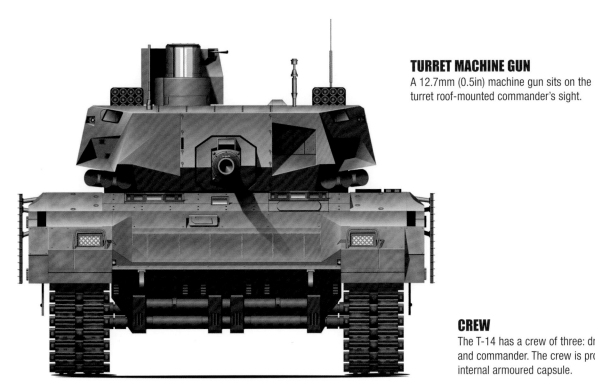

TURRET MACHINE GUN

A 12.7mm (0.5in) machine gun sits on the turret roof-mounted commander's sight.

CREW

The T-14 has a crew of three: driver, gunner and commander. The crew is protected by an internal armoured capsule.

Whippet

36

Designed at a time when tanks were for the most part lumbering monstrosities, the Medium A – or Whippet – was built instead for speed and mobility. It carried only machine guns but was capable of penetrating a defensive line and causing mayhem in the enemy's rear area, pioneering the concept of armoured exploitation.

THE FIRST MEDIUM TANK

Designated Medium A, but also known as the Tritton Chaser (after its designer, Sir William Tritton), the Whippet was a different concept to the large and heavy breakthrough tanks already in service. These had proven that they could punch a hole in an enemy defensive line, but were unable to progress much beyond it due to mechanical issues, slow speed and limited fuel capacity. In theory, cavalry should have been able to exploit a gap made by the tanks, but this would still entail a hazardous crossing of no-man's land under fire from surviving positions. The solution was to create a new form of cavalry, combining the mobility of the horseman with the armoured protection of a tank.

The Medium A was produced to meet this need, and initially featured a rotating turret. This was not an innovation as such; the turret used came from an armoured car. However, the prototype Whippet was the first tank to feature such a system. Production versions instead used a fixed

Edward Patrick Morris, prime minister of Newfoundland, inspects a Whippet tank in July 1918. The design first saw action earlier that year.

SPECIFICATIONS (MEDIUM A WHIPPET)

Dimensions: Length: 6.1m (20ft), Height: 2.74m (9ft), Width: 2.62m (8ft 7in)
Weight: 12.7 tonnes (14 tons)
Engine/powerplant: Two Tylor JB4 petrol engines
Speed: 12.9km/h (8mph)
Armament: 4 x Hotchkiss 7.7mm (0.3in) machine guns
Crew: 3

The Whippet's exhaust was positioned in front of the crew compartment, resulting in fumes sometimes being vented back into the crew space.

MEDIUM MK A WHIPPET

The Whippet mounted four Hotchkiss machine guns, one on each side of its blocky fixed superstructure. Only one gunner was carried, but the commander could also man a gun.

CREW

The Whippet had a crew of three, all concentrated in the fighting compartment at the rear of the tank.

DRIVER

The Whippet was the first tank that could be driven by one man.

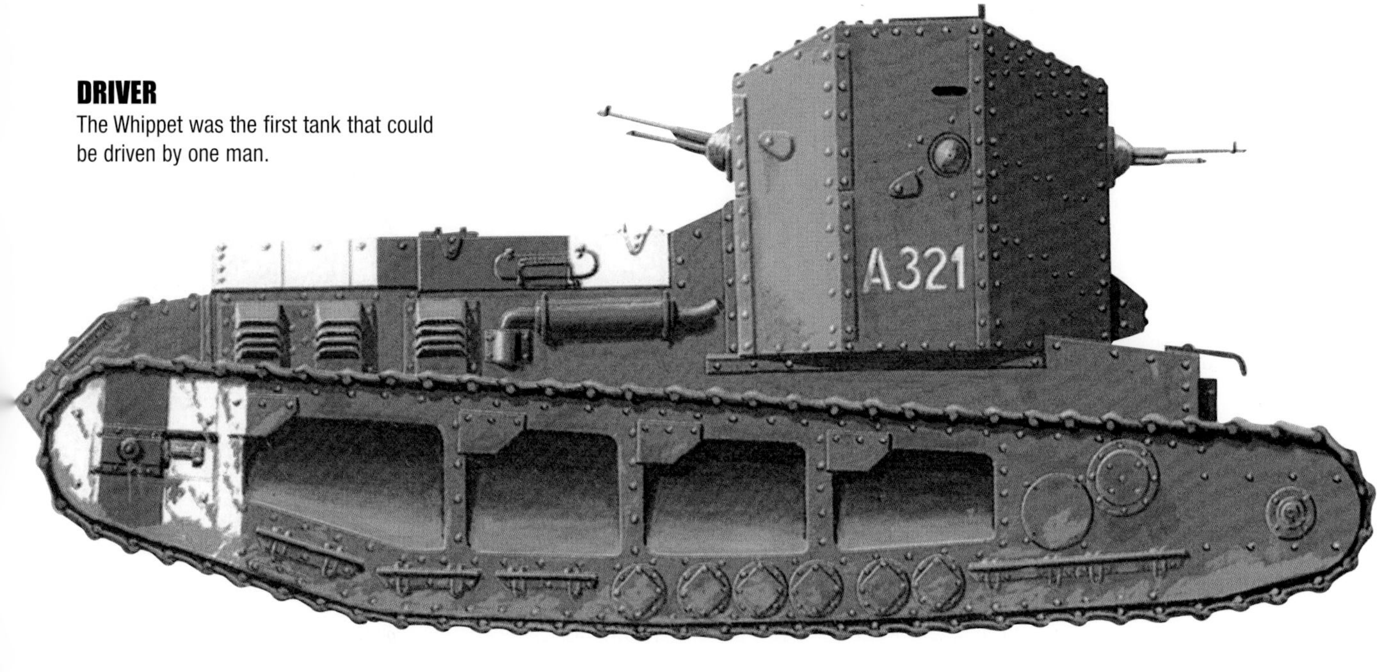

When not in action, the turret-top hatch provided ventilation as well as giving the commander improved vision. Fumes from the engine and guns made the Whippet's crew compartment all but intolerable.

box superstructure with a machine gun on each side, as fabrication of turrets would have held up an already slow production schedule. The three-man crew included only one gunner, making this arrangement highly inefficient even if the commander chose to man one of the guns.

The Whippet was very much a creature of its environment. Large mud chutes directed mud falling from the upper tracks out and down rather than allowing it to clog up the suspension, while the track design itself was well suited to cratered ground and trench crossing. Its name, implying very high speed, was appropriate only in comparison to other tanks.

WHIPPETS IN ACTION

The Whippet was not intended to supplant the existing heavy tank design, but instead to support them and exploit their breakthroughs. The first such exploitation took place in August 1918, when a small force of Whippets was reduced

Japanese Army Whippet tanks halt during a road march. Although primitive, the Whippet demonstrated that tanks could do more than break a defensive line. Armoured exploitation restored mobility to a battlefield previously dominated by trenches and artillery.

to a single tank by breakdowns and terrain hazards. This one Whippet, named Musical Box, was able to overrun an artillery battery and drive away the crews before being cut off behind enemy lines. Thus began a rampage that lasted several hours and inflicted heavy casualties. Musical Box was eventually disabled by a direct hit from a field gun, but in the meantime one tank had demonstrated its ability to severely disrupt enemy operations over a wide area.

A handful of Whippets were captured and went on to influence German tank development. However, the real contribution of the Whippet was to armoured doctrine. The idea of tanks bursting through the enemy line and going on to destroy supply and command centres in an 'expanding torrent' was shown as workable in 1918, although it was not until World War II that it became a reality. In the meantime, Whippets were sent to Russia, where experiments took place with a 37mm (1.4in) gun. The Whippet also served in Ireland, and a very small number were exported to Japan.

KV-85

Created in response to the arrival of the Panther and Tiger on the Eastern Front, the KV-85 was an interim design mating a powerful 85mm (3.3in) gun to the chassis of the KV-1 heavy tank. Theoretically formidable, the KV-85 was plagued by mechanical problems and vulnerable to the heavy guns of German panzers.

A NEW HEAVY TANK REQUIREMENT

Although Joseph Stalin himself was fond of heavy tanks, Soviet doctrine gradually swung away from them. The heavily armoured 'breakthrough tank' was of limited usefulness except against a fixed defensive line or when acting as one. The faster but more lightly protected T-34 was far more important to the defence of Russia than the KV series of heavy tanks. Indeed, efforts had been made to lighten a KV-1 (creating the KV-1S) and thereby give it greater mobility.

The appearance of heavily armoured German tanks caused a review of the move towards lighter tank designs.

GUARDS UNIT

The KV-85 equipped a number of elite Guards regiments in November 1943, as signified by the Guards emblem on the side of the turret.

MAIN GUN

The KV-85 mounted an 85mm (3.3in) gun, a much more powerful weapon than the 76mm (3in) weapon mounted on the KV-1.

ARMOUR

The front armour of the KV-85 was sloped to increase effectiveness. The hull armour was up to 75mm (2.9in) thick, while the turret had armour thickness of 110mm (4.3in).

SPECIFICATIONS (KV-85)

Dimensions: Length: 8.6m (28ft 2in), Height: 2.8m (9ft 2in), Width: 3.25m (10ft 8in)

Weight: 45.9 tonnes (50.7 tons)

Engine/powerplant: V-2 12-cylinder diesel engine

Speed: 42km/h (26mph)

Armament: Main gun: D-5T 85mm (3.3in) gun, 3 x 7.62mm (0.3in) machine guns – co-axial, front hull and turret rear

Crew: 5

The contribution of the KV-series of tanks to the Great Patriotic War (as the Russians referred to World War II) is memorialized by displays like this one, turning a weapon into its own statue.

MACHINE GUN
The turret mounted a rear-pointing 7.62mm (0.3in) DT machine gun.

In particular, there was a requirement for tanks mounting a more powerful gun than the 76mm (3in) that had become standard. Such weapons were available and had been used to good effect by tank destroyers. It was thus decided to create a KV-derived tank armed with an 85mm (3.3in) gun.

The initial prototype mated a modified KV-1 chassis with a turret developed for the KV-1S. There was little room for the 85mm (3.3in) gun, however, and the design proved unsatisfactory. More successful was a vehicle using the turret being developed for the IS-85 heavy tank. This tank went into production designated KV-85.

MIXED SUCCESS

The KV-85 possessed a very potent gun, capable at the time of penetrating any target. However, it was still plagued by mechanical troubles and had limited cross-country performance. The near-invulnerability of the KV-1 at the outset of the war was a thing of the past, as the KV-85 could be penetrated by a range of weapons. The use of the KV-85 as a breakthrough tank meant that it took the brunt of an initial clash, and losses were high.

Ultimately, fewer than 150 KV-85s were manufactured, in part due to the difficulty of obtaining sufficient quantities of D-5T guns. A range of vehicles were using the same 85mm (3.3in) weapon, creating competition in the supply chain. Among the competitors was the IS-85, which was also built in fairly small numbers. The two designs had the same turret, but the IS-85 had a wholly new hull and better armour.

VARIANTS AND THE IS-SERIES

Soviet tank designers experimented with an 'artillery tank' version of the KV-85, mounting a 122mm (4.8in) howitzer, and gun tanks with long 100mm (3.9in) and 122mm (4.8in) main guns. These variants did not go into production, but experimentation with them assisted in the development of the IS-1 heavy tank. The IS-1 started out with an 85mm (3.3in) gun, but later received 100mm (3.9in) and 122mm (4.8in) weapons. The IS-1 was not in production for long before it was replaced by the IS-2, which had a 122mm (4.8in) gun from the outset. Such large weapons were needed to reliably penetrate late-war German heavy tanks, and they set the standard for Soviet tank armament thereafter. The IS-3 appeared in 1945, just too late to take part in the final advance on Berlin. Although different in appearance, the IS-3 had much in common with its forebears, including some mechanical difficulties going all the way back to the original KV-1.

The KV-85G was a KV-1S chassis fitted with a turret designed around the powerful 85mm (3.3in) gun. The standard KV-85 used a KV-1 chassis.

CREW

The KV-85 had a crew of four: commander, gunner, loader and driver. The driving compartment was situated at the front and centre of the hull.

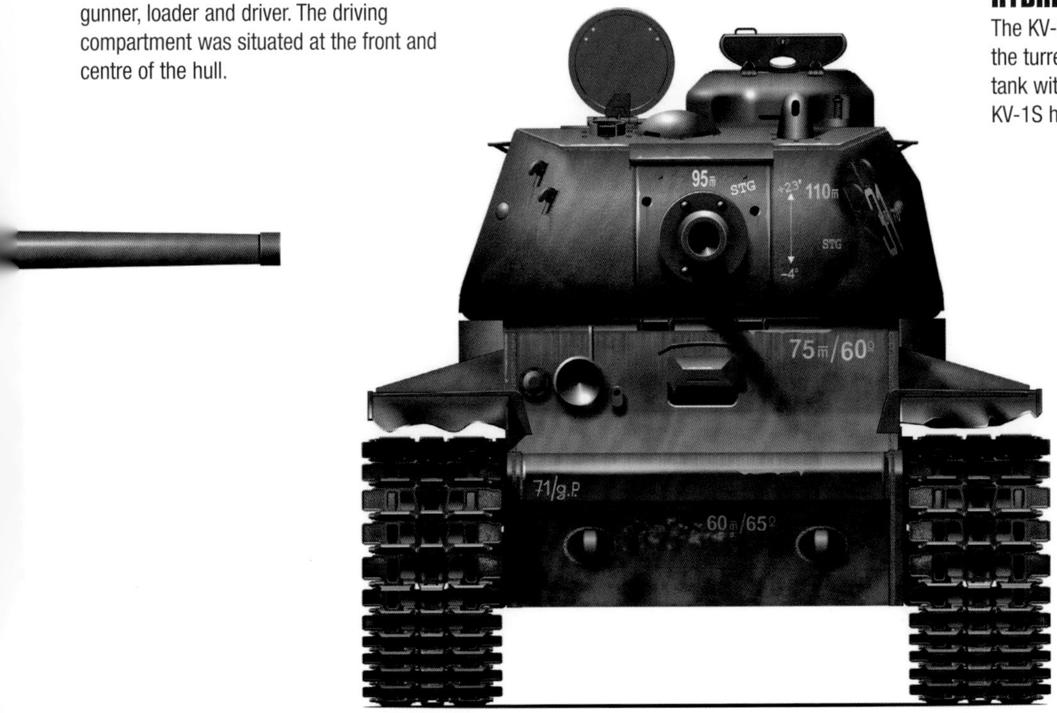

HYBRID

The KV-85 was created by combining the turret and gun of the new IS-85 tank with the chassis of the existing KV-1S heavy tank.

SPEED

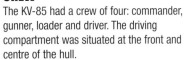

The KV-85 had a road speed of 42km/h (26mph), which was fast for a heavy tank.

M26 Pershing

The M26 was developed as a counter to heavy German tanks in World War II, but arrived only in the closing stages of the conflict. Its 90mm (3.5in) gun could easily penetrate a T-34, which might have been useful if the Cold War had turned hot in the early 1950s.

FALSE STARTS

In the inter-war years, the US military was far more interested in light and medium tanks than heavy models, and assigned a low priority to developing one. The need to tackle heavy German tanks meant that by the middle of World War II development was underway on what would become the M26 Pershing. Another project produced the M6 Heavy Tank, but it was not adopted for service. In addition to reliability issues, the M6 was undergunned for a heavy tank. The T20 series that eventually led to the M26 also mounted a similar gun (75mm/2.9in or 76mm/3in, depending on the variant) until the T25, which was fitted with a far more potent 90mm (3.5in) weapon.

The development of a heavy tank became far more urgent once M4 Shermans began encountering German Panthers and Tigers in Normandy. Thus far, the project had

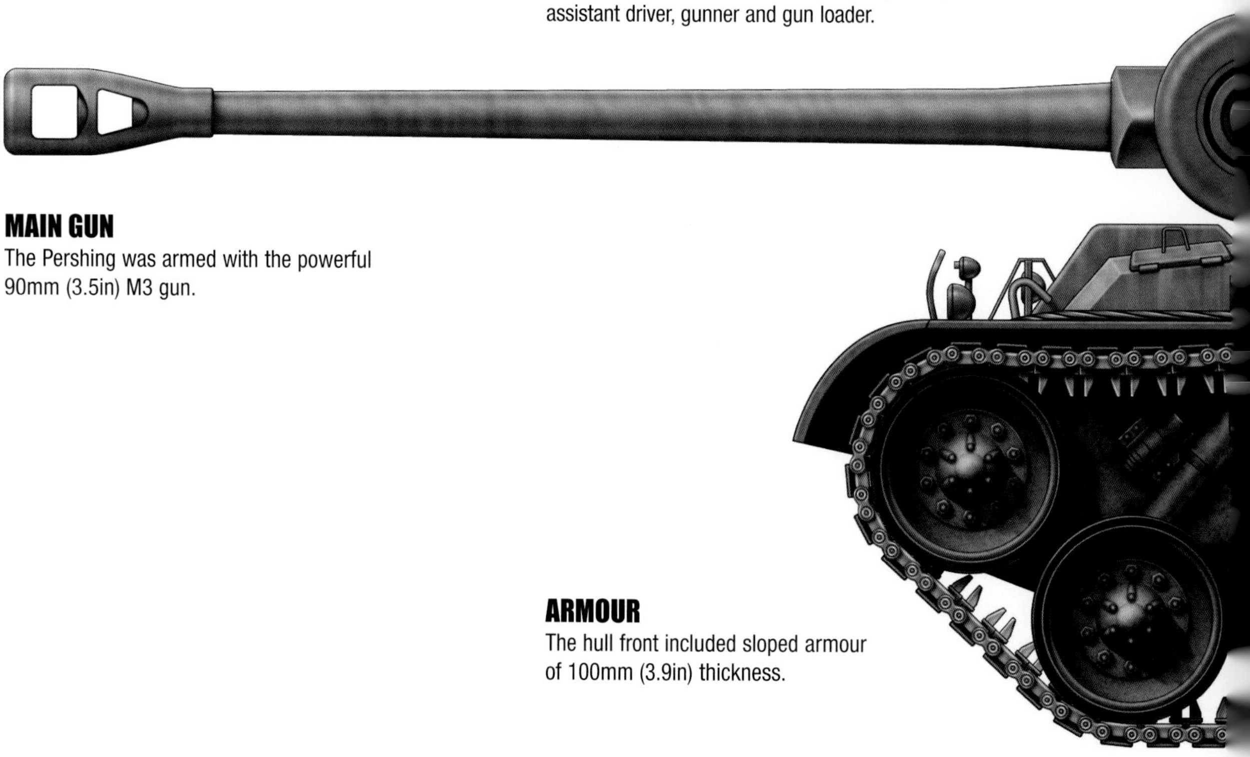

CREW
The M26 had a crew of five: commander, driver, assistant driver, gunner and gun loader.

MAIN GUN
The Pershing was armed with the powerful 90mm (3.5in) M3 gun.

ARMOUR
The hull front included sloped armour of 100mm (3.9in) thickness.

By the end of 1950, more than 300 M26 Pershings had been deployed in Korea. By that time, the majority of North Korean tank forces had been eliminated.

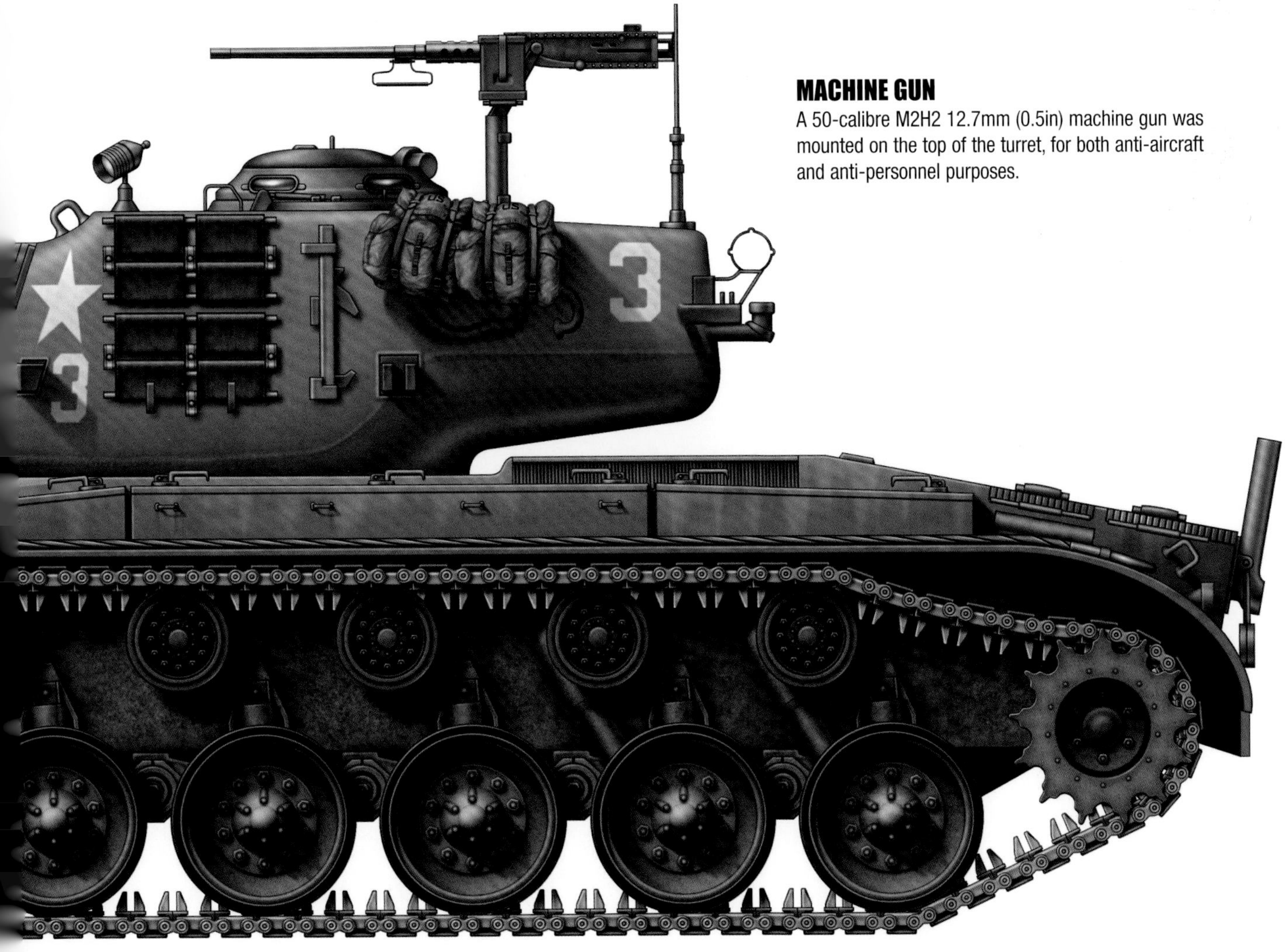

MACHINE GUN

A 50-calibre M2H2 12.7mm (0.5in) machine gun was mounted on the top of the turret, for both anti-aircraft and anti-personnel purposes.

34

The weight of the M26 meant that lighter tanks spearheaded the drive across the Rhine in 1945. The Pershings followed once the far bank was secure.

been used as an opportunity to experiment with various new systems, notably transmission and engines, but it was apparent that a new and heavily armoured tank needed to be put into the field as soon as possible. The T26E3 version was adopted for service as the M26 and went into production in November 1944.

PERSHINGS IN THE FIELD

The first M26 Pershings arrived in Europe in early 1944 and proved effective against the German Tiger. However, a more powerful round had to be developed to reliably penetrate the Königstiger, necessitating a change to the gun. Additional armour was also added as an expedient, and was standardized on the M26A1 that went into production after the end of the war.

By the time the Pershing entered combat in Europe the Axis forces were more or less completely defeated, and few actions occurred. Similarly, a small number were sent to assist in the capture of Okinawa but arrived too late. At the outbreak of the Korean Conflict in 1950, a handful of Pershings were rushed into action to try to stem the tide of defeat. Others followed in much larger numbers, but saw little combat against other tanks. On the occasions they did meet, Pershings proved entirely superior to T-34s in North Korean service. The Pershing did struggle with the Korean terrain, however, and was supplanted by the more mobile M46 Patton.

SPECIFICATIONS (M26 PERSHING)

Dimensions: Length: 8.61m (28ft 3in), Height: 2.77m (9ft 1in), Width: 3.51m (11ft 6in)

Weight: 37.3 tonnes (41.2 tons)

Engine/powerplant: Ford GAF 8-cylinder petrol engine

Speed: 48km/h (30mph)

Armament: Main gun: 90mm (3.5in) M3 gun, Co-axial: 7.62mm (0.3in) Browning M1919 machine gun, Turret top: 12.7mm (0.5in) M2 machine gun, Bow: 7.62mm Browning M1919 machine gun

Crew: 5

ALWAYS TOO LATE

The M26 Pershing has acquired a reputation of always being just too late to make a difference. Even in Korea, by the time

The M26 Pershing encountered T34/85s in Korea, where it proved equally capable of destroying them and withstanding hits from their guns.

it was deployed in significant numbers there were few enemy tanks left for it to fight. It stood ready in Europe to repel a Soviet invasion that never came, passing into Belgian service after being phased out by the US military. However, the Pershing marked a maturing of US tank design, which led to the M48 Patton.

While some of the concepts explored during the development of the Pershing did not work out, others were proven and remain in use today. The Pershing had a much lower hull profile than the M4 Sherman, although height to the turret top was almost exactly the same. The M26 also lacked the slab sides that made a clean contact by an enemy shell much more likely on an M4 than on later tanks.

Stingray

Stingray and Stingray II were developed by Cadillac-Gage for the export market. The intent was to provide the mobility and firepower of a larger and far more expensive tank on a lightly armoured hull. Although the project was not a marketplace success, the concept seems entirely viable.

LIGHTWEIGHT AND INEXPENSIVE

While various armoured platforms existed that could carry lighter weapons, it seemed in the early 1980s that a gap in the market existed for a light tank mounting a full-sized gun. In theory, such a vehicle would provide users with a credible armoured warfare capability at a modest price, enabling significant numbers to be fielded, or a cash-strapped government to field at least some tanks. There was also the consideration that fast-reaction forces would want a vehicle that was easily air-transportable but delivered real firepower.

Creating such a vehicle naturally resulted in some compromises. The Stingray used many components that were already available, and was technologically unsophisticated. This was a potential asset in other ways than purchase cost – a simpler vehicle could be maintained by less-well-trained personnel, and would incur lower through-life costs to keep it running.

The Stingray's armament was the proven L7 105mm (4.1in) rifled gun that was developed in Britain. At the time of the Stingray's entry to the marketplace, this gun was effective against any tank in the world. Even today it remains a credible threat, especially combined with the ability to rapidly outflank a heavier tank force. Armour was much lighter than that of a main battle tank, offering protection against armour-piercing heavy machine-gun ammunition in the frontal arc and small-arms fire elsewhere.

As a fire support platform or armoured reconnaissance vehicle the Stingray was entirely adequate and, although its electronics were not at the cutting edge of available technology, they were appropriate to their task. The stabilized gun was supported by a fire control computer, with thermal imaging and night-vision equipment available for the crew.

SPECIFICATIONS (STINGRAY)

Dimensions: Length: 9.3m (30ft 6in), Height: 2.55m (8ft 4.5in), Width: 2.71m (8ft 10.5in)

Weight: 18.9 tonnes (20.9 tons)

Engine/powerplant: Detroit 8V-92TA diesel engine

Speed: 70km/h (45mph)

Armament: Main gun: L7A3 105mm (4.1in) rifled gun, Co-axial: 7.62mm (0.3in) machine gun, Turret top: 12.7mm (0.5in) machine gun

Crew: 4

CREW

The Stingray has a crew of four: the driver, who sits in the hull front; and a commander, gunner and gun loader/radio operator, who sit in the turret.

MAIN GUN

The low recoil version of the British Royal Ordnance L7 105mm (4.1in) rifled gun is the tank's main asset: it is powerful, and shares most of its ammunition with NATO stocks.

ARMOUR

The Stingray's strength is its speed and manoeuvrability, which has meant it is lightly armoured, with just 23mm (0.9in) maximum on the hull and turret.

The only export success achieved by the Stingray was with the Royal Thai Army, which bought 106 models. This did not prevent other versions from being developed and offered for sale.

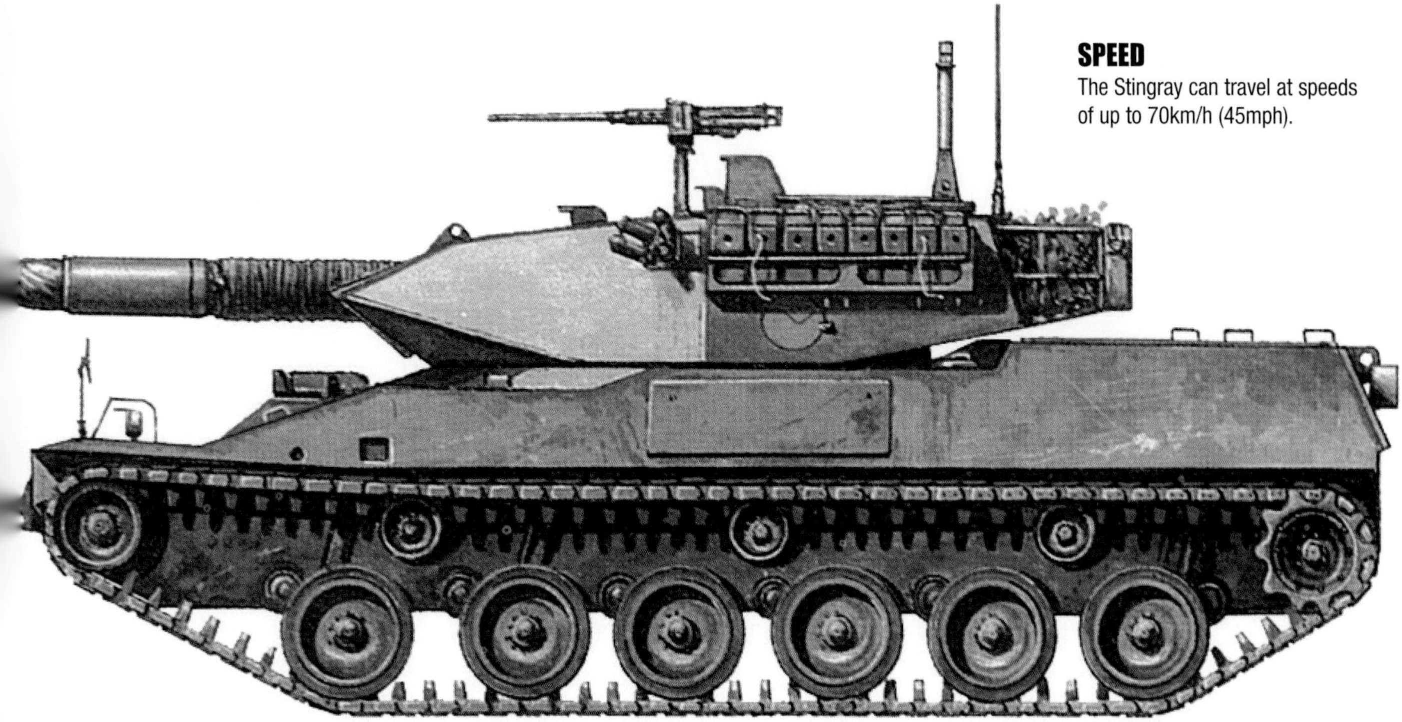

SPEED

The Stingray can travel at speeds of up to 70km/h (45mph).

33

Thai army Stingrays line up in two-tone camouflage. It may be that the changing nature of warfare results in renewed interest in vehicles like the Stingray. Any armoured capability is better than no armoured capability.

STINGRAY II

Towards the end of the 1980s, the Stingray achieved its only export success with an order from the Royal Thai Army. Variants and developed versions took part in a number of competitions and selection processes but ultimately were unsuccessful in finding buyers. Nevertheless, Stingray II was developed in the early 1990s. In addition to more advanced fire control systems, Stingray II was given improved suspension and thicker

armour. Although still only proof against 23mm (0.9in) cannon rounds, this could be augmented by appliqué sections.

The redesigned Stingray could also carry the turret developed for the fire support version of the LAV-25 used by the US Marine Corps. This included an autoloader for the 105mm (4.1in) gun, reducing the four-man crew of the original Stingray to three. Experiments with other armament indicated that it was possible to squeeze a compact 120mm (4.7in) gun into the turret. Stingray II reached the prototype stage, but was discontinued due to poor marketplace prospects. Renewed interest in lighter armed vehicles in recent years suggests that a similar low-weight, low-cost, air-transportable tank might eventually emerge. However, the armament/protection balance might be different, since such a vehicle might be expected to deal with low-intensity warfare situations rather than attempting to take on heavily armoured tanks.

T-72

The T-72 marked a return to the principles of simplicity and ease of manufacture for Russian designers. It was produced in very large numbers and remains in service today with many nations worldwide. Its 125mm (4.9in) gun can fire both conventional shells and guided anti-tank missiles.

DESIGNED FOR MASS PRODUCTION

In the mid-1950s, Soviet tank designers began work on a new main battle tank with some new features. Entering service as the T-64, this tank was the first Russian design to use composite armour, and had an autoloader to reduce crew requirements. Although advanced for its time, the T-64 was complex and slow to manufacture. Thus, even before the T-64 had entered service, a new tank, eventually designated T-72, was being developed.

The T-72 was designed from the outset to be cheaper and simpler than the T-64, and was built in huge numbers. At least 25,000 T-72s were constructed and supplied to Warsaw Pact members as well as to export customers worldwide. In appearance and general characteristics it followed standard Russian practice, with a low silhouette and rounded turret. Ergonomically it was also typically Russian, being cramped and uncomfortable to operate. Although the T-72 required a smaller crew than the T-64, this did not translate to more working space; instead, the tank was made smaller. This did improve survivability by presenting a lower and smaller target. The T-72 was built around its 125mm (4.9in) gun, capable of firing advanced anti-tank ammunition or guided missiles. Spaced composite armour provided good protection on the original 1973 model, and has been enhanced with panels of explosive reactive armour (ERA) to defeat shaped-charge weapons.

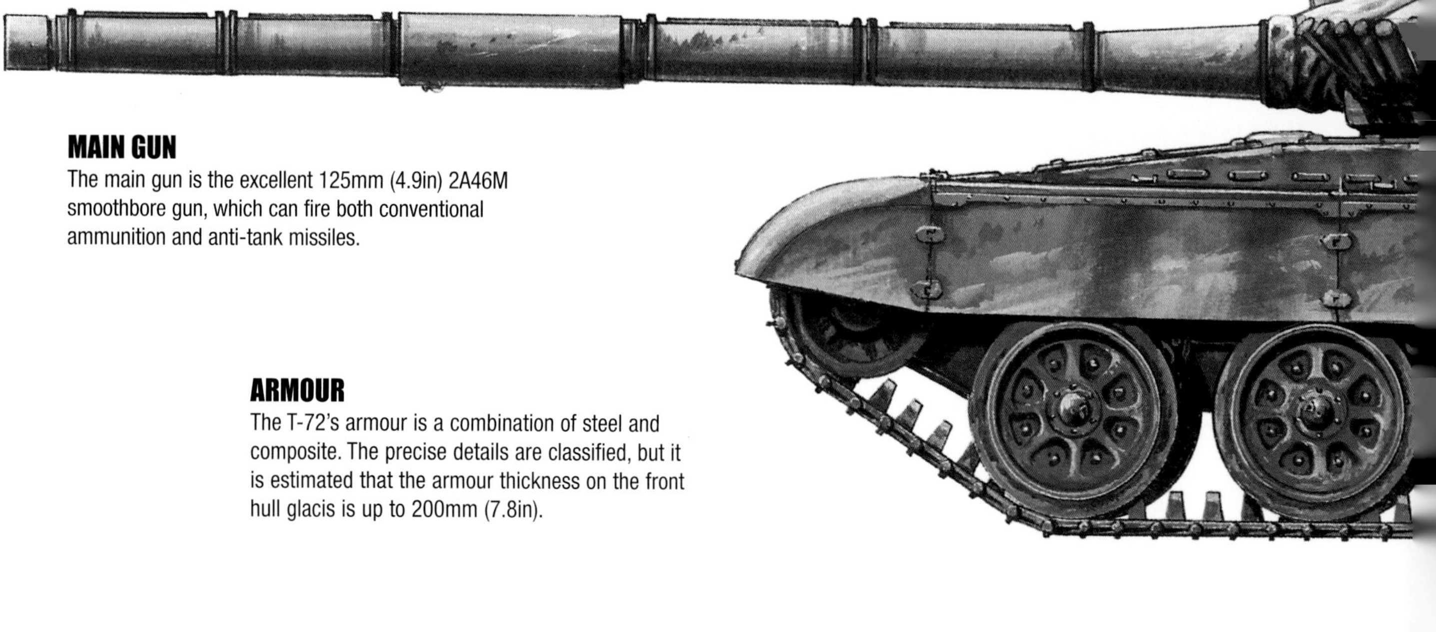

MAIN GUN

The main gun is the excellent 125mm (4.9in) 2A46M smoothbore gun, which can fire both conventional ammunition and anti-tank missiles.

ARMOUR

The T-72's armour is a combination of steel and composite. The precise details are classified, but it is estimated that the armour thickness on the front hull glacis is up to 200mm (7.8in).

SPECIFICATIONS (T-72)

Dimensions: Length: 9.53m (31ft 3in), Height: 2.22m (7ft 3in), Width: 3.59m (12ft 9in)

Weight: 40.6 tonnes (44.8 tons)

Engine/powerplant: V46 V12 diesel engine

Speed: 60km/h (37.3mph)

Armament: Main gun: 2A46M 125mm (4.9in) smoothbore gun (can launch Svir anti-tank missiles or conventional ammunition), Co-axial: 7.62mm (0.3in) machine gun, Turret top: 12.7mm (0.5in) machine gun

Crew: 3

The T-72 and its derivatives remain a potent symbol of Russian military power, and have taken part in May Day parades in Moscow for many years.

MACHINE GUN

A 12.7mm (0.5in) NSVT machine gun is mounted on the commander's cupola for anti-aircraft defence.

32

Armenia took delivery of around 150 export-model T-72M tanks, codenamed 'monkey' by NATO observers. 'Monkey' has become a slang term for downgraded export versions of other weapon systems.

POLISH PT-91

Poland was one of three countries to build the T-72 during the Cold War period. Following the break-up of the Soviet Union, Poland developed its own version of the T-72, the PT-91.

UPGRADE

Changes from the T-72 include a new and more powerful engine and an automatic gun loader. The main gun remains the same 125mm (4.9in) 2A46MS smoothbore.

VARIANTS AND EXPORTS

Like most similar tanks, the T-72 was upgraded during its service life. The mid-1980s T-72B received improved armour and electronics, including enhanced targeting systems for the gun and a new laser-guided anti-tank missile. The latest upgrade, appearing in 2013 and featuring advanced electronics and sighting systems, was designated T-72B3. However, not all variants were improved. Downgraded export versions lacking the missile launch capability and with reduced NBC (nuclear, biological, chemical) protection was offered for sale. Downgrades are usually for one of two reasons: to prevent the transfer of sensitive technologies, or to create a cheaper version to increase the number of possible export customers.

In addition to serving as the basis for Russian designs such as the T-90, the T-72 has been manufactured by several countries or used as the basis for locally produced tanks. The Polish PT-91 was derived from the T-72M1, an export version that has achieved some export success of its own. Meanwhile, Romania produced a version with an improved engine and enhanced armour. Other former Warsaw Pact members built their own variants. India also adopted the T-72M, designating it Ajeya. A quantity were purchased directly from the Soviet Union, after which local production began.

COMBAT OPERATIONS

The T-72 has seen action in several conflicts, notably in the Middle East. It performed well against Western-supplied tanks in the Iran–Iraq war of the 1980s, but was outmatched in the 1991 Gulf War. T-72s proved vulnerable to anti-tank missiles, although these were export versions with less effective armour than those in Russian service. Encounters between T-72s and the US M1 Abrams were very one-sided.

T-72s also saw action in the Balkans in the 1990s, and have performed well in asymmetric warfare situations where they came under attack with rocket-propelled grenades and improvised explosive devices. Although now a little dated, the design is sound and capable of being upgraded; given the large numbers built, continued service is certain for the foreseeable future.

ARMOUR

This PT-91 is fitted with additional explosive reactive armour (ERA) in the form of hundreds of tiles. These are estimated to increase the armour protection by 30–70 per cent.

Char B1

The French Char B was one of the best-protected tanks in the world at the outbreak of World War II. Its unusual design was intended to provide both anti-tank capability and infantry support on the same vehicle, but was not well suited to the task it faced in 1940.

CHAR DE BATAILLE

In the 1930s, French tank designers recognized that, along with punching holes in a defence line, tanks might have to engage other armoured vehicles. A mixed armament offered possibilities, but the multi-turreted tanks appearing at the time proved ineffective. A simpler and more practical solution was to create a heavily armoured breakthrough tank equipped with a heavy gun for infantry support and a lighter but higher-velocity weapon in the turret.

A hull-mounted gun made sense for infantry support, as the tank would be advancing towards a static target. However, the Char B made virtually no provision for traverse – the weapon was aimed and fired by the driver, who also had a fixed machine gun aimed in the same manner. He was assisted by a loader, but had to bring the ponderous vehicle to bear in order to use his weapons. The steering system was complex and prone to technical issues, further compounding the problem.

The turret-mounted 47mm (1.8in) gun did not produce a high enough muzzle velocity to penetrate thick armour, but was effective against lighter vehicles using high-explosive ammunition. The commander of the tank operated this

Although almost invulnerable to German tanks, the Char B1 was not well handled tactically or strategically. Many of the tanks were abandoned after being outflanked and bypassed.

ASSETS

The Char B1 had two formidable assets: its thick armour and good firepower, which made it a match for any tank on the Western Front in 1940.

CREW

The Char B1 had a crew of four: driver, main gunner, secondary gunner and commander.

A Char B during the early stages of the invasion of France. Clearly a product of 'Great War thinking', the Char B's size, shape and speed made it unsuited to mobile warfare.

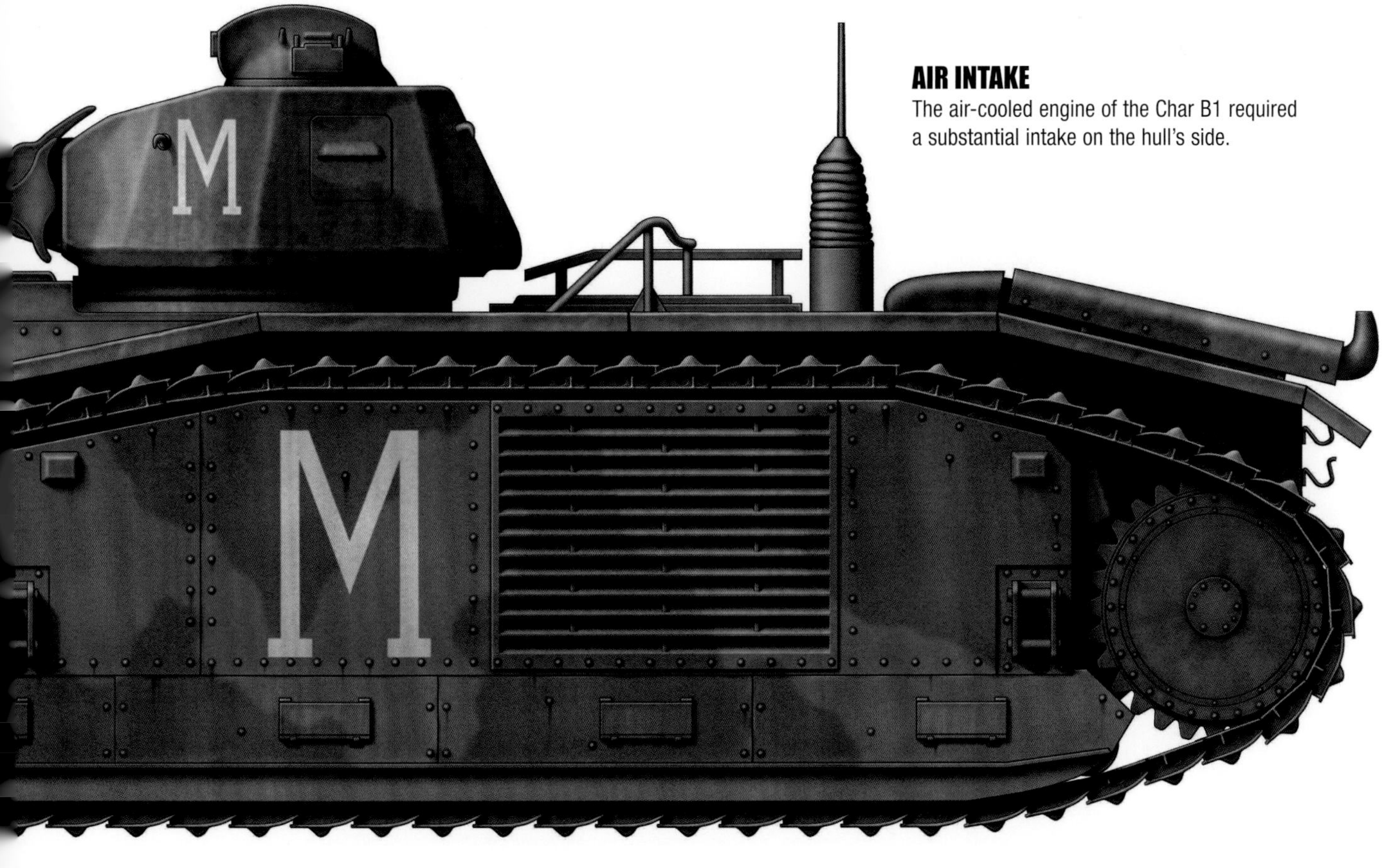

AIR INTAKE
The air-cooled engine of the Char B1 required a substantial intake on the hull's side.

31

SPECIFICATIONS (CHAR B1-BIS)

Dimensions: Length: 6.52m (21ft 5in), Height: 2.79m (9ft 2in), Width: 2.5m (8ft 2in)

Weight: 29 tonnes (32 tons)

Engine/powerplant: 6-cylinder Renault petrol engine

Speed: 28km/h (17.4mph)

Armament: Hull-mounted: ABS SA35 75mm (2.9in) gun and 75mm (2.9in) machine gun, Turret-mounted: 47mm (1.8in) SA35 anti-tank gun and 75mm (2.9in) machine gun

Crew: 4

weapon with some assistance from the radio operator. This arrangement reduced the efficiency of an already limited weapon.

In 1935, the improved Char B1-bis entered service. Along with a larger engine and thicker armour, it featured a longer turret gun that improved accuracy. A further upgraded model, designated B1 Ter, reached the prototype stage before war broke out.

IN DEFENCE OF FRANCE

French armoured warfare doctrine was very poor in 1940, although in any case the short operating radius of the Char B limited how it could have been used. The tank was deployed in its intended role during the Saar offensive of September 1939, where it supported a successful French advance that was halted by a change in French plans rather than serious opposition.

By the time of the German invasion of France, the Char B force was concentrated in reserve formations intended to support other forces. They were badly handled at the strategic level but performed well in action. Indeed, the Char B was immune to most anti-tank weapons; the Panzer IV with its 75mm (2.9in) gun posed a threat, but only at close range. Many Char Bs were destroyed after putting up a stiff fight, but they were deployed in 'penny packets' and became little more than isolated points of resistance.

The capabilities of this very well-protected tank were demonstrated when a lone Char B destroyed 13 enemy tanks and withdrew from the engagement intact despite receiving more than 100 hits. Others took part in counterattacks that were locally successful in many cases, but ultimately failed to halt the Axis advance. Captured Char Bs were used by the occupying forces against the Allied landings in Normandy; after the liberation of France, a handful were returned to their national forces. These were primarily used in mopping-up operations against pockets of resistance – a role to which they were well suited.

GUNS

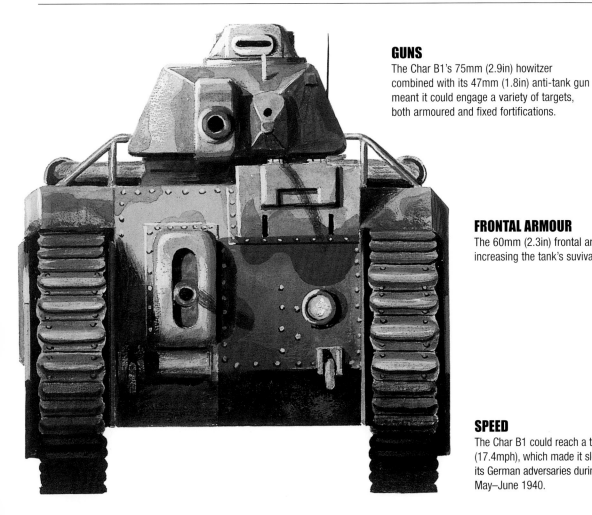

The Char B1's 75mm (2.9in) howitzer combined with its 47mm (1.8in) anti-tank gun meant it could engage a variety of targets, both armoured and fixed fortifications.

FRONTAL ARMOUR

The 60mm (2.3in) frontal armour was sloped, increasing the tank's suvivability.

SPEED

The Char B1 could reach a top speed of 28km/h (17.4mph), which made it slower than most of its German adversaries during the campaign of May–June 1940.

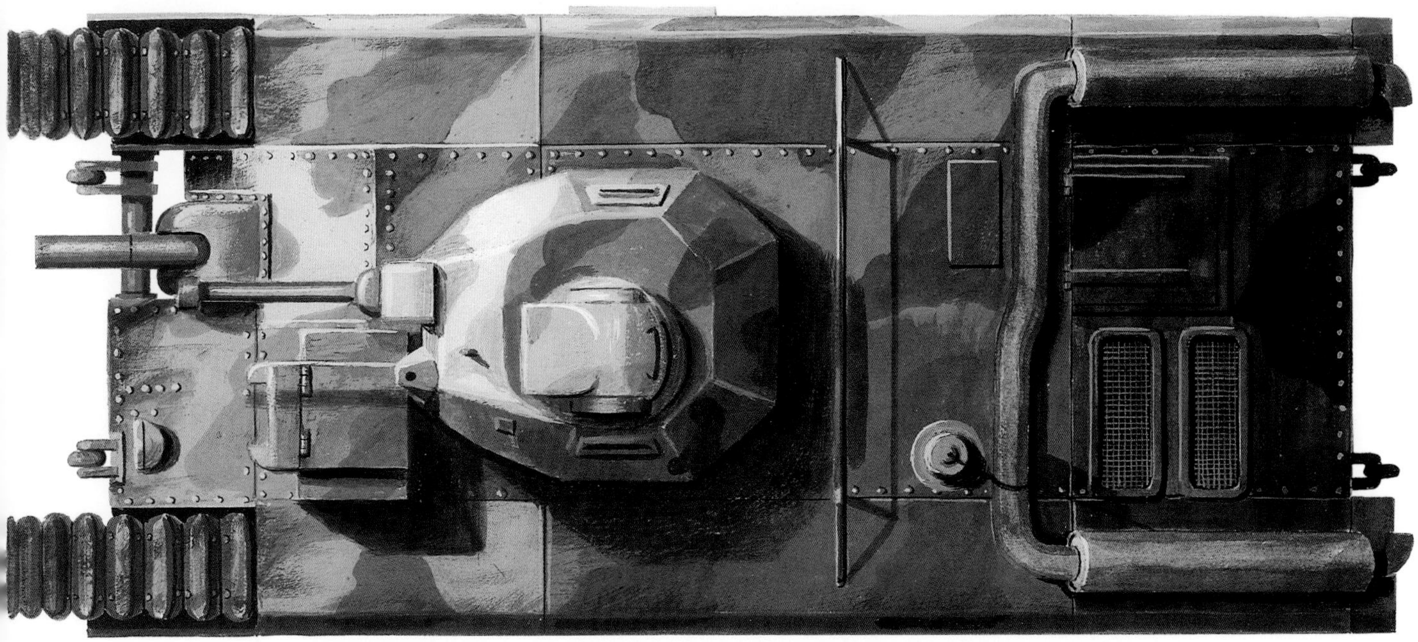

Panzer III

The Panzer III was Germany's first medium tank design. It was intended to operate alongside the Panzer IV, with the two designs complementing one another. In the event, the PzKpfw III was phased out of service in the middle of World War II, with the IV taking over both tanks' intended roles.

WORKHORSE OF THE ARMOURED FORCES

While the British, who had pioneered armoured warfare, largely neglected tank development in the inter-war years, Germany – which had been on the receiving end – took a far greater interest. The earliest designs, PzKpfw I and II, were intended as an interim measure only; the intent was always to build an infantry-support tank with a big gun and a lighter, faster vehicle for exploitation and mobile warfare.

This vehicle was designated PzKpfw III, and was produced in variants lettered from A to N. The first four models (Ausf A–D) were for development purposes, with the Ausf E and nearly identical F entering mass production in 1939–40. Upgrades continued, with some Ausf F models mounting a 50mm (1.9in) gun. The Ausf L variant was an

PANZER III AUSF F

Some Ausf Fs were armed with the more powerful 50mm (1.9in) gun.

An early-model Panzer III crossing water. The Ausf M model and onwards featured a deep-wading capability to improve obstacle crossing.

SPECIFICATIONS (PANZER III AUSF F)

Dimensions: Length: 5.38m (17ft 8in), Height: 2.45m (8ft 0.5in), Width: 2.91m (9ft 7in)

Weight: 17.4 tonnes (19.2 tons)

Engine/powerplant: Maybach HL120 TRM V12 petrol engine

Speed: 40km/h (24.9mph)

Armament: Main gun: 37mm (1.4in) KwK anti-tank gun, Co-axial: MG34 7.92mm (0.3in) machine gun, Turret top: MG34 7.92mm (0.3in) machine gun

Crew: 5

COLOUR

This Panzer III has been camouflaged by applying *dunkelgelb* (dark yellow) paint over the grey base coat.

CREW

The Panzer III had a crew of five. The three-man turret included a gunner and loader, freeing up the commander to direct the tank in combat.

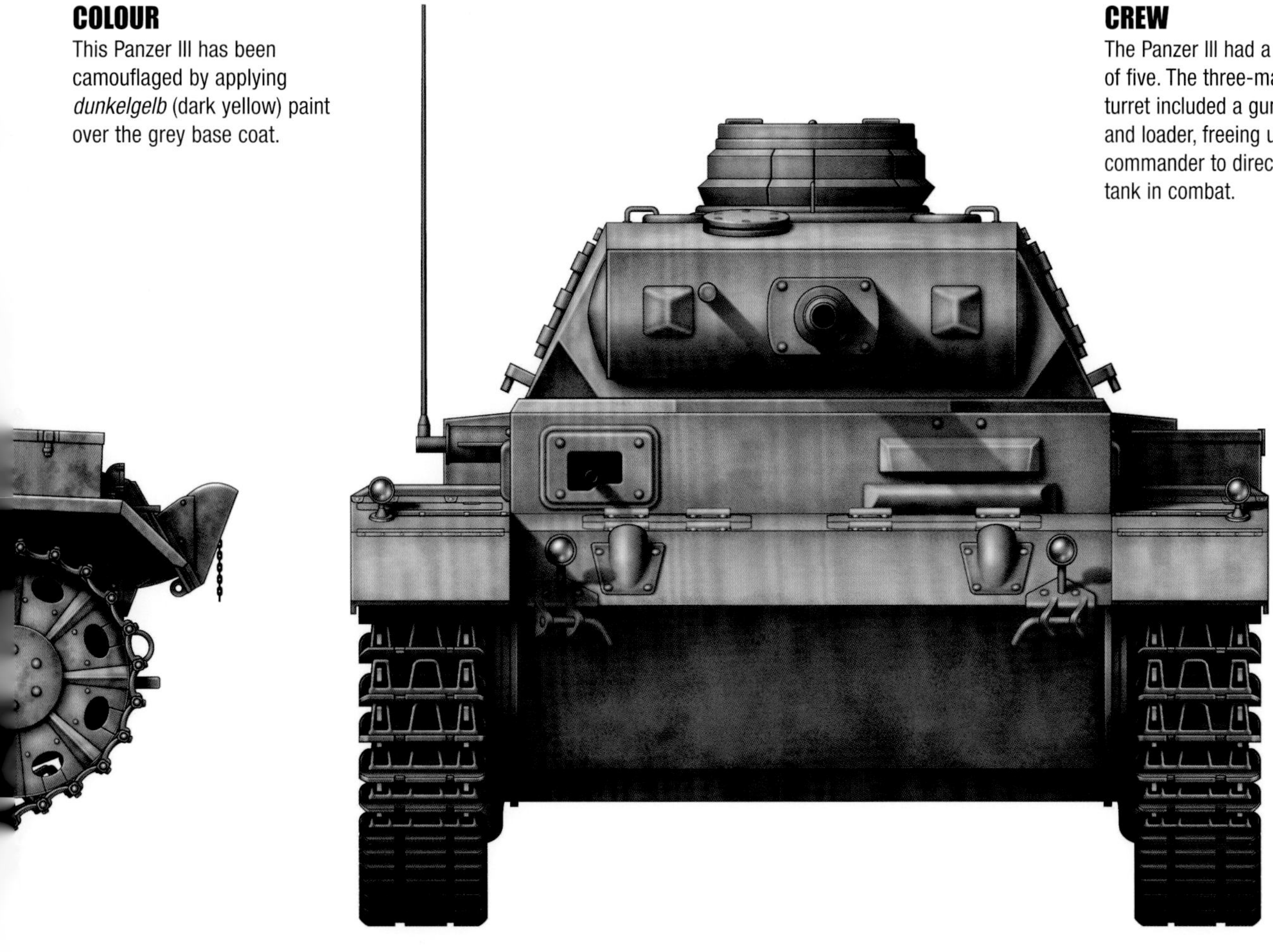

upgraded J, with enhanced armour protection, while the last model, Ausf N, was a conversion to use a low-velocity 75mm (2.9in) gun as an infantry support platform.

The decision to arm what would become the Panzer III with a 37mm (1.4in) gun was made for economic and logistics reasons – the standard infantry anti-tank gun of the time could be adapted for tank use, requiring no new production for guns or ammunition. The 50mm (1.9in) gun, fitted from 1941 onwards, was the largest that the Panzer III's small turret ring would permit and was barely adequate to deal with mid-war Soviet tanks. Once this weapon was no longer adequate, the PzKpfw III became obsolete.

SERVICE ON ALL FRONTS

The PzKpfw III saw action in Poland and Norway, but was not really tested until the invasion of France. Its 37mm (1.4in) gun proved useless against heavily armoured French Char B and British Matilda tanks, but aggressive tactics and good use of mobility, compounding strategic errors on the part of the French, enabled the Panzers to overcome their tough opponents. The incorporation of an intercom system meant that German tanks were on the whole better handled by their crews than those of their opponents. The Panzer III also encountered Matildas in North Africa, and again struggled to penetrate their armour. Against other tanks, however, the 37mm (1.4in) gun was adequate.

On the Eastern Front, Panzer IIIs mounting the new 50mm (1.9in) gun were superior to the early-war BT and T-26 tanks fielded by the Red Army. They were outmatched by the T-34 and did not handle the harsh conditions encountered in Russia very well. Heavy losses and the cessation of production ensured that by the late-war period the Panzer III had become uncommon. It continued to serve in small numbers right to the end, fighting in Italy, Normandy and within Germany against the Allied advance.

The Panzer III chassis was used for the Sturmgeschütz (StuG) III assault gun, of which more than 9000 were constructed. The StuG III was originally intended for infantry support and armed with a short-barrelled 75mm (2.9in) gun. Later models received a longer gun and could take on tanks using HEAT (high-explosive anti-tank) ammunition. These guns were often pressed into service as ersatz tanks, making up numbers in an armoured formation.

German troops capture a town supported by Panzer IIIs. The Panzer III was the primary German gun tank during Operation Barbarossa, but was becoming obsolete even then.

PANZER III AUSF J

Prior to the invasion of Russia, many Panzer IIIs were upgraded with the new 50mm (1.9in) KwK38 L/42 gun.

WINTER CAMOUFLAGE

This Ausf J has had a coat of whitewash applied over the top of the grey base layer for operations in Russia during the winter of 1941–42.

German troops and a Panzer III move through the Libyan desert. The Afrika Korps was primarily equipped with Panzer IIIs in 1941, but suffered heavy losses. Few remained by 1943.

M3 Stuart

The American M3 light tank was named Stuart by the British, who took it into service. It was sufficiently well liked that it gained an additional unofficial name: the Honey. Numerous variants were fielded, including command and personnel-carrier versions; the chassis was also used for a number of experimental projects.

CHANGING DOCTRINE

The United States, like most nations, considered the tank to be an infantry support system during the inter-war years. Indeed, tracked armoured fighting vehicles used by cavalry units were known as combat cars; officially the cavalry did not use tanks. The M1 Combat Car, equipped only with machine guns, was intended for traditional cavalry tasks such as scouting and screening, and stood little chance of survival if it encountered anti-tank weapons. Nevertheless, it was innovative in one way, as it was the first tank to mount an anti-aircraft machine gun on the turret top.

The M2 that followed was little better suited to armoured warfare, but after the fall of France in June 1940 a new 'cavalry tank' was ordered and doctrine evolved rapidly. The idea of armoured forces operating independently of infantry took hold, and the M3 was developed to suit this style of

RELIABILITY
The M3 Stuart was well liked for its ruggedness and reliability. It was also easy to drive and operate.

MAIN GUN
All models of the Stuart were armed with a 37mm (1.4in) gun, which was too weak for tank-to-tank combat.

An early M3 smashes through a wooden obstacle during training. Even a light tank could demolish most structures by driving into them.

SPECIFICATIONS (M3A1 STUART)

Dimensions: Length: 4.52m (14ft 10in), Height: 2.31m (7ft 7in), Width: 2.24m (7ft 4in)

Weight: 11.5 tonnes (12.7 tons)

Engine/powerplant: Continental W-670 radial petrol engine

Speed: 58km/h (36mph)

Armament: Main gun: M5 or M6 37mm (1.4in) gun; up to five M1919 7.62mm (0.3in) machine guns in co-axial, turret top and hull mountings

Crew: 4

CAMOUFLAGE

This M3 served with the British in North Africa in 1942. The light grey and brown disruptive camouflage pattern was ideal for desert warfare.

ARMOURED RECONNAISSANCE

The M3's speed made it very suitable for an armoured reconnaissance role, especially in North Africa.

29

The curious sponson-mounted machine guns are clearly visible on this early model M3. The weapons were deleted on later models.

warfare. It was still a reconnaissance unit rather than a battle tank, but now carried a 37mm (1.4in) gun backed up by a rather unusual set of sponson-mounted machine guns. These were later deleted.

WARTIME SERVICE

The first M3s entered service in 1941, with many delivered to Britain under lend-lease. These saw action in North Africa, where they were prized for their mobility and reliability. The gun was found to perform poorly against armour, even compared to other 37mm (1.4in) weapons of the day. The M3A1 arrived in 1942 in time to take part in the Operation Torch landings in North Africa. The high and slab-sided shape of the M3, combined with thin armour, proved to be a liability in combat against highly skilled German forces equipped with excellent anti-tank weaponry. By late 1943, sufficient medium tanks were available that the M3 could be transferred to a more suitable role as a reconnaissance asset for heavier formations.

M3s sent to Russia were not well suited to the conditions they encountered there. Their narrow tracks were not ideal for mud and snow, both of which were available in abundance. The M3 fared better in the Pacific theatre, where its light weight and mobility enabled it to operate in the jungle. Japanese tanks could also do so, but the M3 proved superior on the occasions that they met. More commonly, Stuarts provided fire support and engaged enemy strongpoints during the 'island hopping' warfare.

POST-WAR PROLIFERATION

The M3A2 got no further than a design study, but the A3 variant went into production with better armour than the original. It was built until 1943, after which it was supplanted by the M5 light tank. At the war's end, the US had large numbers available that were surplus to requirements. These went into service with various nations, seeing action in Asia, Africa and Central America. Although obsolete by the standards of the major powers, M3s soldiered on in many nations. The last recorded use in action was in 1969, but some Stuarts remained operational for more than 20 years after that.

An M3 preserved as a museum piece. There may still be a few serving in obscure corners of the world.

SOVIET SERVICE

Large numbers of M3s were supplied to the Red Army under the lend-lease agreement but were not popular with their crews.

MACHINE GUNS

The M3A1 came equipped with four 7.62mm (0.3in) M1919A4 Browning machine guns: one on the turret, as well as three further machine guns in the front hull.

Tiger II Königstiger

The Königstiger, popularly known as 'King Tiger' by the Allies, was intended to be a war-winning superweapon capable of sweeping lesser armoured vehicles from the battlefield. In many ways it represented a return to the concept of a short-ranged 'breakthrough tank' better suited to destroying fixed defences than engaging in mobile warfare.

BORN TO BE KING

The PzKpfw VI Tiger was designed to be able to withstand almost any anti-tank weapon on the battlefield, but by 1943 the Red Army was fielding large numbers of vehicles equipped with powerful 85mm (3.3in) guns capable of killing any tank in the Axis arsenal. With no prospect of matching the Allies in terms of numbers, designers working on a successor to the Tiger were ordered to create a vehicle sufficiently superior to its opponents that it could field to redress the balance.

Both Henschel and Porsche produced prototypes, with Henschel winning the production contract. The design drew heavily on experience with the Panther, incorporating sloped armour. The chassis was based on an elongated version of the Tiger and had similar overlapping road wheels. With the usual confusion surrounding wartime German arms procurement, some components were put into production before the final design was agreed. As a result, the first production units were given turrets produced to the original specifications and associated with the Porsche design rather than the Henschel-designed turret of later examples.

SPECIFICATIONS (PZKPFW VI AUSF B KÖNIGSTIGER)

Dimensions: Length: 10.26m (33ft 8in), Height: 3.09m (10ft 1.5in), Width: 3.75m (12ft 3.5in)

Weight: 63.3 tonnes (69.8 tons)

Engine/powerplant: Maybach HL230P30 V12 petrol engine

Speed: 38km/h (24mph)

Armament: Main gun: 88mm (3.4in) KwK43 L/56 gun, Co-axial: 7.92mm (0.3in) machine gun, Hull-mounted: 7.92mm (0.3in) machine gun

Crew: 5

FRONTAL ARMOUR
The frontal armour of the Tiger was 150mm (5.9in) thick and sloped 50mm (1.9in).

SIDE ARMOUR
The sides of the tank had armour 80mm (3.1in) thick.

The extremely long 88mm (3.4in) gun of the Königstiger gave a high muzzle velocity, increasing both accuracy and penetration.

28

The sloped armour of the Königstiger, more reminiscent of the Panther than the Tiger, maximized the protection it offered.

Armament suitable for the new tank was already available in the form of a long 88mm (3.4in) gun that had proved very effective aboard tank destroyers. A modified version was created, with a shorter recoil distance to enable it to fit in a turret. The end result was an extremely well-protected tank with an excellent gun, but since it was heavier than a Tiger and used the same powerplant, mobility was compromised.

KING TIGERS IN ACTION

Production was slow due to the complexity of the King Tiger and further disrupted by Allied bombing. Thus, fewer than 500 Königstigers were built. Although it proved resilient and highly effective in combat, not least due to advanced sights matched to a very accurate gun, the King Tiger was hampered by excessive fuel consumption, and in any case faced an impossible task. Vastly outnumbered by Allied tanks, King Tigers were also a priority target for tank-hunting aircraft armed with rockets capable of penetrating its upper surfaces. Some were eliminated by large-scale heavy bomber attacks. The Königstiger had a chance to show what it could do during the Ardennes Offensive, or 'Battle of the Bulge'. This was a hugely over-ambitious plan to punch through the Allied forces and deny them the port of Antwerp. This would have severely hampered Allied operations, but there was never any real prospect of success. Nevertheless, in December 1944 the offensive opened and achieved near-total surprise. Around 90 Königstigers were available for the operation, although propaganda footage suggests there were far more.

German fuel reserves were very low at the outset of the operation, and retaining mobility required the capture of Allied supply dumps. Even had this been accomplished, the slow Königstiger was not well suited to a fast exploitation after a breakthrough; counterattacks or fallback positions would have halted the tanks even if fuel supplies had been adequate. Although they were effective in combat, many Königstigers were abandoned for lack of fuel.

Similarly, on the Eastern Front a lack of mobility allowed Soviet tanks to engage the King Tiger from the flanks where it could be killed by a well-placed 85mm (3.3in) shell. Others suffered breakdowns. Even the 15:1 ratio of kills to losses claimed by some units was insufficient to stem the tide of Allied tanks pushing towards Germany.

An SS Panzer tank battalion made up of formidable Tiger IIs gathers. The Königstiger featured in many propaganda films and photographs, creating a greatly inflated impression of its numbers.

SHAPE

The elegant and clean lines of the Königstiger create an impression of power and menace.

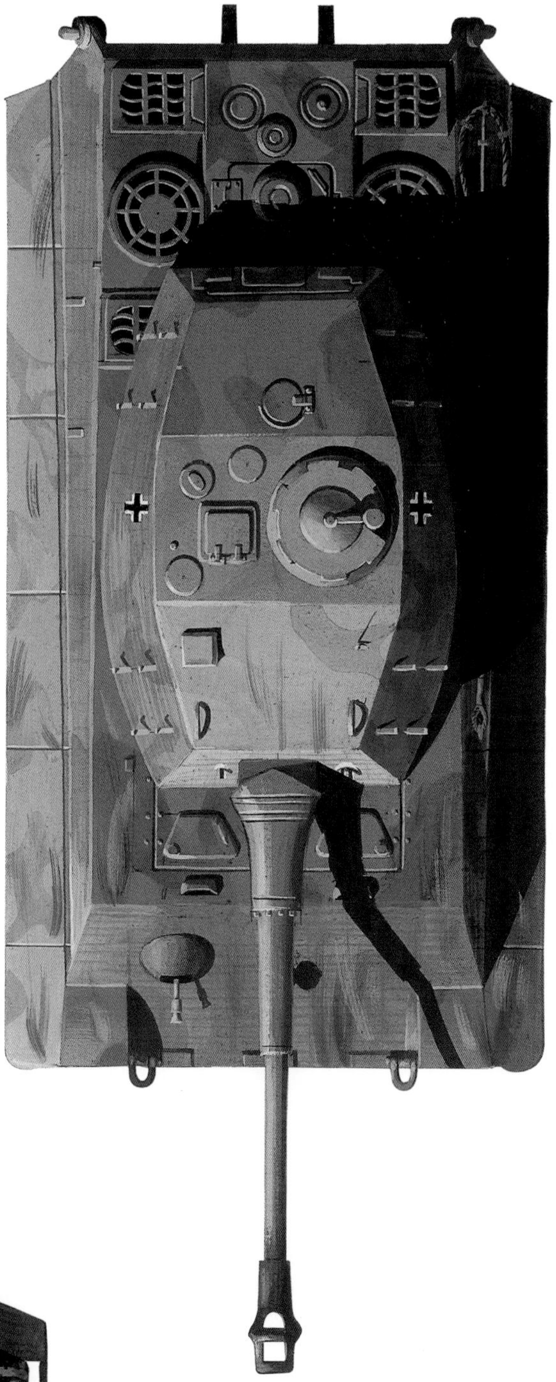

SLOPED ARMOUR

Unlike the Tiger I, the Tiger II had sloped sides on both the turret and hull, increasing its invulnerability to the majority of Allied anti-tank guns.

Chieftain

27

The Chieftain was the first British tank to mount a 120mm (4.7in) gun. Its design emphasized protection and firepower over other qualities, creating a tough and formidable tank that later served as the basis for specialist vehicles such as bridgelayers and engineering vehicles. As is often the case, these outlasted the gun tank in service.

CENTURION'S SUCCESSOR

The Centurion, armed with a 105mm (4.1in) gun, emerged at the end of World War II. It proved more than capable of defeating contemporary Soviet tanks, which were its likely opponents in any major future war. However, as protection improved, it became obvious that a bigger gun would be needed by the next British main battle tank. This was not merely about the amount of explosive that could be packed into a shell; some advanced ammunition types required a larger calibre to accommodate them. Early Chieftains were underpowered and suffered from some serious mechanical defects. The multifuel engine was troublesome, produced a lot of smoke and never delivered the power output originally hoped for. Indeed, the Chieftain was slower than the preceding Centurion, although it was better armed and protected. This was in part due to the extreme sloping of the frontal glacis, made possible by a curious reclining driving position. Overall, although many nations preferred greater speed, the Chieftain delivered what the British Army wanted at the time – an extremely well-protected tank mounting a world-class gun.

TURRET ARMOUR
The turret was protected by 195mm (7.7in) of armour, angled at 60 degrees.

SPECIFICATIONS (CHIEFTAIN MARK 5)

Dimensions: Length: 10.87m (35ft 8in), Height: 2.89m (12ft), Width: 3.66m (12ft)

Weight: 49.1 tonnes (54.13 tons)

Engine/powerplant: Leyland L60 multifuel engine

Speed: 48km/h (30mph)

Armament: Main gun: 120mm (4.7in) L11A5 rifled gun, Co-axial: 7.62mm (0.3in) machine gun, Turret top: 7.62mm (0.3in) machine gun

Crew: 4

The Chieftain was one of the earliest tanks to have a thermal sleeve on its gun barrel, reducing distortion due to heating.

EXPORT SUCCESS OUTSIDE EUROPE

As well as going into British service, the Chieftain was offered on the export market. European nations generally preferred the contemporary Leopard, but the Chieftain found favour in the Middle East, often in variant form with

CAMOUFLAGE

This two-tone disruptive pattern camouflage was designed for operations in Northwest Europe.

MAIN GUN

The Chieftain was armed with the powerful 120mm (4.7in) L11A5 gun with a laser rangefinder.

a local name. The largest order went to Iran, with Jordan and Kuwait also taking deliveries. Interest from Israel came to nothing due to political considerations, resulting in the Israeli development of the Merkava.

The Chieftain did not perform well in the Iran–Iraq war of the 1980s, mainly due to poor maintenance. The post-revolution Iranian military lacked the skills required to keep technologically sophisticated weapon systems in working order. The Iranian Chieftain force thus suffered heavy losses from mechanical breakdowns. This did not reflect upon the Chieftains in British service; the Chieftain was well regarded and generally considered a very potent weapon system.

VARIANTS AND DEVELOPED VERSIONS

The Chieftain was upgraded repeatedly during its period of service, sometimes requiring a rebuild and on other occasions receiving improved electronic systems that were much easier to integrate. The Mk5 was the last large-scale production version; later models were upgrades to existing vehicles. The Mk10 received an armour upgrade known as the Stillbrew Crew Protection Package, which used an early form of composite armour to enhance protection against kinetic energy penetrator rounds.

The Chieftain was also used as a testbed for Chobham composite armour, which would become standard on its replacement, the Challenger. Indeed, Challenger grew out of a Chieftain variant. Originally the intent was for joint development between Britain and Germany to create a replacement for the Chieftain. This project was eventually cancelled, requiring an extension to the Chieftain's service life and development of a new British tank.

Work had already begun on such a tank, commissioned as Shir 2 by Iran. Based on the Chieftain, the Shir 2 project became Challenger 1, continuing the tradition of emphasizing extremely heavy protection rather than speed. Challenger was given Chobham armour, which was developed and tested using the Chieftain as a base. Like the Centurion before it, the Chieftain was outlived in service by its engineering vehicle variant, although this too has been retired.

CHIEFTAIN 900

A variant model, the Chieftain 900 included the Chobham armour that later featured on the more modern Challenger tank.

A preserved Chieftain on display at a tank show. Note the extreme slope of the glacis (main frontal armour) plate.

ENGINEERING VEHICLE

The Chieftain AVRE (Armoured Vehicle, Royal Engineers) could deploy a fascine (bundle of sticks) to quickly fill a trench or ditch.

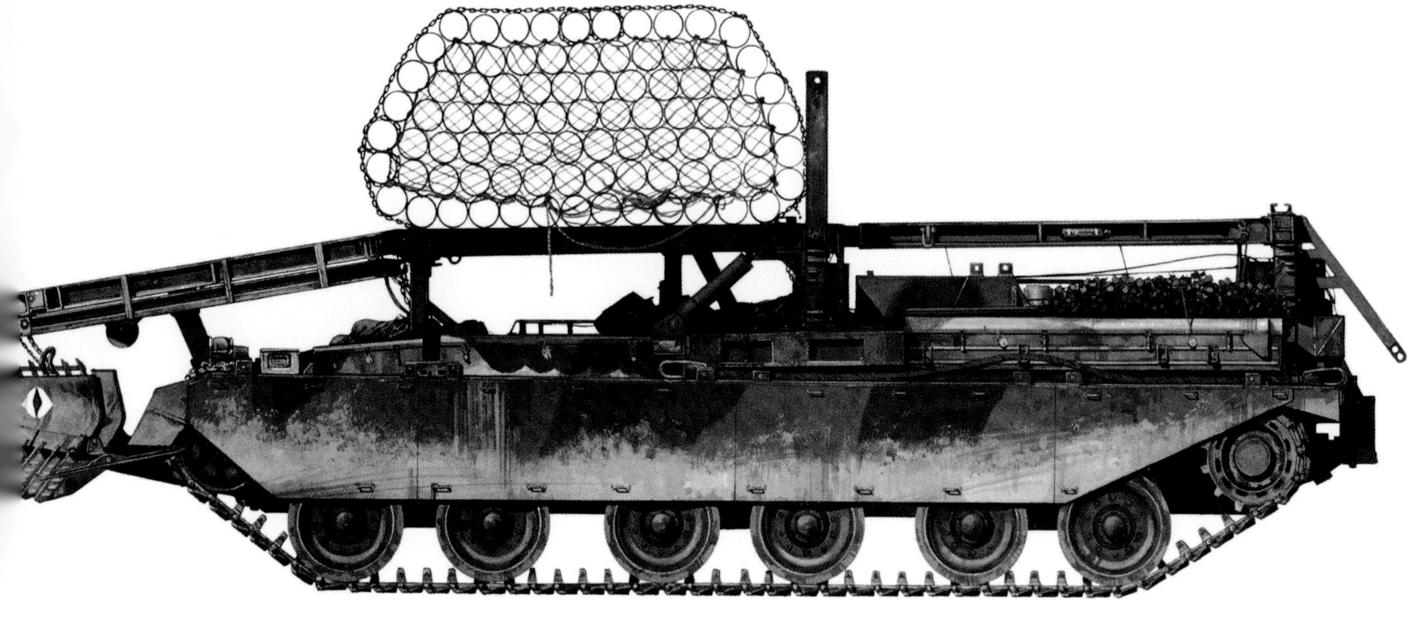

PT-76

26

From the outset, the PT-76 light tank was designed as a reconnaissance platform that could overcome the obstacle posed by bodies of water, giving it the ability to cross rivers or lakes without any preparation. It has found favour in Indonesia, where difficult terrain cut by many watercourses makes conventional armoured operations problematic.

COLD WAR LIGHT TANK

The Red Army used a succession of amphibious light tanks from the early 1930s onwards, culminating in the T-40, which was introduced in 1941. Armed only with a heavy machine gun, the T-40 was fully amphibious and driven through water by a propeller. Production was curtailed in favour of a non-amphibious version initially designated T-40S and then T-60. The T-60 was simpler to build, which was critical at a time when large numbers of tanks were needed, and it mounted a more powerful armament.

MAIN GUN

The PT-76 was armed with a 76mm (3in) gun, which was adequate when dealing with light armoured vehicles and infantry positions.

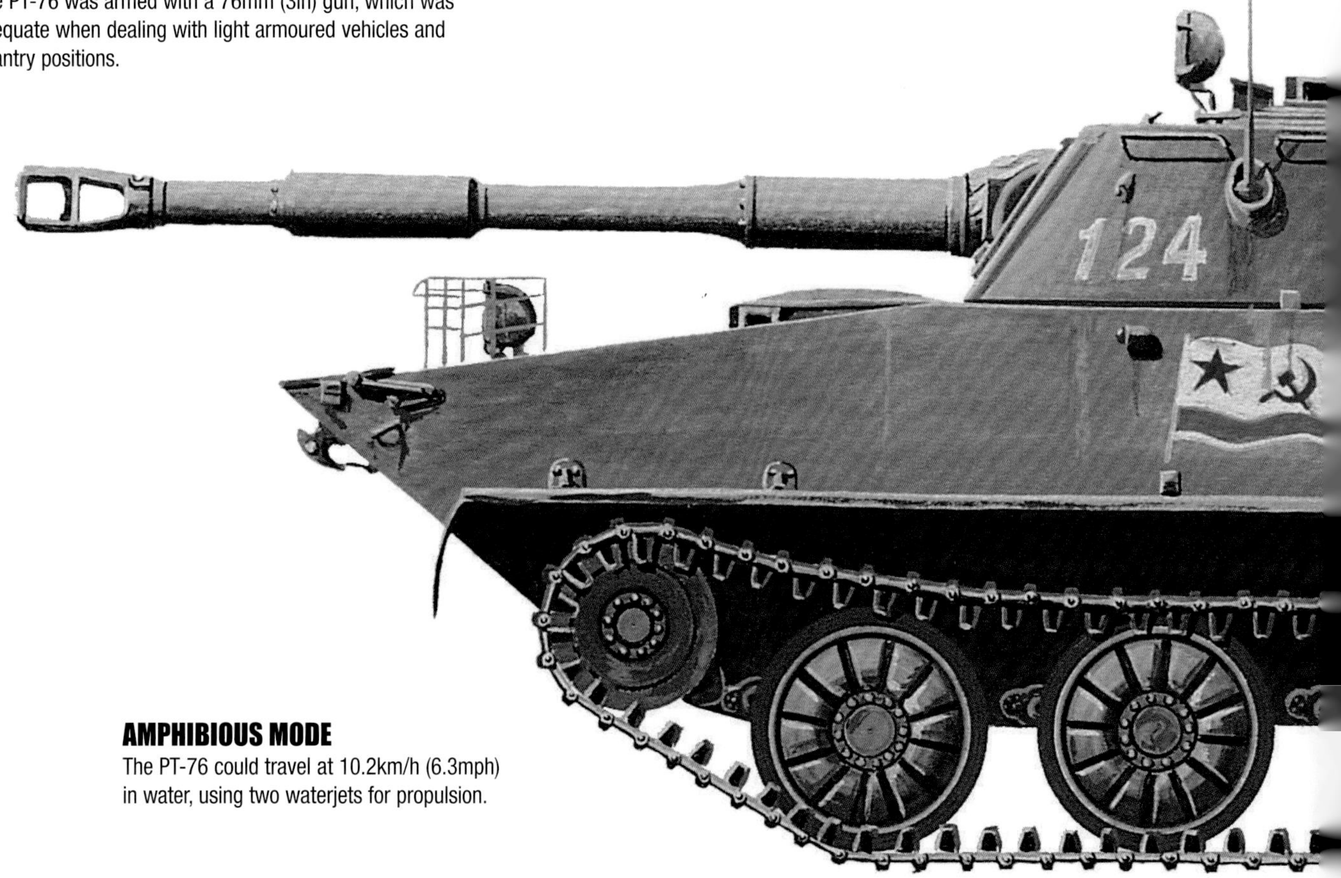

AMPHIBIOUS MODE

The PT-76 could travel at 10.2km/h (6.3mph) in water, using two waterjets for propulsion.

SPECIFICATIONS (PT-76)

Dimensions: Length: 6.91m (22ft 8in), Height: 2.26m (7ft 5in), Width: 3.14m (10ft 3.5in)

Weight: 12.5 tonnes (13.8 tons)

Engine/powerplant: V6 diesel engine

Speed: 45km/h (28mph)

Armament: Main gun: 76mm (3in) D-56T rifled gun, Co-axial: 7.62mm (0.3in) SGMT machine gun

Crew: 3

The PT-76 saw action with the North Vietnamese Army (NVA) during the Vietnam War. Its thin armour was a real liability against US firepower.

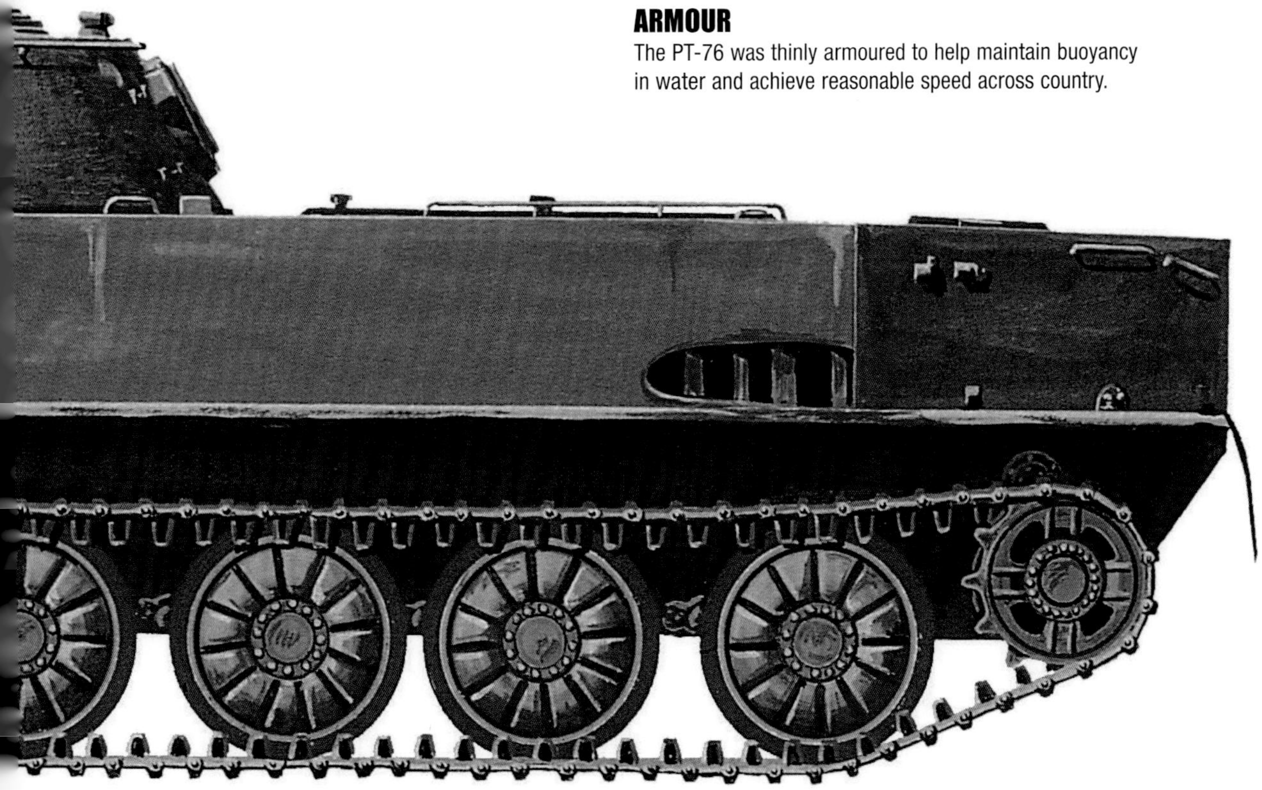

ARMOUR
The PT-76 was thinly armoured to help maintain buoyancy in water and achieve reasonable speed across country.

26

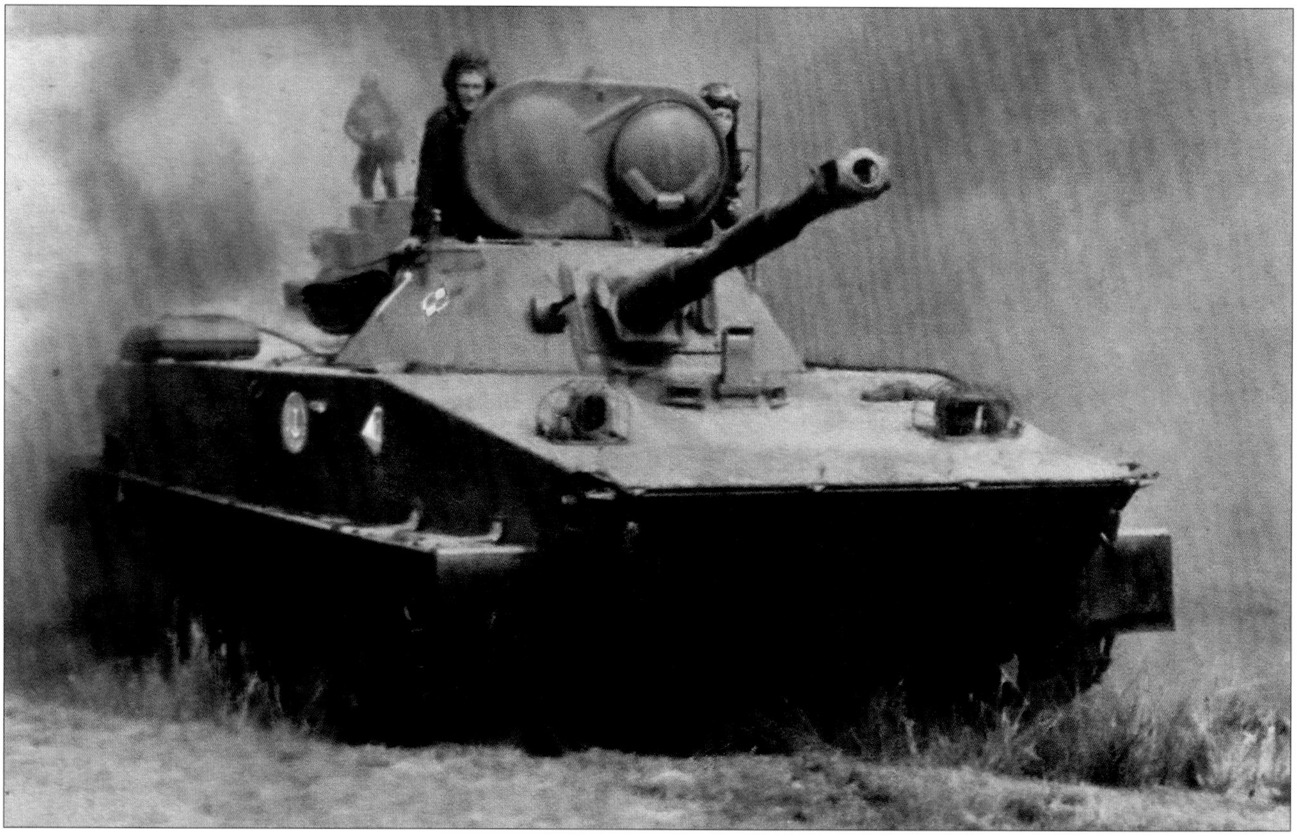

The PT-76's turret houses the commander and the loader, who share a large double hatch. The commander also operates the radio and the main gun.

The PT-76 has proven highly useful in amphibious operations, but is vulnerable in the direct assault role due to its thin armour.

Interest in an amphibious light tank was renewed after the war, resulting in the PT-76 entering service in 1952. Very lightly armoured – the hull was proof against small-arms fire only – the PT-76 mounted an effective 76mm (3in) gun and had an innovative water-jet propulsion system, giving it good mobility in water. The boat-shaped hull provided a relatively large target for a light tank, but a low silhouette compensated somewhat for this.

VARIANTS AND UPGRADES

A series of upgrades from 1957 to 1959 resulted in the PT-76B, which gained an NBC protection system and an improved main gun. Sighting and electronics systems were also upgraded. Around 12,000 PT-76Bs were produced up to 1967. Numerous derivatives were also developed, including missile launchers and support vehicles, as well as experimental projects that met with mixed success. China attempted to develop a similar vehicle based on the PT-

Not all retired tanks are scrapped or end up as museum pieces. This PT-76 has simply been abandoned to its fate.

76, but ultimately went with a different design. In Russian service, the PT-76E was created by a comprehensive upgrade and modernization package. This replaced the 76mm (3in) gun with an advanced 57mm (2.2in) cannon, greatly enhancing lethality against even quite well-armoured targets. Improved engines and control systems resulted in better operability and cross-country performance.

Other operators have benefited from 'Westernization' of the PT-76. Since the end of the Cold War, it has become increasingly common to mix weapon systems of Eastern and Western origin. Thus, an upgraded PT-76 is available with a 90mm (3.5in) Cockerill gun and advanced electronic systems.

WORLDWIDE SERVICE

The PT-76 was a huge export success, with around 7000 vehicles taken into service worldwide. Although only a handful remain in Russian service, large numbers of PT-76s are still operated worldwide. The design has seen combat in numerous conflicts, from Vietnam in 1959 to Chechnya at the end of the 20th century.

The PT-76 saw extensive combat in Angola from 1966 onwards, and proved effective against Pakistani light tanks during the India–Pakistan wars of 1965 and 1971, although encounters with heavier tanks had a predictable result. Iraqi tanks were used in the Iran–Iraq war, but were outmatched in 1991 and 2003 against Western forces.

Not surprisingly, the PT-76 has been most effective in amphibious operations. Egyptian marines made a crossing of the Great Bitter Lake in the 1973 Yom Kippur War against Israel, and the Indonesian military has used the tanks in several amphibious operations.

With significant numbers still serving all around the world, there is a solid market for upgrades and refurbishments, which in turn makes it likely that the PT-76 will remain in service for some years to come.

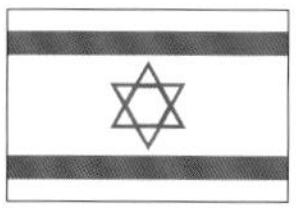

Merkava

The unusual design of the Israeli Merkava main battle tank draws on years of hard-won experience. The engine is located in front of the crew, with space at the rear of the fighting compartment for a handful of additional personnel or a small quantity of cargo.

INDIGENOUS DESIGN

At its creation just after World War II, the modern nation of Israel inherited quantities of Western military equipment, and has traditionally procured arms in the West. This was not without its problems, as the complex politics of the Middle East have at times resulted in nations declining to sell to Israel. This was the case at the end of the 1960s, causing a plan to obtain a new main battle tank from Britain to fall through.

Plans were thus drawn up for a locally produced tank that had to combine survivability with ease of maintenance. Where possible, components were based on those already

TURRET
The low, wedge-shaped turret reduced the tank's silhouette, making it a smaller target.

MAIN GUN
The Merkava mounts a powerful 120mm (4.7in) MG253 smoothbore gun capable of penetrating any tank it is likely to encounter.

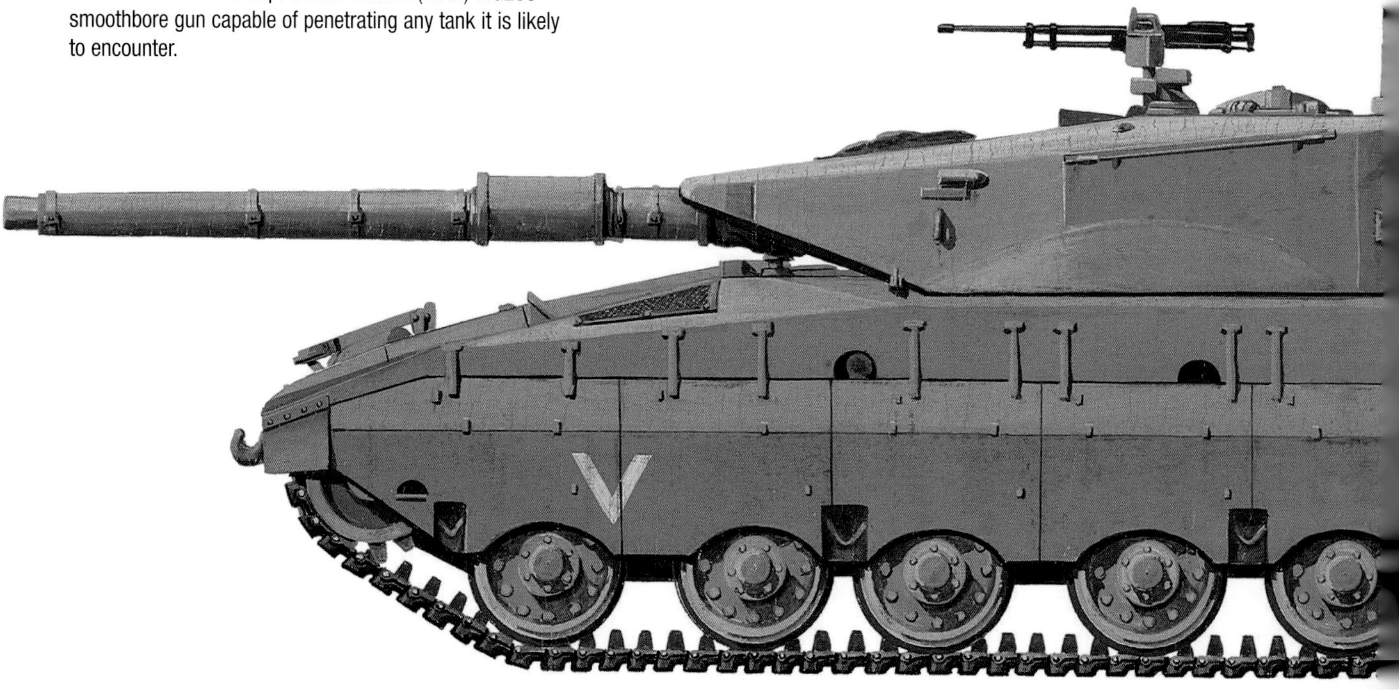

SPECIFICATIONS (MERKAVA MK III)

Dimensions: Length: 7.6m (24ft 11in), Height: 2.64m (8ft 8in), Width: 3.7m (12ft 1.5in)

Weight: 55.3 tonnes (61.02 tons)

Engine/powerplant: Teledyne AVDS 1790 9AR V12 diesel engine

Speed: 55km/h (34.2mph)

Armament: Main gun: 120mm (4.7in) smoothbore gun, Co-axial: 7.62mm (0.3in) machine gun, 60mm (2.3in) mortar (smoke or CS gas rounds), Additional: 2 x 7.62mm (0.3in) machine guns or 1 x 7.62mm (0.3in) and 1 x 12.7mm (0.5in) machine gun

Crew: 4

The Merkava was developed to meet the unique needs of the Israeli Defence Force, notably a high level of crew survivability.

MERKAVA III

This Merkava III includes one turret-mounted 7.62mm (0.3in) FN-MAG machine gun for defence against infantry, and a larger front-mounted 12.7mm (0.5in) M2HB heavy machine gun intended for defence against attack helicopters.

TRACKS

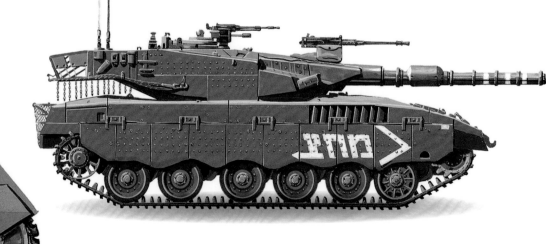

The tracks of the Merkava were developed from the Centurion, which served extensively with Israeli forces.

in service elsewhere, but the new tank, produced by a project named Merkava ('Chariot') and given the same name, did have some unusual features.

The Merkava's turret is very narrow, presenting a small target to whatever gun is aimed at it. Frontal protection is increased by placing the engine in front of the crew, with additional protection provided for critical systems. Another unusual feature is the ability to carry a small infantry squad, who access the vehicle through doors at the rear. This has allowed some Merkavas to be turned into fully combat-capable 'tankbulances'.

PERFORMANCE AND UPGRADES

The Merkava Mk I, armed with a 105mm (4.1in) gun, might be considered underpowered by the standards of European tanks. However, its tactical mobility on poor terrain was good enough and it was not expected to travel far under its own power outside combat. Experience in Lebanon in the early 1980s influenced the Mk II, which retained the same gun but offered enhanced protection against shaped-charge weapons. Sub-marks added more armour and upgraded the electronics.

Introduced in 1989, the Merkava Mk III was distinguished by improved transmission and powerplant along with a 120mm (4.7in) smoothbore gun. Further modifications eventually led to the current Merkava Mk IV model, with an upgraded gun and the capability to carry modular add-ons as necessary. All versions carry a 60mm (2.3in) mortar, used to deliver smoke or tear gas projectiles.

LOW-INTENSITY COMBAT

In Lebanon, the Merkava proved superior to the T-62s it encountered, but since that conflict it has mainly been threatened by infantry-launched weapons. Rather than the

CREW
The Merkava's driver sits in the hull front, while the gunner, loader and commander are housed in the turret.

Chains hanging from the rear of the turret are intended to detonate warheads before impact. Those on the hull front are more likely used for towing.

CHARIOT
The word Merkava translates as 'chariot' from Hebrew.

SPEED
The Merkava has a road speed of 64km/h (40mph), while it can travel at 55km/h (34mph) off road.

large-scale tank battles of 1967 and 1973, Israeli forces have tended to be involved in 'low-intensity warfare' in recent years. Rocket-propelled grenades and guided anti-tank missiles might be launched at a Merkava at short range, making adequate protection a critical necessity.

One response was the creation of a low-intensity warfare kit, with a remotely controlled machine gun allowing the crew to defend their tank without emerging from behind its armour. The kit also includes protection for sensitive areas such as optics. Very few Merkavas have been seriously damaged by missiles or rocket-propelled grenades, with crew casualties extremely low. This was one of the paramount goals of the project, and it appears to have been a success.

Upgrades and development of the Merkava series continues. A turretless armoured personnel carrier variant exists, along with an armoured recovery vehicle. A self-propelled gun was developed in the mid-1980s, but was not adopted for service.

Scorpion/ Scimitar

24

The Alvis Scorpion was officially designated a Combat Vehicle, Reconnaissance (Tracked), which sums up its intended role. It was the basis for a whole family of military vehicles, including an armoured personnel carrier, a field ambulance and a missile-armed tank destroyer. The Scorpion family was widely exported, with examples still in service today.

AN ARMOURED CAR, BUT WITH TRACKS

In the mid-1960s, the British military requested designs for a light and highly mobile vehicle to serve in the armoured reconnaissance role. At that time, the six-wheel Saladin armoured car and its derivative vehicles were fulfilling a variety of roles with the British Army, and also achieving considerable export success. The Scorpion was in many ways similar to the Saladin; both mounted a 76mm (3in) gun offering good offensive capabilities against the sort of targets a light tank could reasonably be expected to engage. Like the Saladin, the Scorpion was to be the basis for a family of derivative vehicles.

FV101 SCORPION

A classic light tank, the engine is at the front with the turret set to the rear of the vehicle.

MAIN GUN

The 76mm (3in) L23A1 main gun can fire up to six rounds per minute and has a range of 2200m (7217ft).

SPECIFICATIONS (SCORPION)

Dimensions: Length: 4.79m (15ft 8.75in), Height: 2.01m (6ft 10.75in), Width: 2.24m (7ft 4in)

Weight: 7.3 tonnes (8.078 tons)

Engine/powerplant: Jaguar 4.2-litre petrol engine

Speed: 80km/h (50mph)

Armament: Main gun: 76mm (3in) L23A1 gun, Co-axial: 7.62mm (0.3in) machine gun

Crew: 3

The Scorpion entered British service in 1972, and was widely exported. The design included a degree of amphibious capability using a flotation screen, and also an NBC protection suite. Like most British armoured vehicles, the Scorpion was equipped with a boiling vessel for the

The Scimitar, armed with a 30mm (1.1in) cannon, has outlived the Scorpion in service. Its cannon can penetrate a T-62 main battle tank.

ARMOUR

The armour thickness is just 12.7mm (0.5in) and made of aluminium. The Scorpion's extensive use of aluminium armour reduced weight but provided only limited protection.

This Scorpion has been heavily camouflaged, using foliage to break up its angular outline and blend in with the natural background.

preparation of meals and hot drinks. Ground pressure was extremely low, enabling the Scorpion to cross terrain that might bog down even personnel on foot.

VARIANTS AND DERIVATIVES

The standard Scorpion, with its 76mm (3in) gun, was followed into service by a range of derivative vehicles. Among these was the Scimitar, intended for the same general role as the Scorpion but armed with a 30mm (1.1in) RARDEN cannon. The Scimitar is still in service, having undergone an upgrade programme. The Striker, on the same hull but armed with Swingfire anti-tank missiles, entered service in 1975 and served until 2005. The Spartan armoured personnel carrier followed in 1978; some were later converted into carriers for the MILAN missile system.

A hybrid vehicle was created in the mid-1990s by adding the turret of a Fox armoured car – also armed with a 30mm (1.1in) RARDEN cannon – to a Scorpion chassis. Designated Sabre, this vehicle was very similar to the Scimitar, but was not a success. The Sabre was withdrawn from service in 2004, while the more expensive Scimitar remains in service.

The Scorpion family was widely exported, with one variant produced specifically for the export market. This was the Scorpion 90, armed with a Cockerill 90mm (3.5in) gun. Reportedly, this weapon's performance against armoured targets is only slightly inferior to the 105mm (4.1in) guns arming many main battle tanks. However, with armour protection limited to small arms all round and heavy machine guns in the frontal arc, the Scorpion 90 is still very much a light tank.

COMBAT SERVICE

Scorpion and Scimitar CVR(T)s were deployed for the 1982 Falklands War. Limited sealift capability and difficult operating terrain precluded the use of heavier armoured vehicles, and in the event the light tanks gave good service. The Scorpion did not fare so well in Iranian hands during the 1980s. Suffering from poor maintenance and low training standards, the Iranian Scorpion force suffered heavy casualties against Iraqi armour.

Scimitars served in Iraq during the 1991 and 2003 conflicts, proving capable of successfully engaging a T-62 with discarding sabot ammunition. Scimitars were also deployed to Afghanistan, resulting in an urgent request for an upgraded version suited to dealing with the current threats encountered there. The Scimitar Mk2 was delivered in 2011, incorporating better armour and protection against mines.

In service since the early 1970s, the Scimitar is due for replacement in British service.

FV107 SCIMITAR

Conceived as a Cold War reconnaissance vehicle, the Scimitar has proven effective in modern counter-insurgency operations.

CREW

The Scimitar has three crewmembers: a driver at the front of the hull, next to the engine, and a commander and a gunner inside the turret.

MAIN GUN

The RARDEN cannon can fire a range of ammunition but is fed by three-round clips, limiting its firepower.

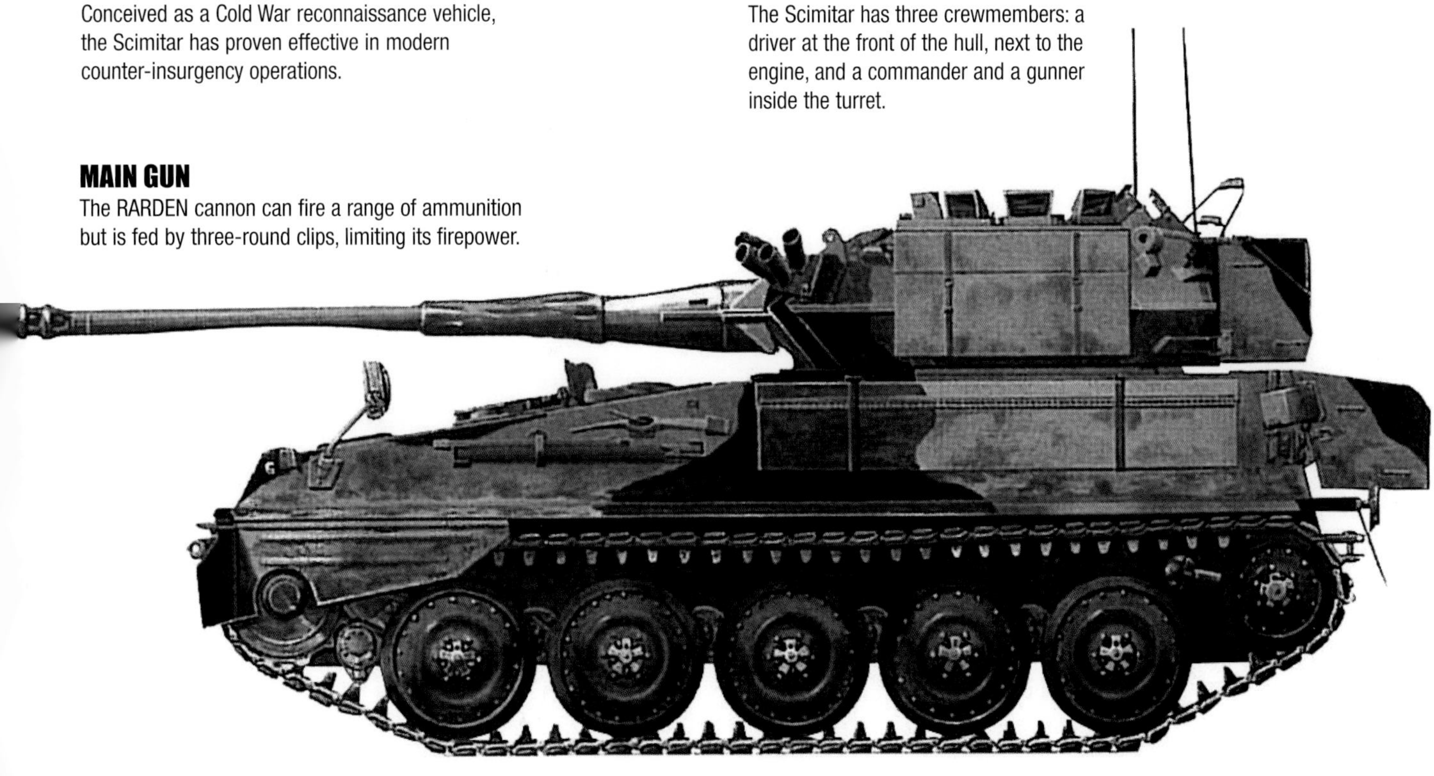

M48 Patton

23

The M48 Patton has seen action in numerous conflicts. It served primarily in an infantry support role during the Vietnam War, and fought Indian tanks during the Indian–Pakistan conflicts. M48s served on both sides of the 1967 Six-Day War, as well as with Iranian forces in their war against Iraq.

A NEW TANK FOR THE POST-WAR WORLD

The end of a major conflict such as World War II normally leaves the combatant nations with sufficient stocks of weaponry to last several years – perhaps even decades with a suitable upgrade programme. However, the outbreak of the Korean Conflict in 1950 demonstrated a need for a more modern tank. The M47 medium tank, named after General George S. Patton, was essentially an upgraded version of the M26 that was hurriedly fielded for service in Korea. It was still essentially a World War II-era vehicle, lacking night-fighting equipment and NBC protection.

The M48, also named 'Patton', was a new design, with a longer and lower chassis and a new turret mounting a 90mm (3.5in) gun. The M48's armour and powerplant were also improvements on those of the M47. Rushed into service in Korea, the M48 suffered from some early defects but rapidly matured into an excellent combat tank. Later in its career, the 90mm (3.5in) gun was upgraded to a 105mm (4.1in) weapon to deal with the new generation of Soviet tanks then appearing.

WORLDWIDE SERVICE

US forces made extensive use of the M48 during the Vietnam War, including a flamethrowing variant designated M67. The chief threats faced in this conflict were from mines and infantry-launched anti-tank weapons rather than the guns of other tanks, although after the US withdrawal M48s in South Vietnamese hands fought against a variety of Soviet-supplied tanks. Pakistani M48s proved effective against Indian tanks in 1965 and 1971, but attacks on anti-

The M48's searchlight was aligned with the main gun for target illumination. It could be used in white light or infrared mode.

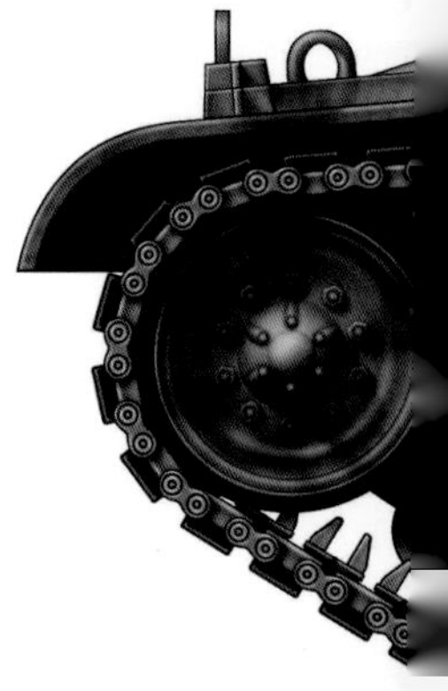

MAIN GUN
A 105mm (4.1in) M68 cannon was installed in the later model M48A5.

M47 PATTON MEDIUM TANK

Developed in the early 1950s, the M47 was the primary tank of the US Army and the basis for the M48.

MAIN GUN

The M47 was armed with an M36 90mm (3.5in) gun.

COMMANDER'S CUPOLA

A 12.7mm (0.5in) Browning heavy machine gun is fitted inside an enclosed cupola.

23

tank positions proved costly. Fortunes in the Six-Day War varied – Israeli M48s proved very effective, whereas their Arab opponents tended to underperform. This was due in no small part to training and highly effective cooperation with air support. Spain and Germany also bought large numbers of M48s, with German M48s eventually being replaced by the indigenous Leopard main battle tank. Systems developed for the Leopard were also used to upgrade the M48, while many users developed specialist variants such as bridgelayers, mine-clearance vehicles or anti-aircraft vehicles.

DEVELOPED VERSIONS

The main problem faced by early M48s was a very short operating radius. This was rectified on the M48A3 version, which had a more powerful diesel engine. However, it

SPECIFICATIONS (M48A5)

Dimensions: Length: 9.31m (30ft 6in), Height: 3.01m (10ft 1in), Width: 3.63m (11ft 11in)

Weight: 43.7 tonnes (48.2 tons)

Engine/powerplant: Continental AVDS-1790-2 12-cylinder diesel engine

Speed: 48km/h (30mph)

Armament: Main gun: 105mm (4.1in) M68 rifled gun, Co-axial: 7.62mm (0.3in) machine gun, Turret top: 12.7mm (0.5in) machine gun

Crew: 4

A heavily camouflaged M48 on manoeuvres in Europe. Shooting from a position of concealment was a standard Cold War NATO tactic.

retained the original 90mm (3.5in) gun; the M48A5, entering service in the mid-1970s, was the first to carry the new 105mm (4.1in) weapon. M48A5s are still in service in several nations today.

Developed and modified versions have also appeared over the years. The Israeli Defence Force modified its M48s, designating them Magach. This name was also applied to modified M60s in Israeli service – the Magach 5 and onwards is based on the M60; earlier numbers are M48s. The most radical M48 variant to appear thus far is the Taiwanese 'Brave Tiger'. Based on an M60 hull, Brave Tiger uses an M48A3 turret fitted with a locally produced 105mm (4.1in) gun. Fire control electronics are derived from the M1 Abrams.

The 'Super M48' was developed in the 1980s as an upgrade package for existing tanks. Based on the German upgrade that created the M48A2GA2, the Super M48 included appliqué armour, stabilization for the 105mm (4.1in) gun and improved powerplant and drive train. It was not a success due to tough market conditions at the time. However, with M48 continuing to serve in many nations it is possible that a new version may eventually emerge.

The M48 did not engage in much tank-versus-tank action in Vietnam, although some PT-76 light tanks were knocked out.

ISRAELI MAGACH 3 M48A2

The Israeli army improved the M48 by adding a larger gun and a better diesel engine.

ESCAPE HATCH

An escape hatch in the belly of the tank gave the crew a chance to get out if disabled and under fire.

Churchill

Despite being designed for an entirely different war (World War I), the Churchill proved very effective in World War II. It was agile and very well protected, if undergunned. Even after becoming obsolete as a gun tank, the Churchill continued to serve in a variety of important roles such as engineering and bridging vehicles.

GREAT WAR-ERA DESIGN

The Churchill was designed as an infantry tank – well protected but not capable of great speed. It was expected that tanks would have to cross wide trenches and would target infantry strongpoints rather than other tanks. As a result, the armament chosen for the early production models was a 2-pdr (40mm) gun in the turret and a 75mm (2.9in) howitzer in the bow. Multi-turret tanks were considered a viable prospect at this time, so multiple main armament was not much of a departure from the norm.

The bow howitzer was deleted from the Churchill MkII model, while the MkIII and MkIV used a more powerful 6-pdr (57mm) main gun. Variants armed with a 95mm (3.7in) howitzer were also fielded. These might be considered close-support platforms or 'artillery tanks' rather than conventional gun tanks. Once it became apparent that the 6-pdr was no longer adequate to deal with well-armoured German tanks, 75mm (2.9in) guns were fitted. A further upgrade to use the 76mm (3in) gun fitted to the Sherman Firefly was considered, but the Churchill's turret ring proved too small for the enlarged turret that would be needed.

WARTIME SERVICE

A critical shortage of tanks in the early months of World War II forced the Churchill to be rushed into production by several constructors. Early models suffered from mechanical defects, although these were rectified and the basic design proved highly useful. Churchills could climb slopes considered impossible by many commanders, and occasionally surprised their enemies by appearing in places where other tanks simply could not go. This was in part due to their track configuration, which extended beyond the hull. Tracks were exposed on early models but later were protected by 'catwalks' and large mudguards.

Churchills underperformed during the 1942 Dieppe raid, but were more successful in the North African and Italian campaigns. Slow speed proved something of a problem in the desert, where long-range mobility was a critical factor, but the Churchill's good protection offset this to some extent. Although outgunned by German tanks, armament upgrades allowed them to remain at least somewhat effective against enemy armour.

SPECIALIST VARIANTS

Despite its early reputation for unreliability, the Churchill was popular with Allied forces and was the best-protected tank available in 1943. It was used as the basis for several specialist vehicles. Notable among these was the Crocodile,

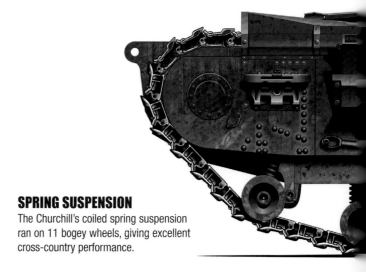

SPRING SUSPENSION
The Churchill's coiled spring suspension ran on 11 bogey wheels, giving excellent cross-country performance.

SPECIFICATIONS (CHURCHILL MKIV)

Dimensions: Length: 7.44m (24ft 5in), Height: 3.25m (10ft 8in), Width: 2.74m (9ft)

Weight: 35.3 tonnes (39 tons)

Engine/powerplant: Bedford 12-cylinder ('twin-six') petrol engine

Speed: 25km/h (15.5mph)

Armament: Main gun: 6-pdr (57mm) Ordnance quick-firing gun, Co-axial: 7.92mm (0.3in) Besa machine gun, Hull-mounted: 7.92mm (0.3in) Besa machine gun

Crew: 5

A column of Churchills (left) passes a force of Shermans during the advance inland after the Normandy landings of 1944.

RED ARMY CHURCHILL IV

This Churchill was used by the Soviet Red Army on the Eastern Front. More than 250 Churchill tanks were supplied to Russia during World War II.

MAIN GUN

The 6-pdr (57mm) main gun was adequate against most enemy medium tanks, but could not penetrate the armour of the German Tiger I or Tiger II.

which was the primary flamethrowing vehicle used by the Allies. Other variants included the 'funnies' used to deal with obstacles during the Normandy landings; 'bobbin' tanks capable of laying a canvas roadway across soft sand; mine-clearance vehicles; bridge- and ramplayers, and fascine carriers for filling in ditches.

The Churchill AVRE – variously given as Armoured or Assault Vehicle Royal Engineers – was capable of carrying out a range of engineering tasks including demolition of fortifications or obstructions using a heavy spigot mortar. This fired a projectile so large it was nicknamed the 'flying dustbin'. Post-war Churchill AVREs used a 165mm (6.5in) demolition gun instead, and served until their replacement in the 1960s by Centurion AVREs. Thus, despite being an imperfect gun tank, the Churchill established a long tradition of armoured engineering vehicles.

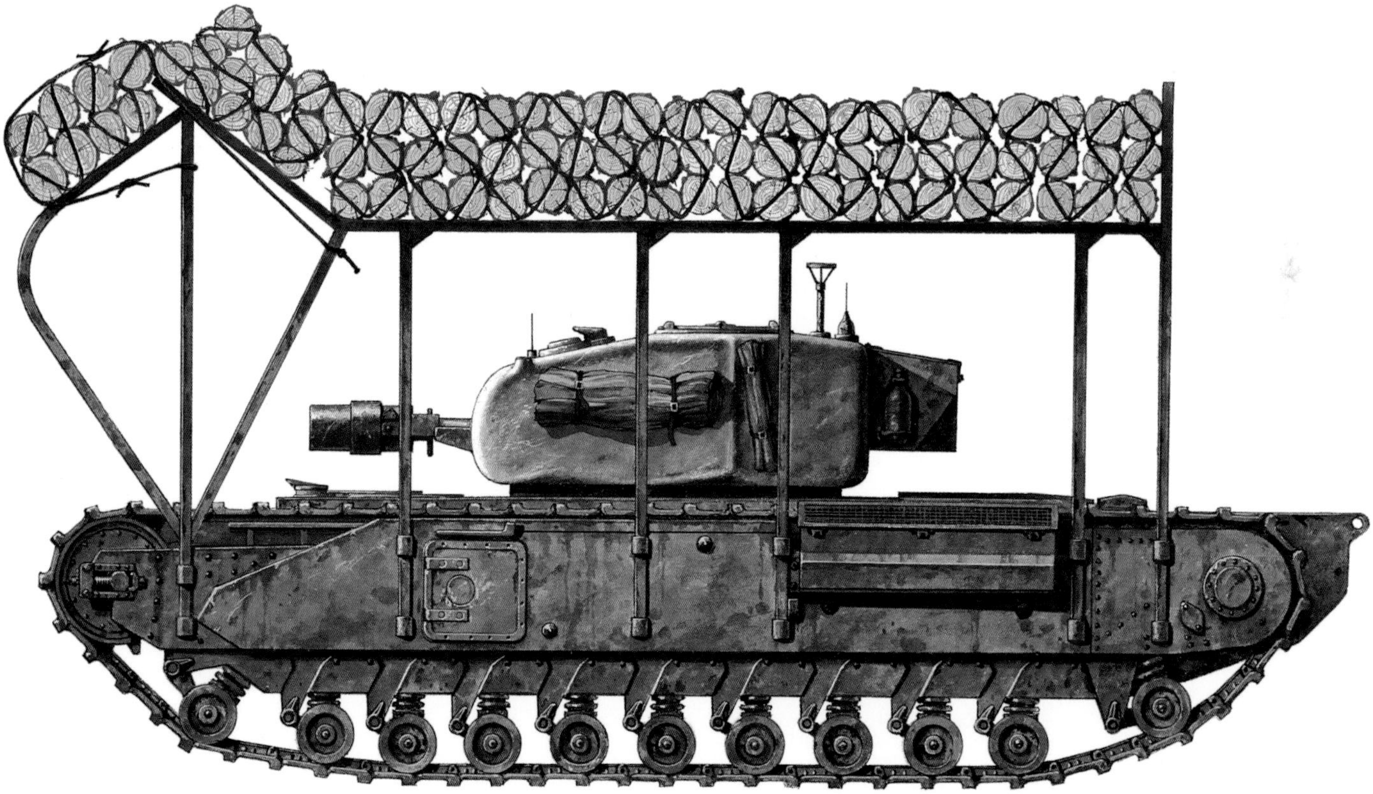

CHURCHILL AVRE

This Churchill carries a log carpet designed to help tanks cross boggy or uneven ground.

A force of British Churchills during the fighting for Italy. The Churchill was highly effective in mountainous terrain.

TRAILER
The Crocodile's armoured trailer carried a total of 1820 litres (400 gallons) of flame fuel.

CHURCHILL CROCODILE FLAMETHROWER
This flamethrower tank could shoot flame up to 91m (298ft). It was ideal for attacking fixed fortifications and bunkers.

Leopard 1

The German Leopard main battle tank was designed early in the Cold War and emphasized speed and mobility over protection. The Leopard was adopted by several European nations and remains in service worldwide, although it has been replaced by the Leopard 2 in the forces of its home nation.

A STANDARD PANZER FOR EUROPE

The onset of the Cold War meant that West Germany had to be rearmed in order to contribute to the defence and security of Europe. Cooperation with France (and later Italy) led to the Standard Panzer, or Europanzer, project. Mobility was to be emphasized rather than attempting to render the new tank invulnerable to the powerful shaped-charge weapons then becoming available in large numbers. The project reached the prototype phase before France withdrew to develop what would become the AMX-30 main battle tank.

Development of the new tank continued in Germany, and in 1963 the Leopard (today normally referred to as Leopard 1) entered service. It was built around the British-designed L7 105mm (4.1in) rifled gun and a multifuel engine and featured an excellent suspension system that, combined with a good power-to-weight ratio, afforded the Leopard excellent cross-country speed.

The Leopard was designed for the Cold War world, in which chemical or nuclear attack was a real possibility. Built from the outset to be sealed against NBC weapons, it was also capable of deep wading using a snorkel tube. Upgraded versions appeared over time, gaining improved gun stabilization, additional armour and enhanced electronics, leading eventually to a modernization programme that created the A5 version. This had additional bolt-on armour and greatly improved electronics over the original, but it retained the 105mm (4.1in) gun. An attempt was made in the 1980s to upgun the Leopard 1 with a 120mm (4.7in) weapon. However, by then the Leopard 2 was available and the project never went beyond the prototype stage.

What had begun as the Europanzer project ended up achieving its aim – a main battle tank for Europe. France went its own way with the AMX-30 and Britain developed the Chieftain, which emphasized protection more than mobility, but although these designs achieved some export success it was the Leopard that armed most European nations. Canada, Brazil and Turkey were among the

MAIN GUN
The Leopard was equipped with a German version of the British 105mm (4.1in) L7A3 L/52 rifled gun.

WEIGHT
The Leopard's good power-to-weight ratio resulted in high speed and excellent mobility.

SPECIFICATIONS (LEOPARD 1)

Dimensions: Length: 9.54m (31ft 3.5in), Height: 2.76m (9ft 0.5in), Width: 3.41m (11ft 2.5in)

Weight: 36 tonnes (39.76 tons)

Engine/powerplant: MTU MB 828 M500 multifuel engine

Speed: 65km/h (40mph)

Armament: Main gun: 105mm (4.1in) L7A3 rifled gun, Co-axial: 7.62mm (0.3in) machine gun, Turret top: 7.62mm (0.3in) machine gun

Crew: 4

A Leopard 1 painted in winter camouflage. An all-white colour scheme would actually stand out against the snow.

MACHINE GUN
The turret was fitted with a 7.62mm (0.3in) Rheinmetall MG3 machine gun.

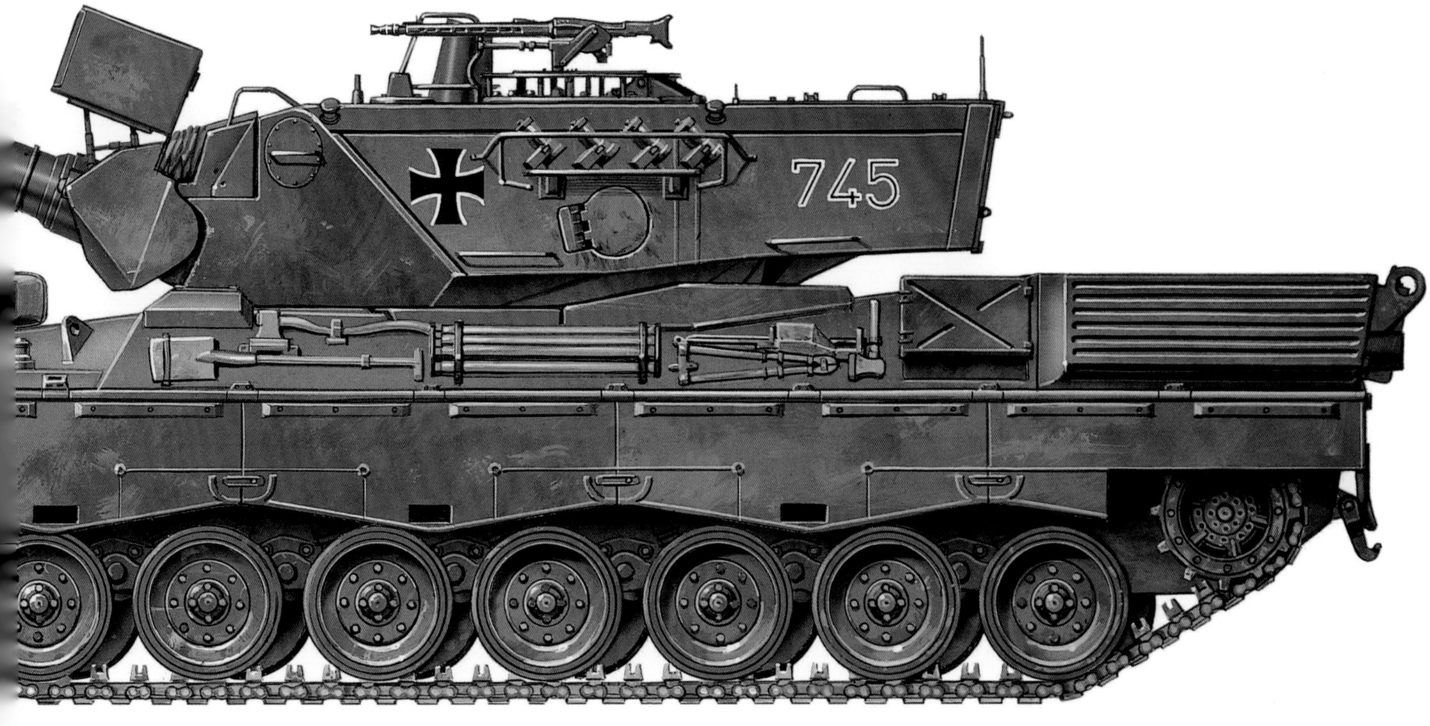

21

The Leopard 1 was conceived to fight a major defensive war in Europe. Mobility was considered the key to survival.

Leopard's users further afield. Some nations obtained vehicles from armies that chose to upgrade to the Leopard 2, prolonging the original's frontline service life.

EXPORT SUCCESS

Although it was a workhorse of numerous military forces for many years, the Leopard saw little combat. Leopards from several nations served in peacekeeping operations in the Balkans. The Danish contingent saw combat, but for the most part the Leopard was a deterrent to combat rather than a participant. The Leopard I has also been deployed to Afghanistan, where it was far more likely to encounter mines or rocket-propelled grenades than to be required to fight other tanks.

As with many successful designs, the Leopard has been the basis for bridgelayers and engineering vehicles. Leopard-derived bergepanzers (armoured engineering vehicles) are operated by several nations that do not use the Leopard itself as a gun tank. The Gepard anti-aircraft platform, mounting twin 35mm (1.3in) cannon on a modified Leopard chassis, served with the German armed forces until 2010 and was exported to several other nations, some of which still operate it.

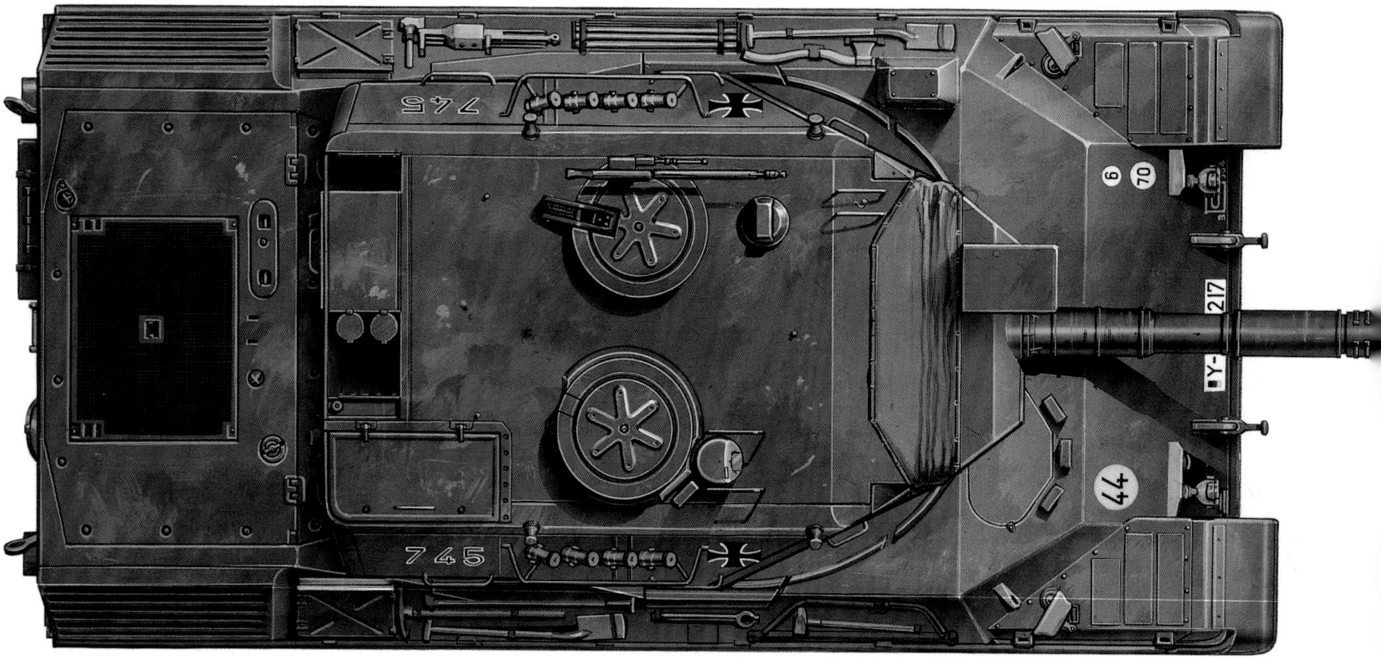

The Leopard 1 has seen service all over the world, but its design has not been severely tested in combat.

TURRET

The turret top had two cupolas, one for the commander and one for the gunner. Both were rotatable and fitted with prismatic vision blocks.

ARMOUR

The front armour of the Leopard was relatively thin at 70mm (2.7in), while the turret was only 60mm (2.3in).

Panzer 38(t)

The Czech LT-38 medium tank was a solid and effective inter-war design. After the German invasion of 1938, it was redesignated Panzer 38 and served in a combat role until 1942. By this time, the Panzer 38 was thoroughly outclassed by more modern tanks and was withdrawn from service.

INTER-WAR CZECH TANKS

Czech tank designers produced two prototypes for what would become the LT-35 medium tank. Both used the same chassis, engine and turret, and were built around the same proven 37mm (1.4in) gun. The design put forward by Skoda was chosen over the more lightly armoured version offered by CKD and went into production. However, it suffered numerous electrical and mechanical deficiencies.

As is the way of things, no sooner had the LT-35 gone into service than work began on its replacement. Designated LT-38, this new tank used well-proven design concepts and built on experience with earlier projects. It

MAIN GUN
The Czech 37mm (1.4in) gun was adequate against early-war tanks, but was obsolete by 1942.

was designed from the outset to be capable of fighting other tanks with its 37mm (1.4in) gun – this was a standard anti-tank weapon in the late 1930s – and to be both easy to produce and to maintain.

IN GERMAN SERVICE

The LT-38 was tough and robust, and sufficiently impressive that it influenced development of contemporary German tanks. After the German invasion of 1938, the LT-35 was redesignated Panzer 35, and the LT-38 as Panzer 38. The latter remained in production at the Skoda works, albeit with some modifications.

The German military was in need of all the tanks it could get, with many units waiting for deliveries of Panzer IIIs. The Panzer 38(t) was equivalent in terms of role and armament, and was supplied to many of these units. The design

SPECIFICATIONS (LT-38/PANZER 38(T) MEDIUM TANK)

Dimensions: Length: 4.6m (15ft 1in), Height: 2.4m (7ft 10in), Width: 2.11m (6ft 11in)

Weight: 8.3 tonnes (9.25 tons)

Engine/powerplant: Praga EPA 16-cylinder petrol engine

Speed: 42km/h (26.1mph)

Armament: Main gun: 37mm (1.4in) KwK L40 or L/45 gun, Co-axial: 7.92mm (0.3in) machine gun, Additional: 7.92mm (0.3in) machine gun

Crew: 4

A Panzer 38(t) in German service demonstrates its very good off-road performance during a training exercise.

WEIGHT
The Panzer 38(t) weighed half as much as a late-model Panzer III.

ARMOUR
The tank's armour protection varied from 8mm (0.31in) to 30mm (1.1in) thickness at the front. Thin armour left the tank vulnerable to almost all anti-tank weapons of its era.

20

The Panzer 38(t) chassis was well designed and reliable, allowing conversion to many other roles after it ceased to be viable as a gun tank. It also offered good cross-country performance.

proved effective in the invasion of Poland, and was still competitive in 1941 when Russia was attacked. The Panzer 35 also served in these campaigns, suffering heavy losses in the advance on Leningrad.

Like the Panzer III, the Panzer 38(t) was outdated by 1942. It was a good early-war tank but had reached the limits of what it could achieve. Its 37mm (1.4in) gun was ineffective against new tanks like the T-34, and could not fire large enough explosive shells to be effective in an infantry support role. In addition, the chassis was too small to carry a larger turret capable of accommodating a bigger gun.

VARIANTS AND SPECIALIST VEHICLES

Although the Panzer 38(t) was withdrawn from combat operations as a gun tank, its reliable and sturdy chassis was very suitable for conversions to other roles. Reconnaissance and anti-aircraft versions were produced, but the most significant conversions were tank destroyers. These used either German 75mm (2.9in) or captured Russian 76mm (3in) guns, solving the problem of mounting a large gun on a small chassis by doing away with a conventional turret. A self-propelled gun, designated Grille, was also produced. Later in the war the name 'Grille' was applied to similar vehicles built on a variety of tank chassis.

Tank destroyers proved effective in their proper role, but being quicker and easier to build they were often added to tank formations to make up numbers. The lack of a quick-traversing turret was a serious drawback in mobile operations, but nevertheless the concept was a success. From mid-1944, the Hetzer tank destroyer, built on a modified Panzer 38(t) chassis, entered service. Much cheaper than the contemporary Jagdpanzer IV, it remained an effective anti-tank platform for the remainder of the war.

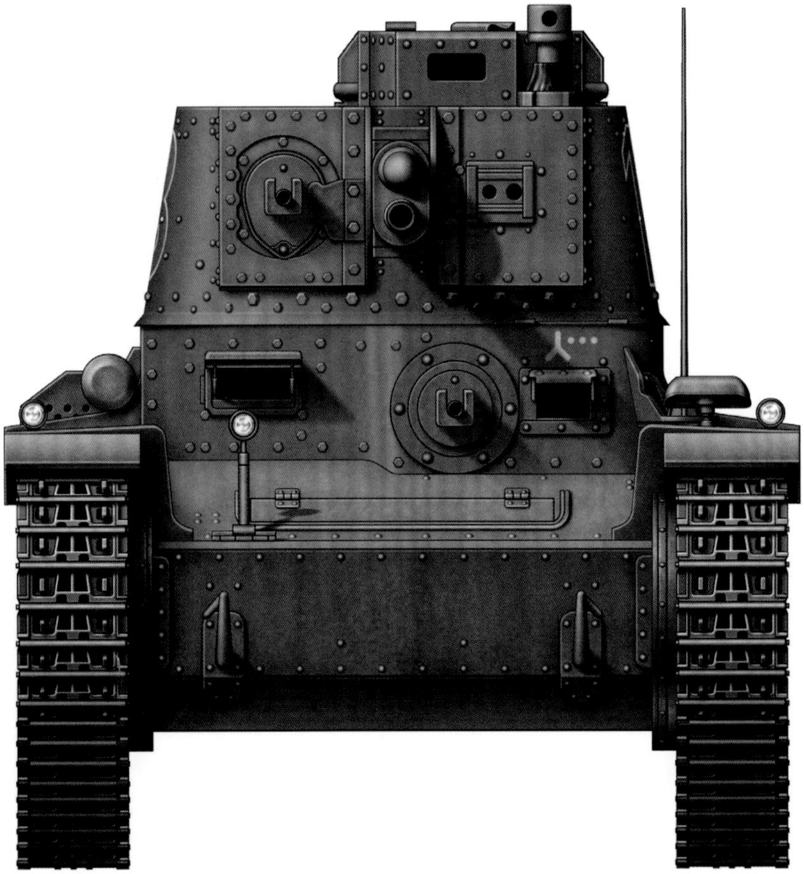

A Panzer 38(t) crosses a pontoon bridge during the invasion of France and the Low Countries in 1940. The light weight of the Panzer 38(t) was an asset when using hastily erected pontoon bridges.

TURRET

The small turret ring of the Panzer 38(t) imposed limitations on how far the gun could be upgraded.

IS-3 Heavy Tank

19

The IS-3 heavy tank fielded an extremely potent 122mm (4.8in) gun, making it the most powerfully armed tank of its day. It also was the first Soviet design to use what became a characteristic feature – the mushroom-shaped turret. Concerns about mobility resulted in the IS-3 being the last Soviet heavy tank design to go into mass production.

HEAVY TANK DYNASTY

The IS-3 can trace its origins back to the KV-1 heavy tank, which gave good service against the German invasion of Russia. Heavy tanks were considered useful in breaking an enemy line or dealing with armoured forces, so while the T-34 became the backbone of Soviet armed forces the heavy tanks still had a place in the order of battle. This was not least because Joseph Stalin (after whom the IS, or JS, series of tanks were named) was very keen on heavy armoured vehicles.

Further heavy tank designs appeared – KV-85, IS-85 and finally the IS series. The IS-1 was based on the KV series, with a larger turret ring to accommodate a more powerful gun. Some IS-1s were retrofitted with a 122mm (4.8in) gun, which became standard on the IS-2. This armament was retained for the IS-3, which had a new turret design and better armour. This move was prompted by the discovery that, for all the potency of the IS-2 'victory tank', it could be penetrated at 1000m (3280ft) by the armament of a Panther or Tiger.

FLAWED DESIGN

The IS-3 went into production very late in the war. The first few examples were rushed westwards to take part in the advance on Berlin, only to arrive a little too late. Reports exist of a skirmish with a small German force, but there is

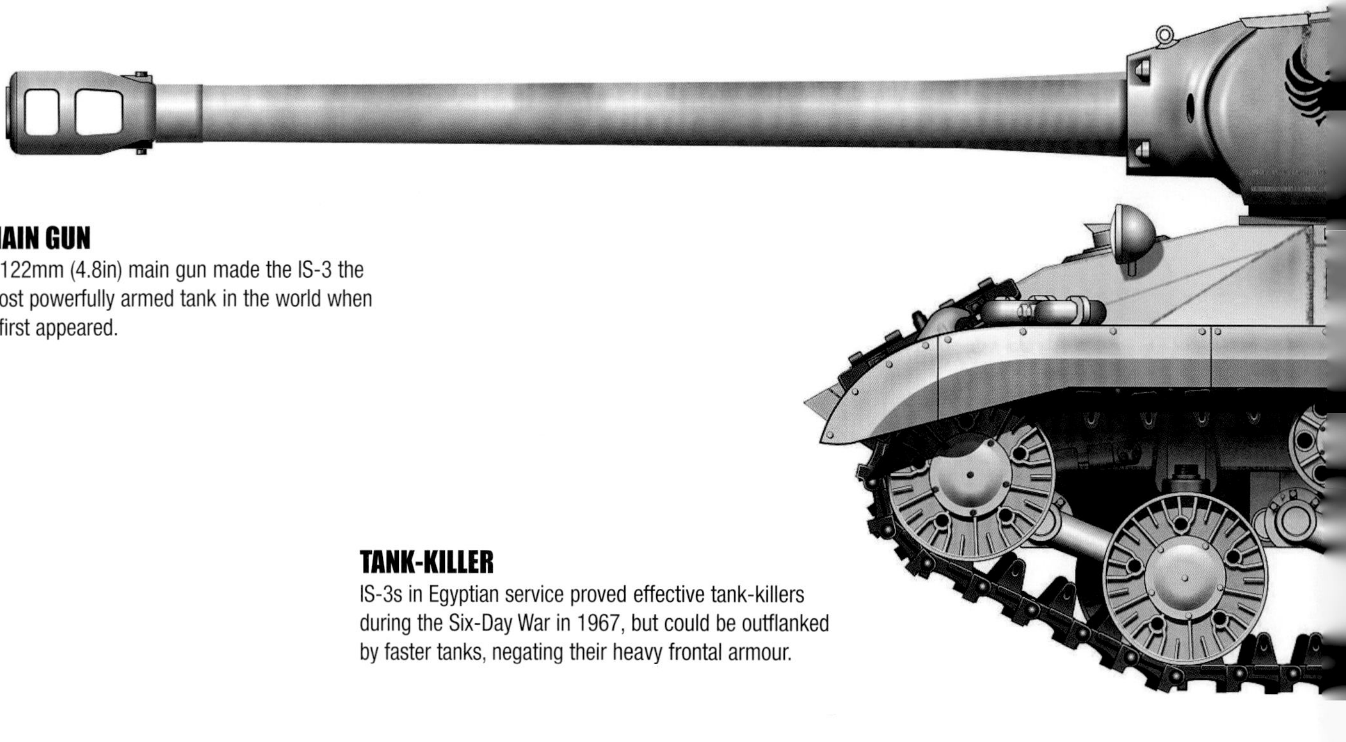

MAIN GUN

A 122mm (4.8in) main gun made the IS-3 the most powerfully armed tank in the world when it first appeared.

TANK-KILLER

IS-3s in Egyptian service proved effective tank-killers during the Six-Day War in 1967, but could be outflanked by faster tanks, negating their heavy frontal armour.

SPECIFICATIONS (IS-3 HEAVY TANK)

Dimensions: Length: 6.81m (22ft 4in), Height: 2.93m (9ft 7.5in), Width: 3.44m (11ft 3.5in)

Weight: 41.2 tonnes (45.5 tons)

Engine/powerplant: V2 IS 12-cylinder diesel engine

Speed: 37km/h (22.9mph)

Armament: Main gun: 122mm (4.8in) D-25 gun, Anti-aircraft mount: 12.7mm (0.5in) machine gun

Crew: 4

Although the IS-3 arrived too late to lead the advance on Berlin, there were real fears that it might lead a new advance westward into Allied-occupied Europe if the Cold War heated up.

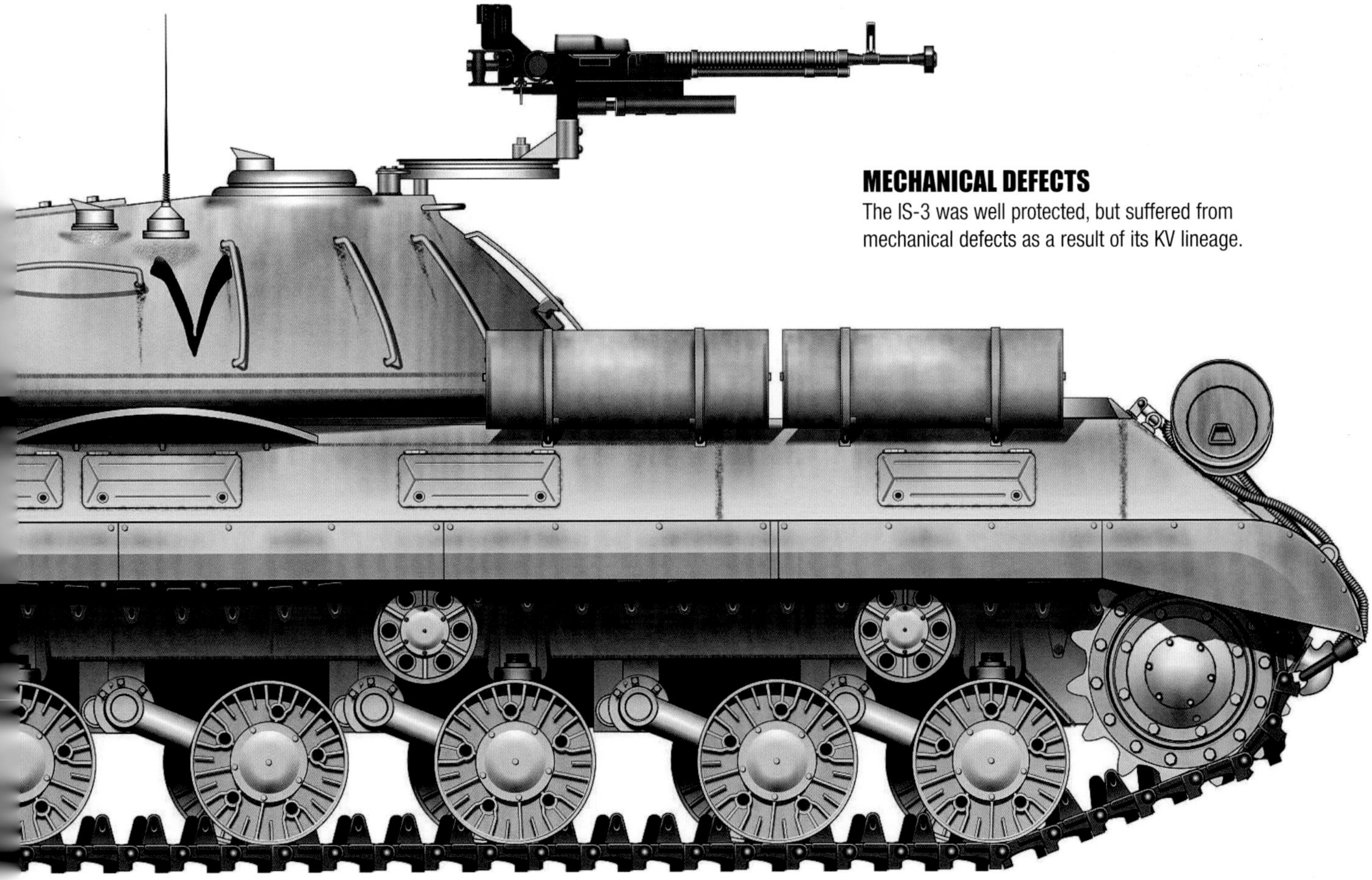

MECHANICAL DEFECTS

The IS-3 was well protected, but suffered from mechanical defects as a result of its KV lineage.

Red Army IS-3s take part in a show of force. Huge parades were a political tool for the Soviet Union; a pointed reminder of its enormous military capabilities.

no clear evidence that this took place. Thus, the IS-3 was conceived in the World War II era but became the most powerful tank of the early Cold War.

Although sufficiently threatening that the Western powers built their own heavy tanks to counter it, the IS-3 was not without faults. Its transmission was based on that of the KV-1 and retained its mechanical difficulties. Similarly, the low turret made the IS-3 a difficult target but limited the depression possible with the main gun. This was not much of a problem in mobile warfare, but prevented the IS-3 from making best use of a hull-down position behind cover. A very limited ammunition supply for the main gun, coupled with a slow rate of fire, imposed further limitations.

IS-3 IN SERVICE

Within a few months of its introduction, upgrades to the IS-3 began to be implemented. These eliminated or reduced most of its faults, creating the IS-3M that served from 1948 onwards. A second round of upgrades took place in the 1950s, with improvements to sighting systems, electrical

GLACIS PLATE

Rather than an angled glacis plate, the IS-3 had a pointed nose, which earned it the nickname 'the pike'.

ATTACK TANK

The IS-3 was designed for spearheading an attack rather than resisting one. Lack of gun depression limited its use in defensive positions.

systems and – most importantly – the engine. The original powerplant, retained from previous heavy tanks, was insufficiently powerful for the greater weight of the IS-3.

Other than the 1956 invasion of Hungary, IS-3s in Soviet hands saw little action. Instead, they exerted a strategic presence during the Cold War standoff. Those supplied to Egypt fought in the 1967 Six-Day War with Israel, where many were captured.

The frontal armour of the IS-3 proved impervious to most Israeli weapons, and in a long-range gun duel the IS-3 had a distinct advantage. However, they were not equipped with a gun stabilizer and could not shoot accurately on the move. With greater mobility and faster-firing guns, Israeli tanks were able to outmanoeuvre the IS-3 and engage it from the flanks or the rear.

ARMOUR

The armour of the IS-3 ranged from 230mm (9in) at the front to 20mm (0.78in) at the rear. Although very tough from the front, the IS-3 was vulnerable to attack from the flank.

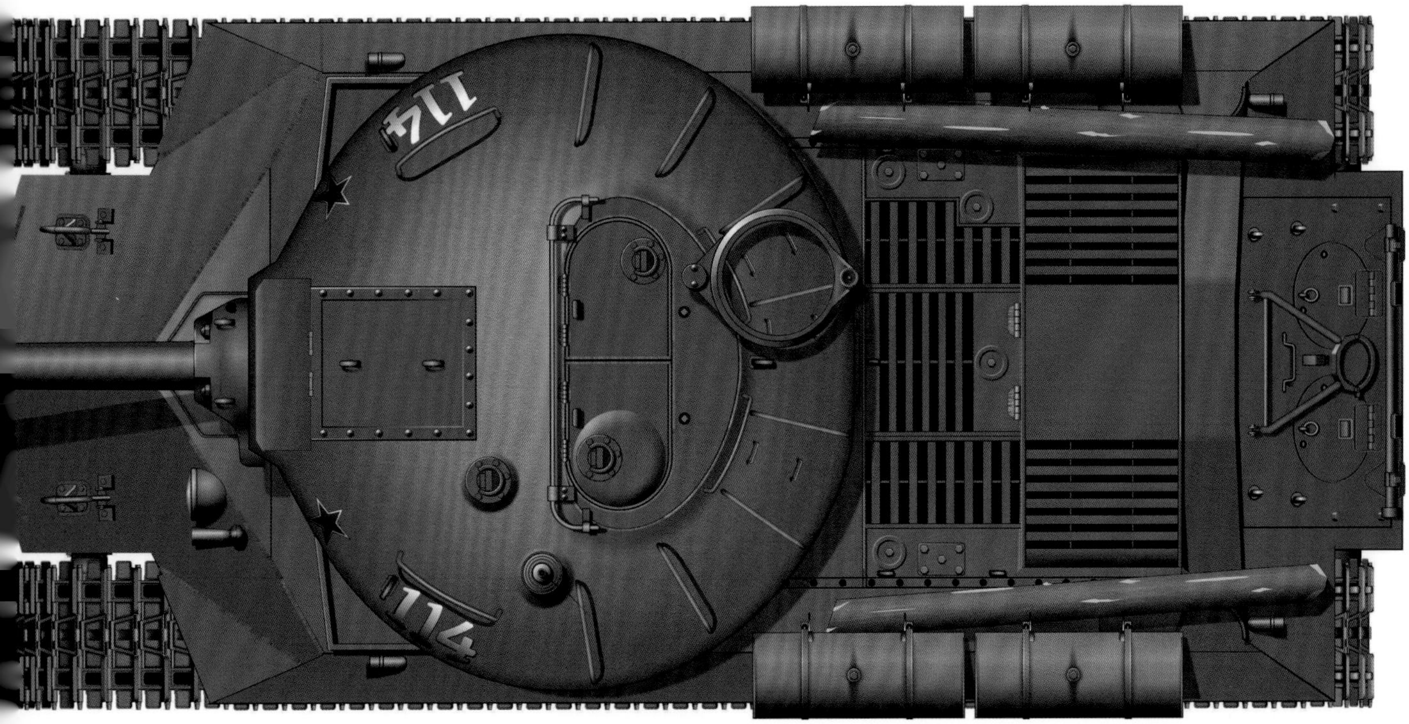

Panzer VI Tiger

18

The PzKpfw VI Tiger inspired such fear that Allied forces were ordered to punish soldiers for saying they had sighted one. However, despite its fearsome reputation and undeniable potential, the Tiger was not quite the wonder-weapon its designers hoped it would be. Mechanical and logistical problems prevented it from achieving its true potential.

BIGGER IS BETTER

The Tiger was conceived as a heavy tank, but not the lumbering monster it eventually grew into. As early as the mid-1930s, German planners realized the need for a tank capable of destroying heavy armoured vehicles such as the French Char 1B. A big gun, of at least 75mm (2.9in) calibre, would be needed, which in turn necessitated a large turret and a heavily armoured hull to protect it. By the end of the 1930s, prototypes from Henschel and Porsche were being tested but development was plagued by mechanical troubles, many of which originated from Hitler's insistence on more armour.

What was to have been an effective and practical heavy tank design gradually became more and more overloaded, requiring complex technical solutions. Among these was the interleaved suspension, which was prone to clogging with mud and required the removal of the outer road wheels for rail transport. Two sets of tracks had to be provided – one for strategic movement and transportation, and a wider set for combat operations.

TIGER IN SERVICE

The Tiger first saw action in late 1942. Its effectiveness was greatly reduced by mechanical troubles, but by early

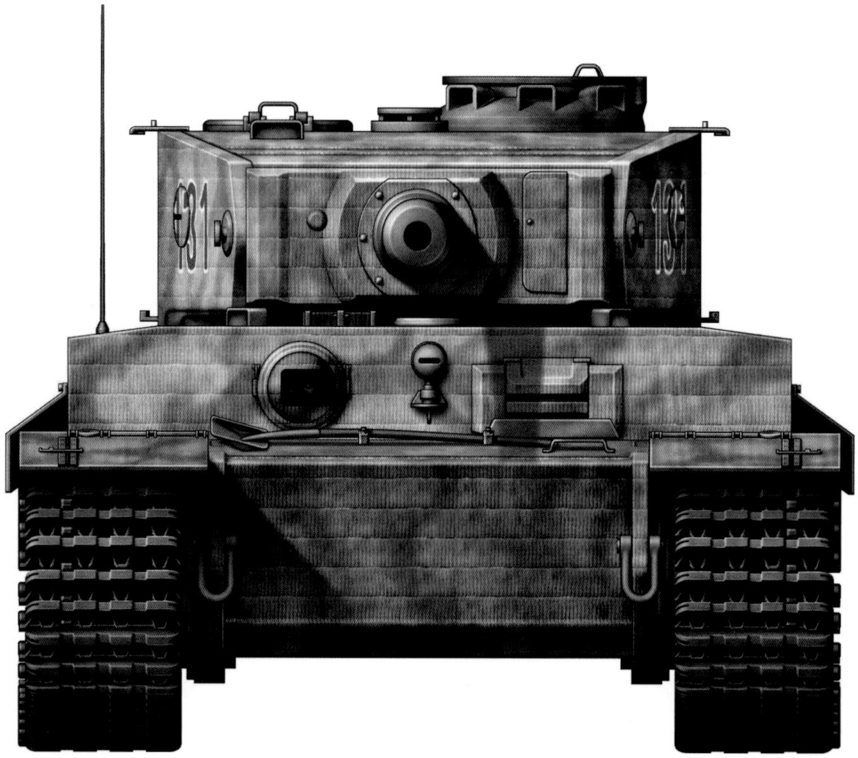

MAIN GUN

The 88mm (3.4in) main gun was one of the most potent tank-killers of its day.

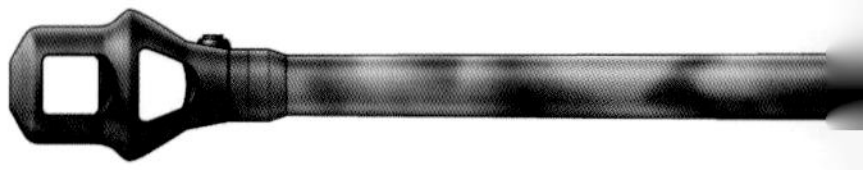

SHAPE

The blocky shape of the Tiger, reminiscent of the Panzer IV, makes inefficient use of its armour thickness.

SPECIFICATIONS (PANZER VI TIGER)

Dimensions: Length: 8.45m (27ft 8.5in), Height: 3m (9ft 10in), Width: 3.56m (11ft 8in)

Weight: 50.8 tonnes (56 tons)

Engine/powerplant: Maybach HL210P45 V12 petrol engine

Speed: 37km/h (22.9mph)

Armament: Main gun: 88mm (3.4in) KwK36 L/56 gun, Co-axial: 7.92mm (0.3in) machine gun, Hull-mounted: 7.92mm (0.3in) machine gun, Additional: 7.92mm (0.3in) machine gun on some examples

Crew: 5

German crew stand outside their Tiger during the fighting for Northwest Europe in 1944. The Tiger was most effective when acting as a mobile anti-tank emplacement. Effective use of foliage for camouflage enabled the tank to strike from ambush positions.

the following year these were largely rectified. However, production was slow and expensive, severely limiting the number of Tigers available. Its fuel consumption was also very high, which became a serious problem, since German supplies became increasingly disrupted as Allied bombing raids damaged German industry and infrastructure.

ROAD WHEELS
Interleaved road wheels reduced ground pressure at the cost of complexity and a tendency to become clogged.

18

A Tiger crew examining their tank somewhere on the Eastern Front. Tiger units frequently acted as a 'fire brigade', dealing with one crisis after another.

With its powerful gun and very heavy armour the Tiger was an unpleasant surprise for the Allied troops it encountered, enabling several commanders to become 'aces' by destroying at least ten enemy tanks. However, by mid-1943 the tide was turning and the German army was increasingly on the defensive. Rather than fighting in a breakthrough role, Tiger-equipped units were rushed from one crisis point to another, resulting in serious logistical troubles and increasingly frequent breakdowns.

In addition to the Eastern Front, Tigers fought in North Africa but arrived too late to prevent defeat there. In Sicily and Italy, the Tiger force suffered from a lack of maintenance and technical support. They also experienced serious mechanical problems, although the tanks were very effective whenever they encountered the enemy.

NORMANDY AND BEYOND

A force of Tigers was deployed to meet the Allied invasion of Normandy, but had to operate under heavy air attack and suffered accordingly. On the defensive or making

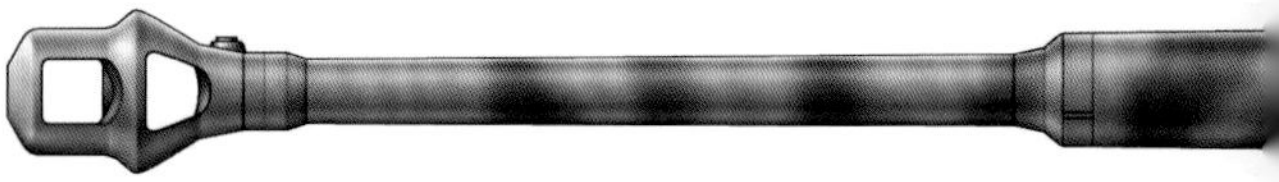

DESIGN

In many ways, the Tiger represented the culmination of pre-war thinking. Its blocky design was supplanted by more efficient sloped and curved armour, such as that used on the Panther and T-34.

ARMOUR

The front hull of the Tiger was 100mm (3.9in) in thickness, while the turret was 120mm (4.7in) – substantially thicker than most of its adversaries.

The Tiger possessed reasonable cross-country mobility, but was too heavy for many bridges.

local counterattacks, the Tiger proved deadly enough to inspire what became known as 'Tiger Terror'. However, in the cluttered terrain of Normandy it was prone to being outmanoeuvred by faster Allied tanks. The very slow traverse of a Tiger's turret was often insufficient to track a fast-moving target, and while kill-ratios in some actions exceeded 20 to 1, there were simply too many Allied tanks for a successful defence.

The Tiger was deployed in increasingly small battlegroups, often supported by other tanks and assault guns as the war went on. With fuel in short supply and forced to make numerous retreats, the Tiger's limitations began to outweigh its undeniable advantages. The resources expended on developing a super-tank might better have been spent on a humbler but far more numerous vehicle – the Tiger could win battles, but it could not alter the outcome of the war.

PANZER ACE

The '007' identifies this tank as that of the 'panzer ace' Michael Wittmann. Wittmann was credited with at least 120 'kills', mainly on the Eastern Front in a Tiger tank.

T-54/55

The Soviet T-54 underwent a series of upgrades and modifications until it was more or less a different tank. This gained it the designation T-55. Existing T-54s were then upgraded until they were more or less identical to the T-55, creating the potentially confusing T-54/55 designation.

T-54

The T-54 epitomized the Soviet Union's policy of quantity over quality. It was designed for simplicity of operation and manufacture, with little concern for the comfort of the crew. This approach suited the military structure of the Soviet Union, with its very large conscript armies. More sophisticated vehicles might have required longer and more advanced training that was not possible under the circumstances.

Development can be traced back to an experiment mounting a 100mm (3.9in) gun on a converted T-34. This was not a success due to the gun's recoil, so a new tank, designated T-44, was developed. After much modification this became the basis for the T-54, which was given improved armour before going into mass production. Modification and improvement continued during production, including a new turret, gun stabilization system and infrared systems for night fighting.

ALL-ROUNDER

The tendency to upgrade T-54s to T-55 standard has made them virtually indistinguishable. A classically Russian design in terms of both appearance and function, the T-54/55 gave reasonable performance at a low cost.

SPECIFICATIONS (T-55)

Dimensions: Length: 6.45m (21ft 2in), Height: 2.4m (7ft 10in), Width: 3.27m (10ft 9in)

Weight: 32.1 tonnes (35.4 tons)

Engine/powerplant: V-54 12-cylinder diesel engine

Speed: 48km/h (30mph)

Armament: Main gun: 100mm (3.9in) D-10T gun, Co-axial: 7.62mm (0.3in) machine gun, Additional: 7.62mm (0.3in) and 12.7mm (0.5in) machine guns on some models

Crew: 4

This T-55 is in Croatian army service. More than 80,000 T-54/55s have been produced and served in at least 50 armies around the world.

T-55

The T-55 entered service in 1958. Developed from the T-54, it combined all the upgrades made thus far, adding NBC protection for the crew. Experience with the T-54 indicated that it was underpowered and suffered mechanical problems as a result. This was rectified by fitting a new engine, with additional fuel storage to increase operating radius. Armament was more or less the same, although

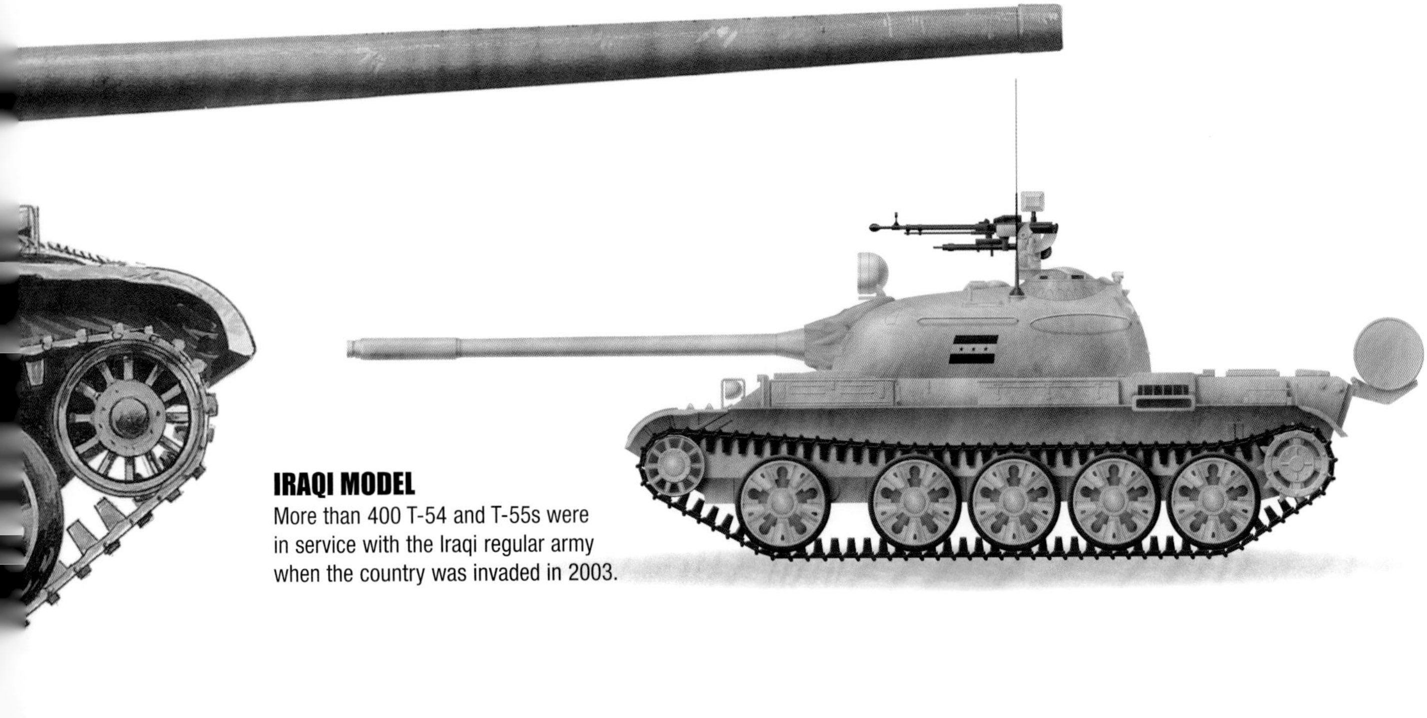

MAIN GUN
The 100mm (3.9in) main gun was a powerful weapon in the early Cold War era.

IRAQI MODEL
More than 400 T-54 and T-55s were in service with the Iraqi regular army when the country was invaded in 2003.

the effectiveness of the main gun was increased by using improved day and infrared sights.

Upgrades continued throughout the T-55's service life, including another improved engine, enhanced NBC protection, additional armour and a better gun stabilization system. Panels of explosive reactive armour (ERA) were retrofitted to protect against the increasingly common threat of infantry-launched shaped-charge weapons. The T-55M6 version is virtually a new tank, with an elongated hull and a new turret as well as improved internal systems.

T-54/55 IN SERVICE

Estimates vary of how many T-54/55s have been built. A figure of around 60,000 within the Soviet Union is widely accepted, with possibly as many as 20,000 more built in other nations – notably Poland and Czechoslovakia. Chinese Type 59 and Type 69 tanks were also derived from the T-54, and have been exported to several nations.

In addition to being the mainstay of the Soviet armoured forces for many years, the T-54/55 has also been widely exported. It found favour with many operators for its simplicity of use, although its awkward internal layout and cramped fighting compartment placed limits on how effective it could be. In short, the T-54/55 enabled its users to obtain armoured warfare capabilities for a relatively small outlay but prevented them from attaining the high levels of capability attained by well-trained users of more sophisticated tanks. Despite this limitation, the T-54/55 could take on any Western tank available at the time it entered service, and even today remains an effective fighting vehicle.

T-54/55s have seen active service in Russian hands from the 1956 invasion of Hungary onwards. Despite new designs becoming available, the need for large numbers of tanks kept the T-54/55 from being fully retired. Exported examples fought in the Arab–Israeli wars and the Iran–Iraq war of the 1980s, the Vietnam War, clashes between India and Pakistan as well as many other conflicts including various civil wars. This is not surprising given the ubiquity of the design, and since upgrade kits are still being manufactured it seems likely that the T-54/55 family will continue to serve for some years to come.

LONG SERVICE
The T-54/55 equipped many Middle Eastern armies during the Cold War era, with many examples remaining in service today.

GUN DEPRESSION
With gun depression limited to about 5 degrees by the small turret, the T-55 is limited on the defensive. This is less of a problem when operating in the open.

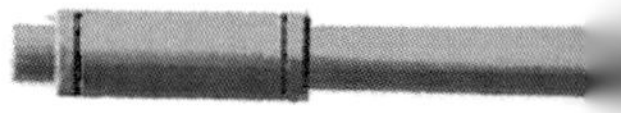

Inadequate stabilization limited the effective range of the T-54/55's gun when firing on the move.

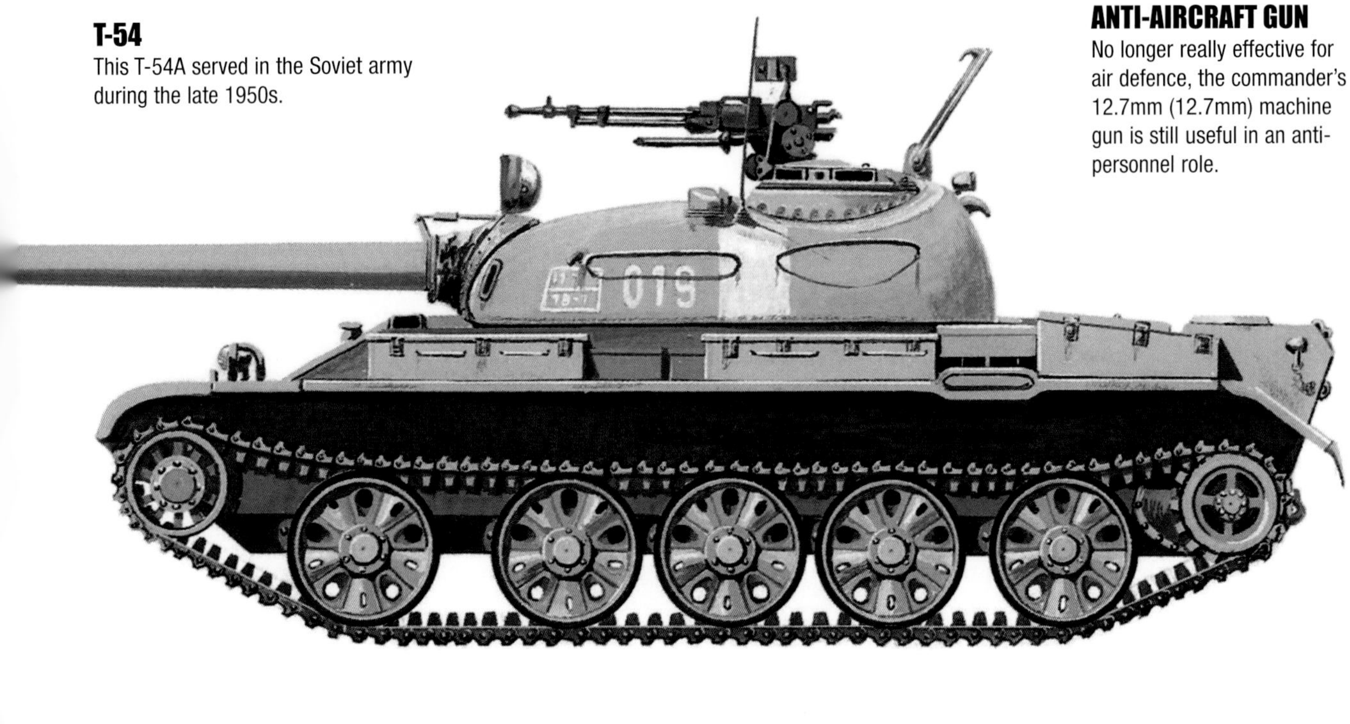

T-54

This T-54A served in the Soviet army during the late 1950s.

ANTI-AIRCRAFT GUN

No longer really effective for air defence, the commander's 12.7mm (12.7mm) machine gun is still useful in an anti-personnel role.

Panzer I and II

16

Although very lightly armed and armoured, the Panzer I and II made up the majority of German armoured strength during the early phases of World War II. These vehicles were hugely influential on the development of armoured warfare tactics and also served as the basis for many important concepts such as self-propelled artillery.

PANZER I

Developed at a time when Germany was prohibited from possessing tanks, the PzKpfw I was the subject of various polite fictions to deflect attention from its true nature. The Ausf A model went into production late in 1934, followed by the Ausf B model in 1936. This had a longer chassis, better suspension and a more reliable engine. Both models were very lightly armoured and armed with a pair of machine guns, and both variants served in the Spanish Civil War, where they encountered Russian-made tanks. Using armour-piercing ammunition, a PzKpfw I could damage a Russian T-26 at close range, but it was clear a more potent weapon was needed.

PANZER II

The PzKpfw II was essentially an enlarged version of the Panzer I armed with a 20mm (0.78in) cannon. Typically loaded with a mix of armour-piercing and high-explosive

PANZER I AUSF B
This Panzer I Ausf B fought in the Polish campaign of September 1939. The Ausf B was slightly longer than the Ausf A model.

Panzer Is ford a river during training. The Panzer I was never intended for more than a reconnaissance role, its light armour and weaponry making it unsuited for armoured combat.

SPECIFICATIONS (PZKPFW II AUSF F)

Dimensions: Length: 4.64m (15ft 3in), Height: 2.02m (6ft 7.5in), Width: 2.3m (7ft 6.5in)
Weight: 8.6 tonnes (9.5 tons)
Engine/powerplant: Maybach HL62TR 6-cylinder petrol engine
Speed: 40km/h (24.9mph)
Armament: Main gun: KwK 30/38 20mm (0.78in) cannon, Co-axial: 7.92mm (0.3in) machine gun
Crew: 3

CROSS-COUNTRY MOBILITY

The Panzer I and Panzer II had high ground clearance to help with cross-country mobility.

MACHINE GUNS

Armed only with a pair of machine guns, the Panzer I Ausf B was never intended as a battle tank.

Panzer IIs and Czech-bullt Panzer 38(t)s advance through the Polish countryside during the invasion of Poland, September 1939. During the invasion of Poland, the Panzer II proved well able to deal with Polish light tanks and tankettes.

shells, the Panzer II's gun was effective against light vehicles as well as infantry positions, and could threaten the light tanks of the day. Later in the Panzer II's career, a tungsten-cored anti-tank round became available. Armour protection was much better than that of the previous design, largely as a result of experience gained in the Spanish Civil War.

The PzKpfw II evolved through a series of models A–F. Other projects were designated PzKpfw II, but were heavily redesigned or wholly different. Among these was a heavy reconnaissance tank designated PzKpfw II Ausf J that, while still armed with a 20mm (0.78in) cannon, was so heavily armoured that it was nicknamed 'baby Tiger'.

PANZER I AND II IN SERVICE

Although intended mainly as a way to gain experience of armoured operations, and far better suited to a light reconnaissance role than serving as a battle tank, the Panzer I had to suffice until more effective vehicles were available in the required numbers. Likewise, the Panzer II, developed mainly as a stopgap, was pushed to the fore and served admirably. This was more due to skilful handling and the effective use of mobility than the capabilities of the tanks themselves, although the Panzer II was entirely

Combined tank-infantry tactics were pioneered with vehicles like the Panzer I, pictured here during fighting for Warsaw in September 1939. The Panzer I allowed Germany to gain experience of operating armoured vehicles on both a small and a large scale.

ARMOUR
The Panzer II had 35mm (1.3in) thick armour at the front, but only 14.5mm (0.57in) at the rear. The sides were 20mm (0.78in) thickness.

DESERT PANZER
A Panzer II wearing desert camouflage and the insignia of the Afrika Korps. Light tanks proved to be effective reconnaissance vehicles in highly mobile desert warfare.

capable of dealing with most tanks possessed by its enemies at that stage of the war.

By the time of the invasion of Russia in 1941, sufficient numbers of heavier tanks were available and the Panzer II had moved to a scouting and screening role for which it was much better suited. It was effective in this capacity, but could take on only the lightest Russian tanks. The Panzer II remained viable longer in North Africa, where its mobility was a huge asset in the desert terrain.

Although some were retained for reconnaissance purposes, by late 1942 most Panzer IIs and virtually all Panzer Is had been removed from the frontlines. Their fates varied – many were used for security duties or crew training, while others were transferred to other Axis nations. Panzer I and II chassis were also used as the basis for a variety of specialist vehicles. These included command tanks, anti-aircraft platforms, ammunition carriers and highly effective light tank-destroyers as well as self-propelled guns that brought together artillery firepower and armoured mobility.

Matilda II

Although woefully undergunnned, the A12 Infantry Tank, or 'Matilda II', proved effective in combat. Its heavy armour was virtually immune to the anti-tank weapons of the day, enabling it to play a vital role in halting the advance of the Afrika Korps and ultimately turning the tide of the North African campaign.

INTER-WAR INFANTRY TANK

The A11 Infantry Tank Mk I, sometimes called the 'Matilda I', was developed in the late 1920s. This was a period when money was in short supply and World War I thinking was very much in evidence. The result was a cheap and reliable tank armed only with a machine gun. This did not make it ineffective or immediately obsolete; the majority of vehicles in the highly successful Panzer campaigns of 1939–40 were PzKpfw I and II, armed with machine guns or 20mm (0.78in) cannon.

The Matilda I was designed for infantry support, with speed considered far less important than armour protection.

MATILDA II

This Matilda II served with the British Expeditionary Force in France in May 1940. Side skirts protecting the Matilda II's flanks had mud chutes similar to those on the World War I Whippet tank.

ARMOUR

Like many other British infantry tanks, this tank was heavily armoured. The front glacis was 78mm (3.1in) thick.

SPECIFICATIONS (A12 MATILDA II)

Dimensions: Length: 5.61m (18ft 5in), Height: 2.52m (8ft 5in), Width: 2.59m (8ft 6in)

Weight: 24 tonnes (26.5 tons)

Engine/powerplant: Twin AEC or Leyland 6-cylinder diesel

Speed: 13km/h (8mph)

Armament: Main gun: 2-pdr (40mm) quick-firing gun, Co-axial: 7.92mm (0.3in) Besa machine gun

Crew: 4

British tankmen of the Royal Armoured Corps train with the Matilda II somewhere in Britain. The small turret hampered the commander, who had to operate the radio and fire the machine gun.

MATILDA I

Slow but heavily protected, the Matilda I (above) was intended for infantry support against static defensive positions. The tank was armed with a 12.7mm (0.5in) Vickers heavy machine gun.

TAIL

Another World War I feature was the 'tail' intended to facilitate trench-crossing.

The resulting tank was tough and served well in France, taking part in the Arras counterattack that briefly halted the Axis advance. After the fall of France, surviving Matilda Is were used for training purposes.

The A12 Infantry Tank Mark II was conceived almost immediately after the Matilda I, and was a more ambitious project. When it proved impossible to upgrade the Matilda I, an almost entirely new design was created. Although still rather slow, the A12 or 'Matilda II' was more mobile than its predecessor and was armed with a 2-pdr (40mm) gun. This was a fairly potent weapon by the standards of the day; the 37mm (1.4in) anti-tank gun was something of an industry standard. The 2-pdr could not fire a large enough high-explosive round to be useful in infantry support, but this limitation was more than offset by very thick armour.

1940 AND LATER

Early Matilda IIs were sent to France, where many were lost in the retreat and subsequent evacuation. It rapidly became clear that they were not built to fight the war now raging – the first batch of Matilda IIs had a 'tail' structure to assist in trench-crossing, which was soon deleted as unnecessary. Production proceeded through five models designated Mark 1 to 5, which can be a little confusing as the design itself was known as Infantry Tank Mark II.

The trench-crossing tail was omitted after the Mk1, with Mk3 and onwards receiving improved engines. The definitive version was the Mk4, produced in 1941–42. However, by this time the limitations of the 2-pdr gun were very obvious and an attempt to up-gun the Matilda using turrets from more recent designs was not a success.

MATILDA MK IV

The Mark IV model, with an improved engine, was the definitive Matilda II.

The Matilda II was used by Australian forces in the Pacific theatre, where they proved virtually invulnerable to Japanese anti-tank weapons.

SOVIET LEND-LEASE

The Red Army was supplied with almost 1000 Matilda IIs under lend-lease, but disliked their lack of mobility.

MATILDA IN ACTION

The Matilda is most commonly associated with the war in North Africa. In the early stages of the campaign it proved near-impervious to Italian and German anti-tank weapons and was not outclassed by the early-model Panzer IIIs and IVs it faced. The only weapon capable of reliably penetrating a Matilda was the 88mm (3.4in) anti-aircraft/anti-tank gun. The Matilda's lack of mobility was a distinct disadvantage here; outflanking or bypassing well-positioned anti-tank batteries was problematic for such a slow vehicle.

By late 1942, the Axis forces in Africa were armed with guns that could penetrate the Matilda's heavy armour, and losses mounted rapidly. Once suitable replacements became available, the Matilda was converted to other roles, such as mine clearance, or withdrawn into reserve. Numerous examples were sent to the Far Eastern theatre, where anti-tank warfare had lagged behind Europe. There, the tank that had been the mainstay of British armoured capability in the early war enjoyed a resurgence both as a gun tank and as a platform for other roles such as the Australian Matilda Frog flamethrowing tank.

KV-1

The Soviet Kliment Voroshilov (KV) heavy tank proved to be almost impervious to the available anti-tank weapons. Despite its limitations, it was a severe obstacle to the advance of German Panzer formations in 1941, and formed the basis for later heavy tank designs, including the IS series.

INTER-WAR HEAVY TANKS

The heavy tank was conceived as a breakthrough weapon. Although short-ranged, it was intended to smash enemy strongpoints and allow lighter forces to advance unchecked. On the defensive, heavy tanks were intended to act as mobile centres of resistance, inflicting heavy casualties on the enemy and forcing them to concentrate their efforts against the most resilient part of the Soviet arsenal.

The KV-1 was developed during the 1930s by a process that produced various unworkable multi-turreted designs. The T-100 and SMK designs were among the more sensible of these, with just two turrets, but proved unreliable and inefficient. However, a version with a single turret was also put forward and proved vastly superior. It went into production as the KV-1, initially using the hull, suspension and transmission of the SMK.

The original intent was to arm this new tank with a high-velocity 76mm (3in) gun, but this was not available in

MAIN GUN
Production delays forced the adoption of a lower-velocity 76mm (3in) gun than had been intended.

A KV-1 advances with infantry support somewhere on the Eastern Front. Although resilient against most German tank guns, the KV-1 could be destroyed by artillery or infantry attack. Cooperation with infantry reduced this risk.

SPECIFICATIONS (KV-1)

Dimensions: Length: 6.68m (21ft 11in), Height: 2.71m (8ft 11in), Width: 3.32m (10ft 11in)

Weight: 38.3 tonnes (42.3 tons)

Engine/powerplant: V2K V12 diesel engine

Speed: 35km/h (21.7mph)

Armament: Main gun: 76mm (3in) L/41 ZiS-5 gun, Additional: 7.62mm (0.3in) machine guns (up to four)

Crew: 5

time so a lower-powered gun of the same calibre was fitted to early KV-1s. Those that received the longer gun were designated KV-1A.

TURRET

Turrets on earlier models, such as this KV-1 Model 1941, were fashioned with welded steel plating. Later models had cast turrets, ensuring better structural integrity.

TRANSMISSION

The KV-1's transmission was unreliable – a fault never fully rectified in derived vehicles.

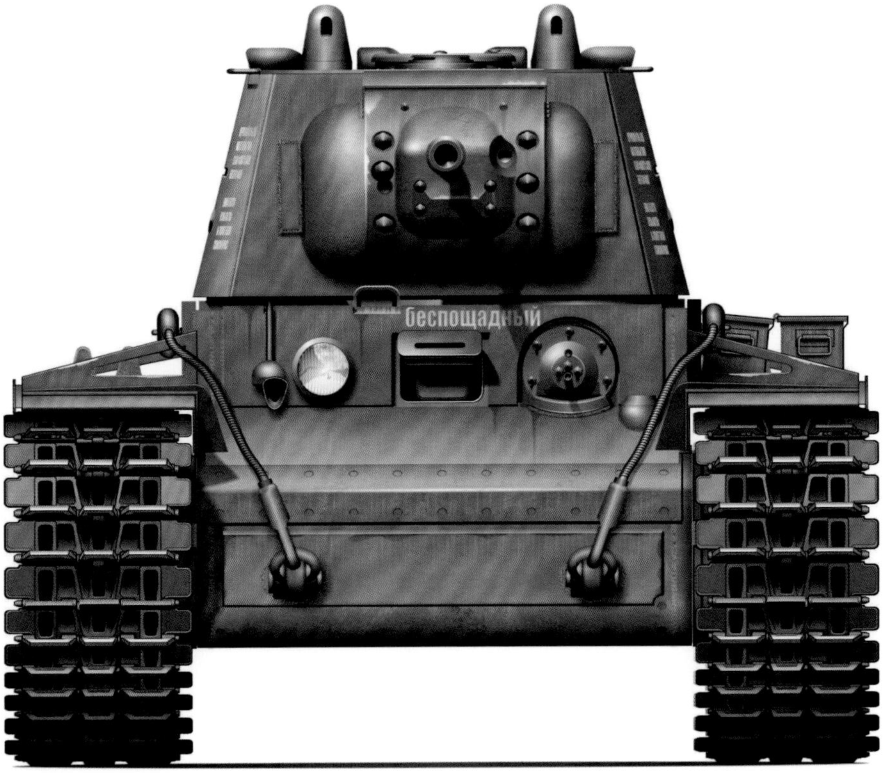

IN DEFENCE OF THE MOTHERLAND

The KV-1 had wide tracks that enabled it to cope with almost any terrain, but it was slow and suffered from poor visibility for the crew. Nevertheless, it was an unwelcome surprise for the advancing German forces in 1941. A lone KV-1 held up a vastly superior force for an entire day, while a handful, fighting from prepared positions, destroyed 43 German tanks in less than an hour.

The KV-1 became a symbol of heroic resistance, and proved very hard to kill. Had it been available in sufficient numbers it might have made the German advance very difficult. Able to shrug off multiple hits from anti-tank weapons, a KV-1 could be immobilized by damage to its tracks or a breakdown of its troublesome transmission. Lacking mobility, many were bypassed and later eliminated by artillery, air attack or tank-hunting infantry.

LATER MODELS AND VARIANTS

Production of the KV-1 was disrupted by the invasion, necessitating a movement of production facilities to safer locations. The KV-1B, or Model 1941, did not enter combat until 1942. It initially had the same gun as the T-34, but was later equipped with a longer-barrelled weapon that was still outranged by the bigger German guns. The KV-1C (Model 1942) version was given increased armour protection but was even slower as a result.

The creation of a 'fast' version, designated KV-1S, produced a lightly protected heavy tank that was no better than a T-34 and more expensive. The final incarnation of the KV-1 was the KV-85, an interim design armed with an 85mm (3.3in) gun. The same weapon was used on the IS-1 heavy tank, which also incorporated many components of the KV-1 series.

The abortive KV-13 programme attempted to combine the KV-1 and T-34 into a single 'universal' tank design, but was unable to fulfil several important design criteria. Another ultimately unsuccessful variant was the KV-2, an 'artillery tank' armed with a 152mm (5.9in) howitzer. Although successfully used to bombard fortifications in Finland, the KV-2 was too slow to be effective on a mobile battlefield. Those that faced the German invasion were hard to kill but relatively easy to bypass and were very prone to mechanical troubles.

The KV-1 was too slow to cope with the fast-moving German advance. Many were lost after being cut off or running out of fuel.

The KV-1 Model 1940 differed from the Model 1939 in that it had a longer gun, giving a higher muzzle velocity.

CAST TURRET

This Model 1941 had a cast turret and additional appliqué armour on the turret and hull.

ARMOUR

The KV-1's armour ranged from 37mm (1.4in) to 110mm (4.3in) on the later models. This made it a heavy and slow-moving tank, but difficult to destroy.

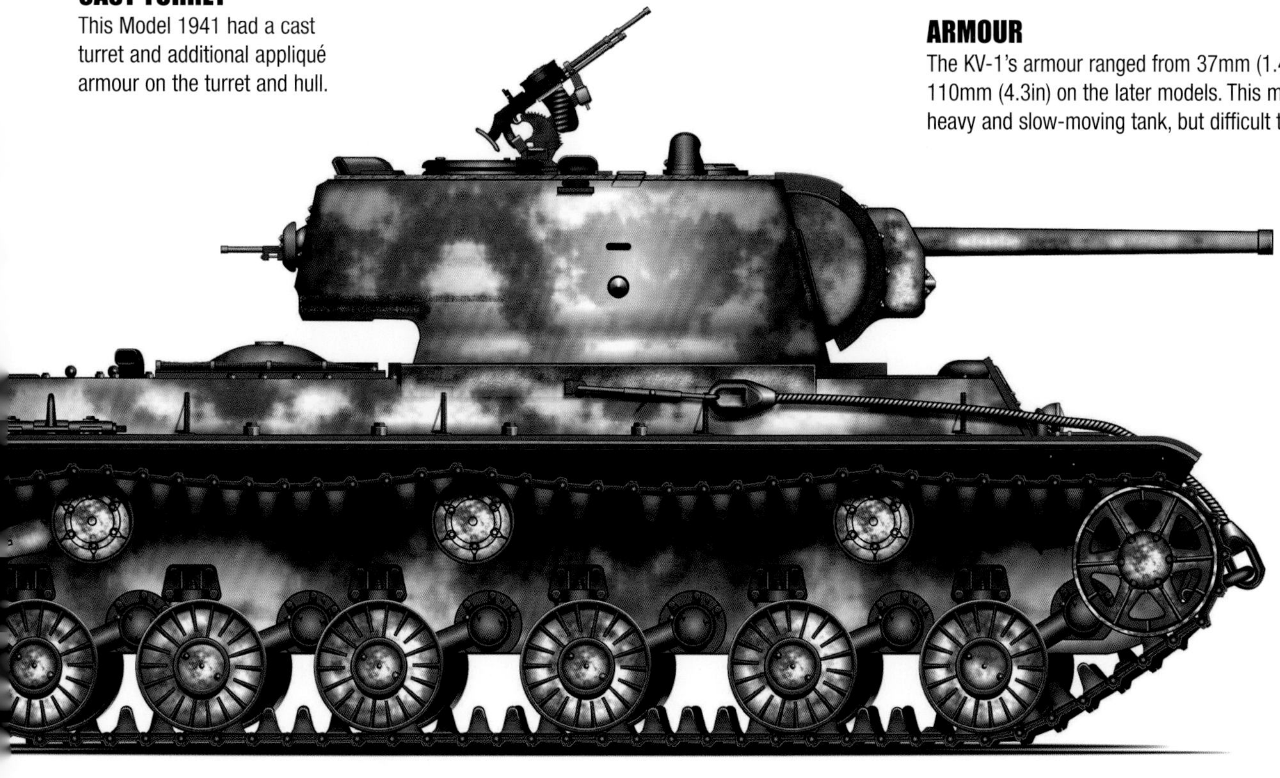

M60 Patton

The M60, unofficially named 'Patton', was the first US vehicle to be officially designated as a main battle tank. It served from 1960 until the late 1990s with the US Army, and remains in service in some nations. More than 15,000 were built and widely exported.

AN UPGRADED M48

The M48 Patton tank was built around a 90mm (3.5in) gun, and performed well in Israeli hands against other tanks. US-operated M48s provided gunfire support during the Vietnam War, but did not engage enemy tanks. One gained the dubious distinction of being the first tank lost to an anti-tank guided missile.

The M48 was well regarded and was produced in large numbers – around 12,000 were built during the 1950s. The M60 was developed from the successful M48 design, and although it included some new components it was very much an evolved version rather than a new design. The M60 proved to be almost infinitely upgradable, contributing to its long service life.

Early models used a very similar turret design to the M48, but from 1963 onwards a new design was implemented, narrowing towards the gun and tapering to the rear. Armament was configured in a manner now very familiar – a main 105mm (4.1in) gun with a co-axial 7.62mm (0.3in) machine gun and a 12.7mm (0.5in)

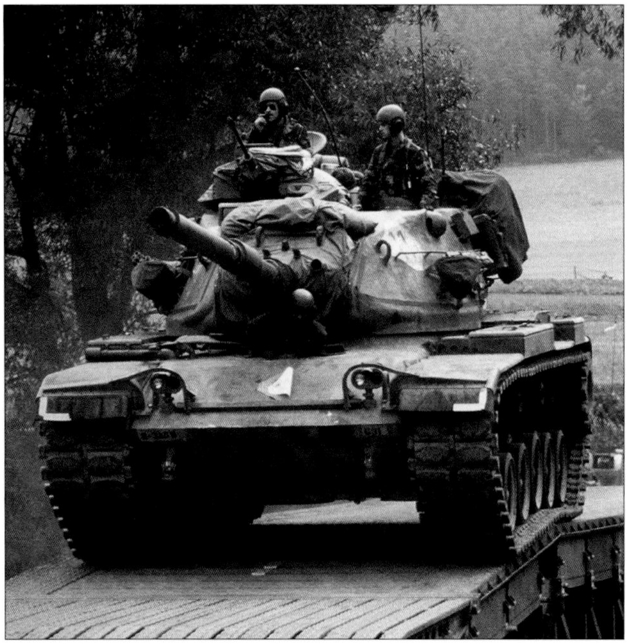

A US Army M60 crosses a girder bridge during exercises in 1983. The M60 Patton was the mainstay of US armoured forces for many years, and even today remains a credible frontline battle tank.

TURRET
The narrow turret design implemented for the A1 variant presents a very small target to the enemy.
GUN STABILIZER
During the 1970s, a gun stabilizer was added to the M60, enhancing on-the-move accuracy.

All-round vision has always been a problem for tank designers. The M60 has an array of optical periscopes that can be swapped for infrared devices at need.

SPECIFICATIONS (M60A1)

Dimensions: Length: 9.44m (31ft), Height: 3.27m (10ft 8.5in), Width: 3.63m (11ft 11in)

Weight: 46.9 tonnes (51.8 tons)

Engine/powerplant: Continental AVDS 1790 2A V12 diesel engine

Speed: 48km/h (29.8mph)

Armament: Main gun: 105mm (4.1in) M68 gun, Co-axial: 7.62mm (0.3in) machine gun, 12.7mm (0.5in) on turret roof

Crew: 4

COMMANDER'S CUPOLA

A 12.7mm (0.5in) M85 Browning heavy machine gun was mounted on the commander's cupola.

A US Marine Corps M60 equipped with add-on reactive armour. The short tubes above the main gun are smoke grenade launchers.

SUPPORT ROLE
The M728's main purpose is to neutralize defensive fixtures and obstacles, such as walls, fences, roadblocks and bunkers, or to destroy enemy-occupied buildings.

ENGINEER VEHICLE
Like many tank designs, the M60 spawned variants, including the M728 Combat Engineer Vehicle.

DOZER BLADE
The M728 is equipped with a dozer blade and armed with a 165mm (6.5in) demolition gun.

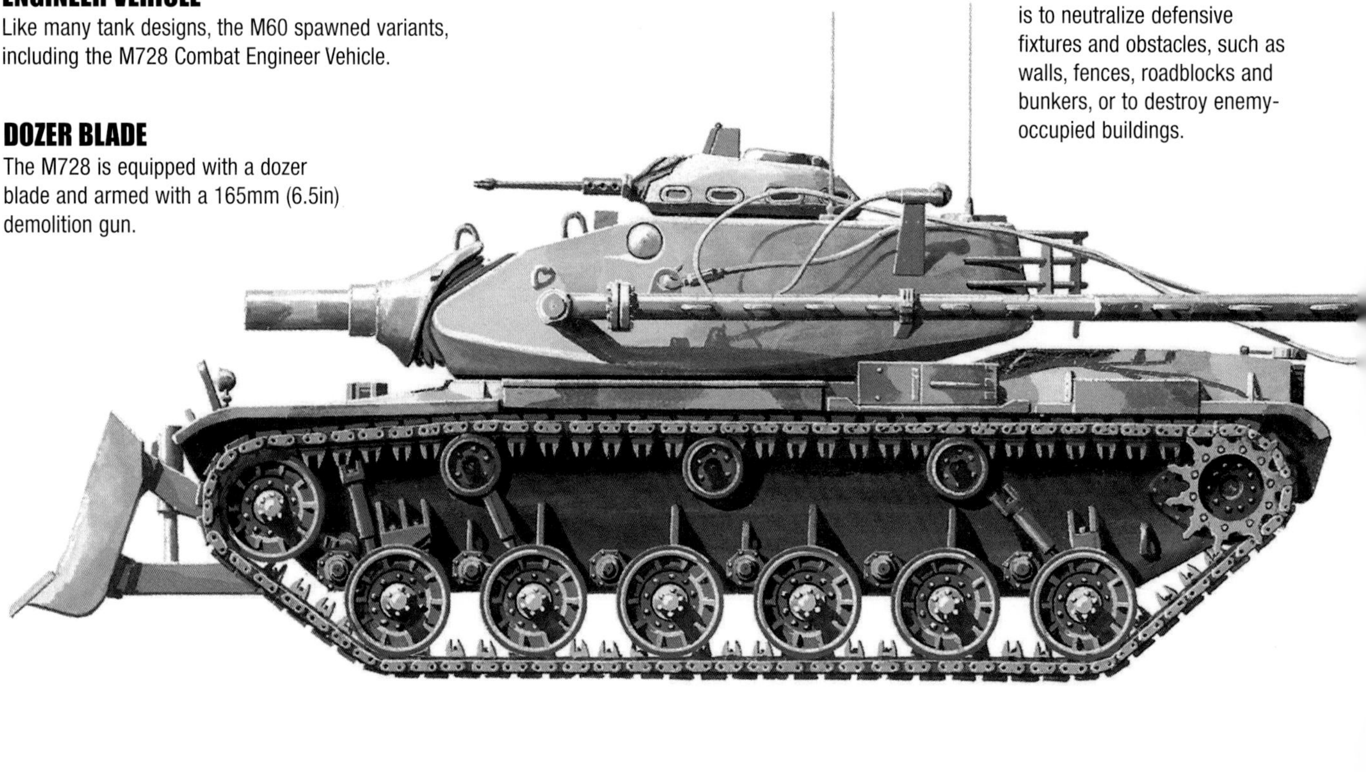

machine gun on the turret top for use by the commander. This gun could be operated from inside the turret if necessary.

Israeli M60s proved superior to Arab-operated T-62s in the 1973 Yom Kippur War, but were vulnerable to guided anti-tank missiles, which were fielded in large numbers. In 1982, Israeli M60s encountered T-72s in Lebanon (and also older designs including some T-34s) and again performed well. No losses to enemy tank guns were reported, although missiles were again a serious threat. Iranian M60s fought Iraqi T-72s during the Iran–Iraq war of 1980–88, although effectiveness was hampered by poor maintenance. The M60 saw relatively little action in US hands, although it was used by the US Marine Corps in the 1991 Gulf War. USMC M60A1s destroyed numerous Iraqi tanks, including T-72s, for the loss of just one M60.

VERSIONS AND VARIANTS

The M60A1 version was the first to receive the new turret, although early M60A1s were constructed with the original design. Other upgrades included a gun stabilization system and a new engine. The A2 variant was an experimental development of the M60 intended to serve until the MBT70 project entered service. In the event, MBT70 did not produce a replacement and the M60A2 also failed to impress. It was built around a 152mm (5.9in) gun that could fire Shillelagh anti-tank missiles or explosive rounds. Like other vehicles using this weapon, the M60A2 was not a success. M60A3, on the other hand, was an excellent tank. Developed alongside the project that would eventually result in the M1 Abrams, the M60A3 was intended to produce a lower-cost vehicle that would still be able to take on the current generation of Soviet tanks. It was revised during production, removing the commander's cupola and thus lowering the tank's silhouette.

Specialist M60 variants, including a combat engineering vehicle, are still in US service, while many overseas users retain the M60 as a frontline tank. The Magach 6 and 7 tanks of the Israeli Defence Force are modified and upgraded M60s, while Jordan has created a version named Phoenix armed with a 120mm (4.7in) gun. Significant numbers of M60A1s and A3s remain in frontline service worldwide.

An M60A1 on manoeuvres in Germany during the 1980s. Although it never took part in a major war in US service, the M60 has seen action worldwide, where it has demonstrated a high level of effectiveness.

Somua S-35

The Somua S-35 was an advanced inter-war design. It was superior in many ways to the German Panzers, mounting a powerful gun by the standards of the time. It was not any deficiency in its design that prevented the Somua S-35 from achieving its potential – it was simply overtaken by events.

CAMOUFLAGE

This S-35 fought in the May 1940 campaign. It is painted in a three-tone, green and brown disruptive pattern camouflage that was popular with French armoured forces at the time.

SIDE HATCH

Lack of turret hatches forced the commander to exit the tank and position himself on the upper surface when not 'buttoned up'.

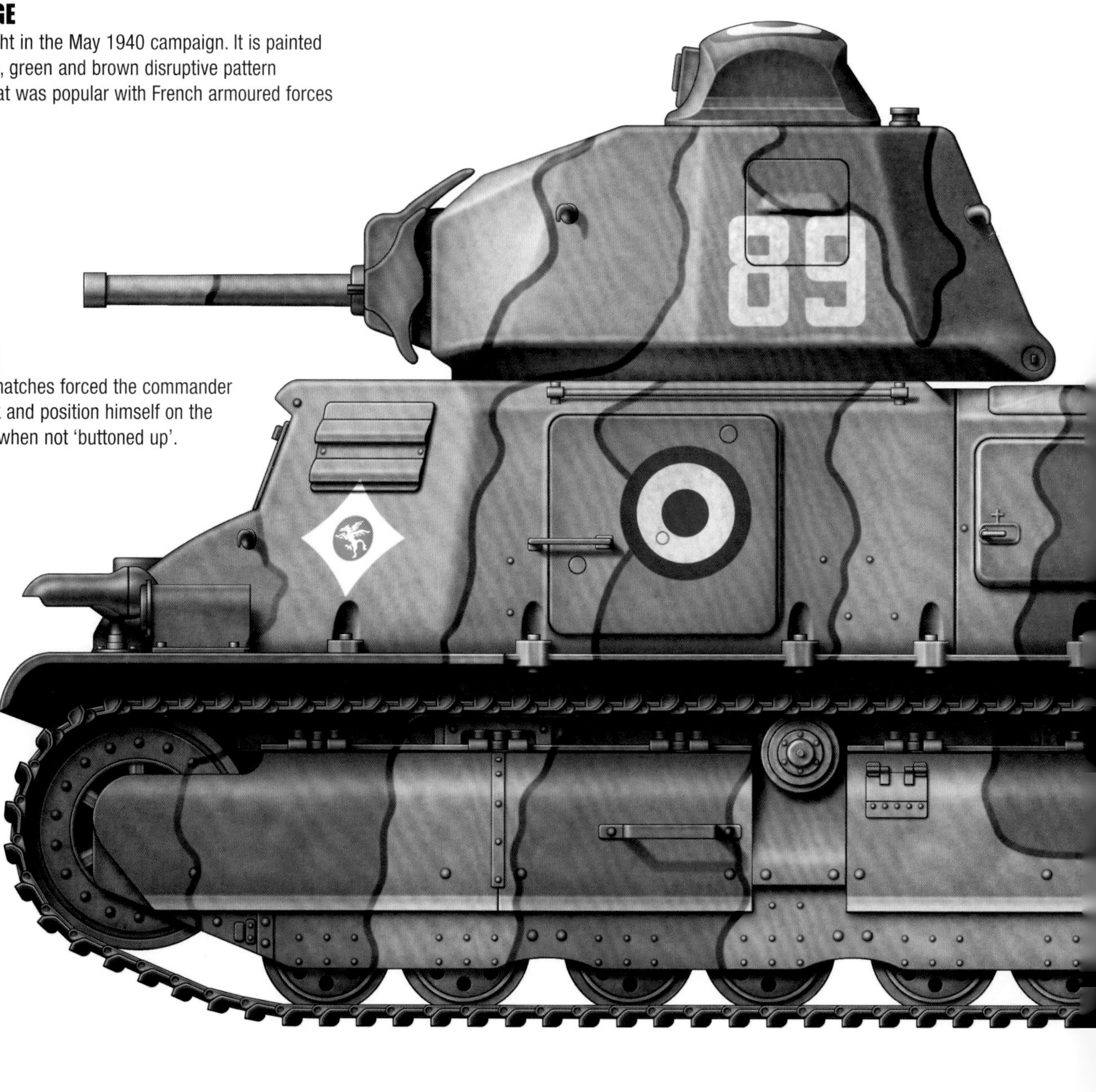

A NEW KIND OF TANK

During the inter-war period, the technology of armoured vehicles advanced rapidly and often ahead of doctrine. Experience in World War I was of powerful 'breakthrough' tanks with limited range and dubious reliability. Advocates of the tank thought it could do far more than help infantry push through static defensive positions, but these theories remained unproven.

The Somua S-35, entering service in 1935, was a new departure for the French army. Up until its introduction, the cavalry were required to refer to their armoured vehicles as automitrailleuse, or armoured cars, whether they had tracks or not. The S-35 was explicitly a cavalry tank, intended to do what cavalry did best. It was fast and had a good operating radius, enabling it to undertake mobile operations. Its 47mm (1.8in) gun was powerful enough to take on any other tank with a good prospect of success.

The S-35 was the first to have a completely cast turret and hull, and was widely regarded as the best medium tank of its time. It was, however, expensive to produce and was available only in limited numbers at the outbreak of World War II.

An S-35 stands knocked out by the roadside somewhere in France. The S-35 proved a tough and capable combatant in 1940, but was overpowered by the better-handled German Panzer forces.

THE FALL OF FRANCE

French armoured warfare doctrine was in its infancy in 1940, and most of the available tanks were dispersed in fairly small numbers as part of infantry forces. Hit hard

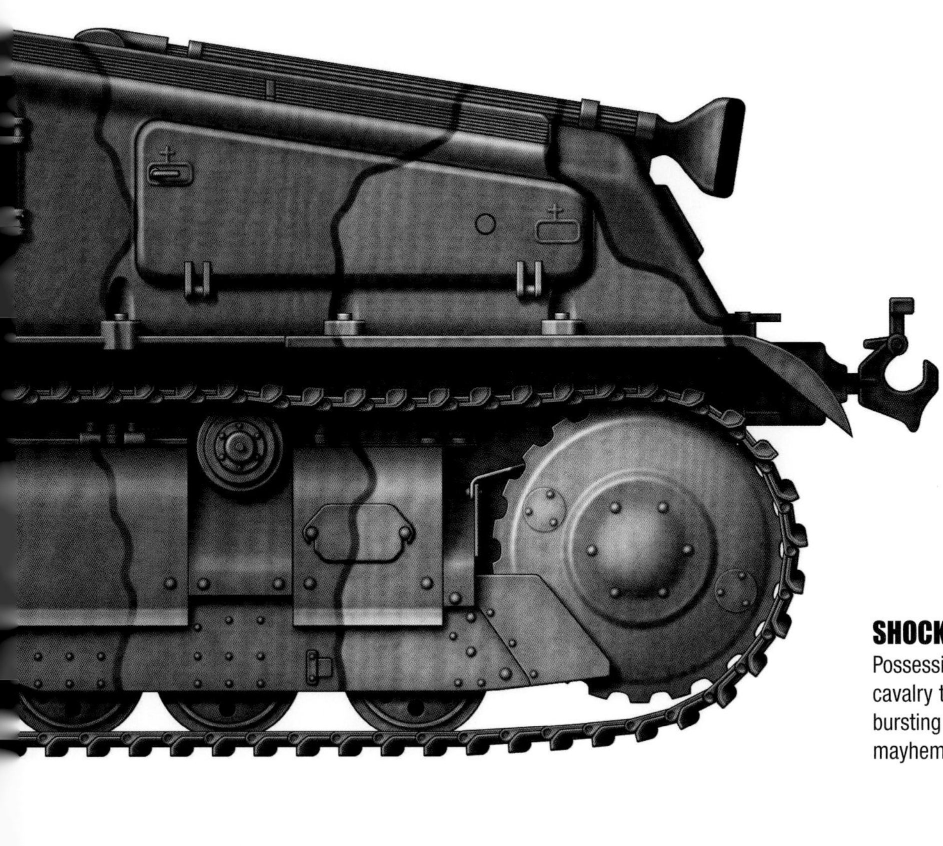

SHOCK ROLE
Possession of a suitable tank allowed the French cavalry to return to its traditional shock role, bursting through the enemy line and causing mayhem.

This museum display piece shows the key characteristics of the S-35; small turret, high sides and a short, low-velocity gun.

by fast-moving Panzer formations, these penny-packets of tanks put up a stiff fight where they could but were overwhelmed. The light armoured divisions did better, notably at the Battle of Hannut on 12–14 May 1940.

French armoured forces were successful in slowing down the German advance and inflicted losses, but were outmatched in both numbers and tactics. Better concentration of force and use of combined arms tactics enabled the German forces to drive the French back. Nevertheless, a determined mobile rearguard action caused near-panic in some German units, which thought they were being assaulted by large tank forces.

S-35 tanks took part in a counterattack by the 4th light armoured division and subsequent rearguard actions. Although individually effective, French tanks were not well employed; armoured forces suffered from a lack of both initiative and coordination. The German advance could not be stemmed, and significant numbers of S-35s were captured.

LATER SERVICE

Some S-35s were taken to North Africa and saw action with the Free French forces. Those captured in the fall of France served with the Axis forces in many areas. Some were assigned to a security or logistics role, while others equipped battlegroups put together to deal with a local situation. A force of S-35s in German hands opposed the Allied landings in Normandy, while others served against the Allies in Italy in the last months of the war.

The S-35 never achieved its potential, largely due to insufficient numbers and an outdated doctrine. Its overall concept was sound, however, and may have influenced the design team working on the M4 Sherman.

SPECIFICATIONS (SOMUA S-35)

Dimensions: Length: 5.38m (17ft 7.8in), Height: 2.62m (8ft 7in), Width: 2.12m (6ft 11.5in)

Weight: 17.4 tonnes (19.2 tons)

Engine/powerplant: V8 petrol engine

Speed: 40.7km/h (25.3mph)

Armament: Main gun: 47mm (1.8in) gun, Co-axial: 7.5mm (0.29in) machine gun

Crew: 3

TURRET
The S-35 used a two-man turret design, increasing efficiency over earlier models.

MAIN GUN
The S-35's 47mm (1.8in) gun was relatively large for a medium tank of its era.

BULKHEAD
Crew protection was increased by a bulkhead between the engine and crew compartments.

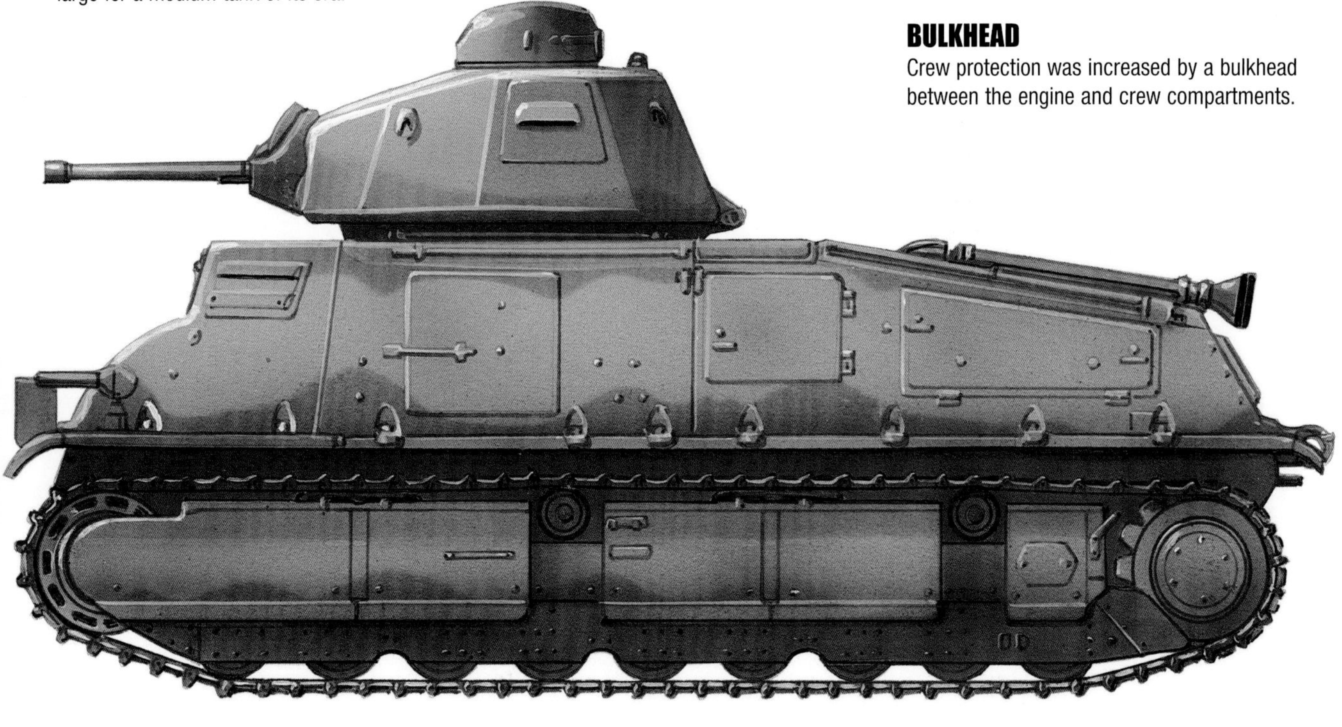

Centurion

Arriving too late to take part in World War II, the Centurion became one of the most successful and influential tank designs of the post-war era. It saw service in Korea and Vietnam, and achieved notable success in Israeli hands. The Centurion has been widely exported, with examples still in service today.

WARTIME EXPERIENCE

Tank design evolved very rapidly during World War II, with several new British tanks turning out to be deficient in some way. The Comet, entering service in late 1944, was developed from the preceding Cromwell and addressed some of that design's deficiencies. Notable among these was an inability to mount a gun capable of penetrating heavy armour. The Comet represented a good balance of protection, firepower and mobility, but a replacement with greater capabilities was required.

Initially designated Cruiser Tank A41, the Centurion was built around the proven 17-pdr (76mm) gun. Specifications

SHO'T CENTURION MK 5
The Centurion was adopted by the Israeli Defence Force as the Sho't ('Whip'). It was upgunned to use a 105mm (4.1in) L7 gun.

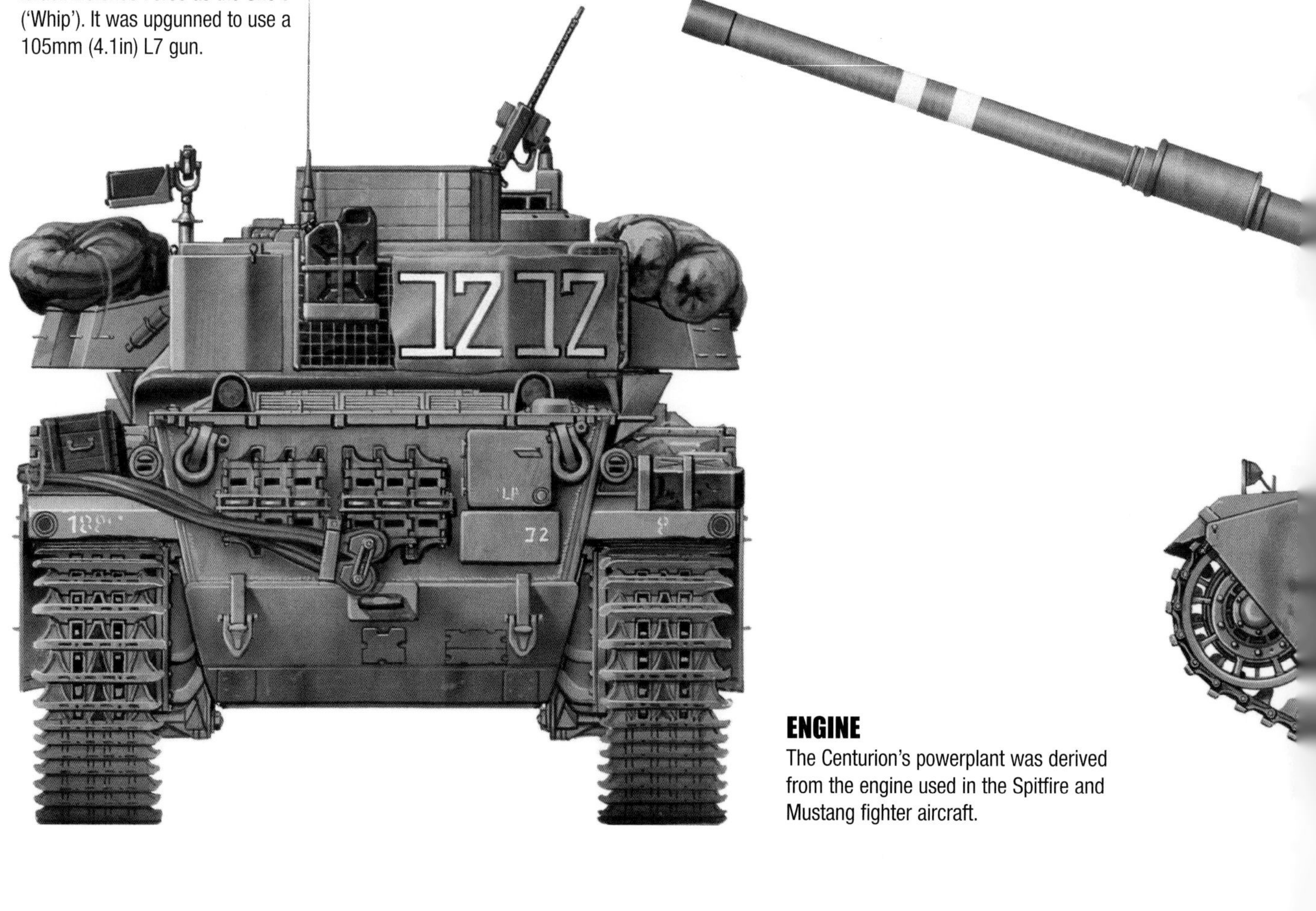

ENGINE
The Centurion's powerplant was derived from the engine used in the Spitfire and Mustang fighter aircraft.

SPECIFICATIONS (CENTURION)

Dimensions: Length: 7.47m (24ft 6in), Height: 3.02m (9ft 11in), Width: 3.40m (11ft 2in)	
Weight: 38.5 tonnes (42.5 tons)	
Engine/powerplant: Meteor V12 petrol engine	
Speed: 35.4km/h (22mph)	
Armament: Main gun: 17-pdr (76mm), Co-axial: 7.92mm (0.3in) Besa machine gun	
Crew: 4	

included a requirement to withstand a frontal hit from an 88mm (3.4in) gun. The Christie-type suspension of the Comet was replaced with a Hortsmann suspension, with an extra road wheel to support an elongated hull. After some development work the A41A model, or Centurion 2, went into production. It was fielded too late to take part in World War II, but became the mainstay of British armoured forces immediately after the war.

POST-WAR SERVICE

Although designed as a wartime cruiser tank, the Centurion developed into a modern main battle tank. Its gun was upgraded to a 20-pdr (84mm) for the Mark 3 model and then to a 105mm (4.1in) weapon on the Mark 5. Unusually, some models of the Centurion mounted a 20mm (0.78in) cannon in addition to its main gun.

The Centurion gave good service in the Korean Conflict, where its mobility and the firepower of its 20-pdr (84mm) gun impressed observers in equal measure. Similarly,

GUN MANTLET

The Centurion's heavily armoured gun mantlet was mounted in a well-protected cast turret.

Australian Centurions attracted praise for their service in Vietnam. In Israeli hands, the Centurion performed admirably against Syrian T-55 and T-62 tanks despite being heavily outnumbered. The spectacular rampage by a handful of tanks – at times down to a lone Centurion – during the 1973 Yom Kippur War has been credited with preventing the collapse of the Israeli defences.

UPGRADES

In its long career, the Centurion was upgraded several times, receiving better electronics, a more powerful engine and improved armour through a succession of 13 models. Not all were a success – the Mark 4 was an attempt to create a fire support vehicle armed with a 95mm (3.7in) howitzer. Although this concept never took off, bridgelayers and engineering vehicles based on the Centurion were still in British service in the early 1990s. An armoured recovery variant served in the 1982 Falklands War, and engineering vehicles took part in the 1991 Gulf War.

Although supplanted in British service by the Chieftain, the Centurion soldiered on overseas. The Israeli Sho't, an upgraded Centurion, entered service in 1970. It was the basis for armoured personnel carriers based on its chassis. Israeli designers also assisted South Africa in developing the Olifant main battle tank, which was derived from the Centurion. Experience in Angola resulted in improved mine protection.

In the mid-1980s, South African Olifants engaged T-34s and T-55s during operations in Angola and were highly successful. While the T-34 was very long in the tooth by that time, the T-55 was a contemporary of the Centurion design. Although the current Olifant Mark 2 has been heavily redesigned, it can trace its lineage back to the last days of World War II.

A surviving Centurion, pictured at a modern military fair. Although the Centurion is out of service, some derived versions are still in use.

Centurions coming ashore from landing craft during the 1950s. The Centurion saw action in the Middle East, the Far East and in Africa.

ENGINEERING VEHICLE

A Centurion engineering vehicle equipped with a mine plough and towing the Viper mine-clearance system.

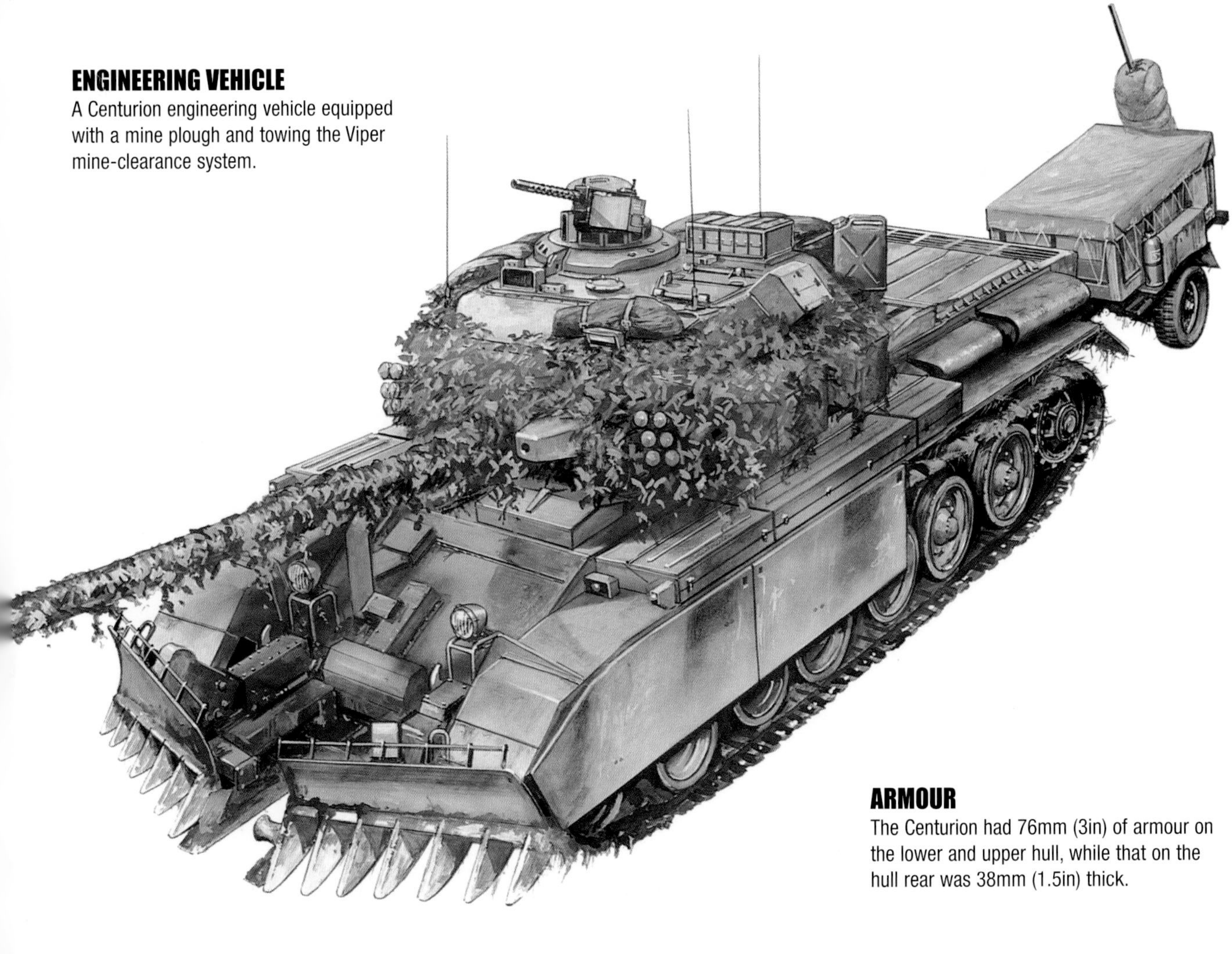

ARMOUR

The Centurion had 76mm (3in) of armour on the lower and upper hull, while that on the hull rear was 38mm (1.5in) thick.

FT-17

The French FT-17 was a highly successful design, remaining in service from 1917 until the end of World War II. It influenced both US and Russian tank design, and was exported to several nations including Finland, Japan and Brazil. It was designed from the outset to be fielded in massed formations.

A SWARM OF TANKS

Early French tank designs were similar to those of other countries – large, cumbersome and heavily armoured gun platforms intended to cross trenches and break a fixed defensive line. These tanks did not perform as well as their designers hoped, not least because their power-to-weight ratio was poor and the hull overhung the tracks, causing them to bog down or become stuck in soft ground.

The FT-17 was a radically different concept to these crawling pillboxes. It was intended to be fast and light (by tank standards at least) and to be cheap enough to deploy in large numbers. Armed with a revolving turret, it could

MAIN GUN
The FT-17 carried a single weapon, either a machine gun or a 37mm (1.4in) gun.

SPECIFICATIONS (FT-17)

Dimensions: Length: 5m (16ft 5in), Height: 2.13m (7ft), Width: 1.71m (5ft 7.33in)

Weight: 6 tonnes (6.7 tons)

Engine/powerplant: Renault 4-cylinder petrol engine

Speed: 7.7km/h (4.8mph)

Armament: 37mm (1.4in) gun or Hotchkiss 8mm (0.31in) machine gun

Crew: 2

Although it looks primitive today, in its day the FT-17 was an impressive and intimidating piece of military technology.

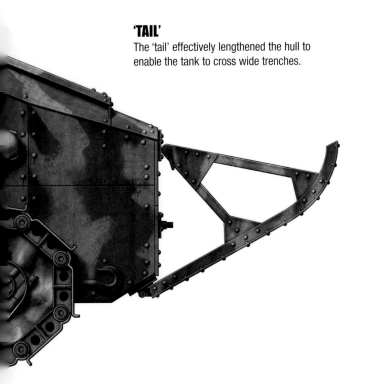

carry a single weapon and still fire in any direction, thus requiring a smaller crew and less hull area than a vehicle mounting multiple weapons. This in turn meant a radical reduction in the amount of hull that had to be armoured.

ARMOUR
Although relatively light, the FT-17 was armoured against machine-gun and small-arms fire.
'TAIL'
The 'tail' effectively lengthened the hull to enable the tank to cross wide trenches.

Military planners were somewhat sceptical of the concept. The idea that tanks should be large and would blast their way across no-man's land with heavy guns had taken root. French tanks before the FT-17 were built around a 75mm (2.9in) gun capable of firing large high-explosive shells. Nevertheless, a prototype was demonstrated and production began in early 1917.

FT-17 IN SERVICE

The FT-17 had a crew of just two men. Most were armed with a machine gun, but a 'male' version with a 37mm (1.4in) gun was also produced. The weapon was loaded and operated by the commander, who stood behind the driver and kicked him in the back to order direction changes. Later the commander was given a rather basic seat in the form of a strap across his compartment.

Despite its primitive nature and some mechanical defects, the FT-17 performed very well in action. Rather than having a few very potent vehicles reaching the enemy lines in a piecemeal fashion, and thus allowing a response with grenades and other anti-tank weapons, FT-17s were fielded in sufficient numbers to swamp the enemy defences. They were not such an easy target as the slab-sided

The FT-17's small turret required the commander/gunner to stand in the hull to operate its weapon.

'lozenge' tanks, but were still largely impervious to machine-gun fire.

Tactics were similar to those used by British tanks, in that the 'male' FT-17s were to engage enemy pillboxes and strongpoints with explosive shells while the 'females' swept the trenches with their machine guns. This system worked well for both the French and American forces.

General George S. Patton commanded a force of FT-17s that were supplied by the French as an interim measure until American-made M1917 tanks (which were a licence-built version of the FT-17) became available.

POST-WORLD WAR I

The US M1917 did not become available before the war's end, but saw service in the inter-war years. As late as 1940, ex-US M1917s were used as training vehicles by the Canadian army, and many were in service around the world. France still had large numbers, some stationed in the colonies. FT-17s saw action in defence of France, Belgium, Yugoslavia and Greece.

Surviving French FT-17s were captured and put into service by German forces. Although enormously outdated, they were still useful as security vehicles, freeing more advanced tanks for combat operations. It has been reported that working FT-17s were encountered during modern operations in Afghanistan – a testament to a simple but eminently workable concept.

CAMOUFLAGE

The FT-17 entered service at a time when camouflage was in its infancy. Nevertheless, measures were taken to conceal tanks where possible.

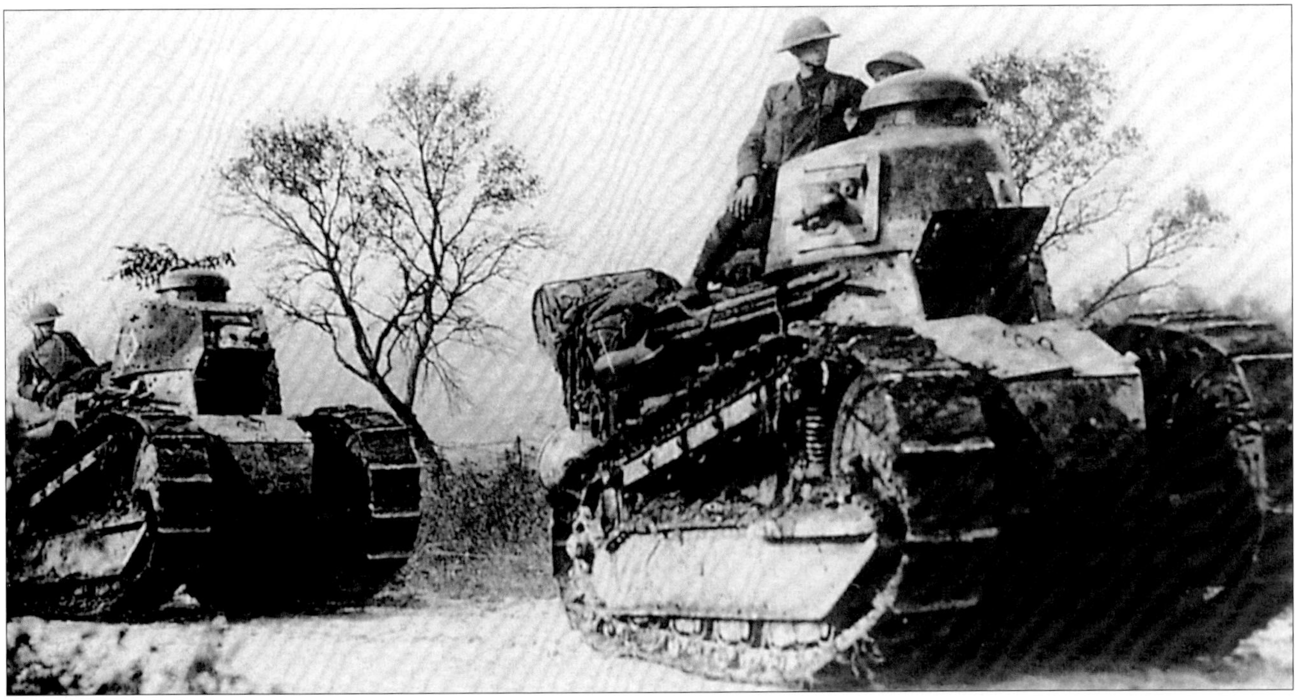

American soldiers ride on the back of FT-17 tanks. The FT-17 was provided to the US tank forces as an interim measure until the US-built version could be fielded.

LAYOUT

The FT-17 fell somewhere between the 'lozenge' type with all-round tracks and the more modern layout used in most designs since.

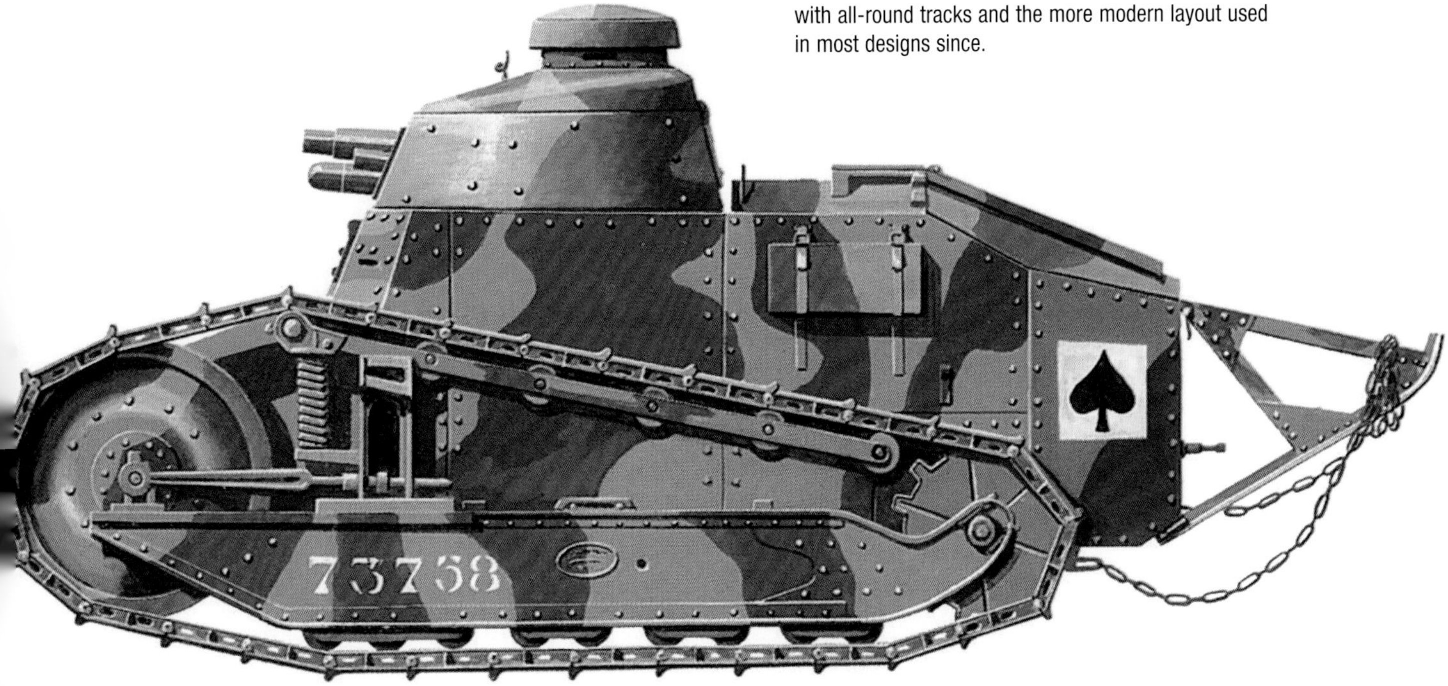

Leopard 2

The German Leopard 2 is a highly effective main battle tank, and has served as the basis of numerous variants and specialist vehicles. The Leopard 2 is in service with several European countries and has been widely exported elsewhere. Development continues, with improved electronics and enhanced protection being added as new technologies become available.

POST-WAR EUROPANZER

Most European nations ended World War II with large quantities of military hardware on hand. This provided the backbone of most militaries for some time, since it was much easier and cheaper to upgrade legacy equipment than to develop new systems. However, the threat posed by a new generation of Soviet tanks required a response.

Germany, Italy and France began a joint project to create a new armoured combat vehicle capable of countering the emerging threat. This 'Europanzer' project, like many international collaborations, failed, but the groundwork was laid for a new German main battle tank. Mobility and firepower were emphasized over armour protection. This decision was influenced by the proliferation of anti-armour weapons; it was felt that providing enough protection to reliably defeat these threats would result in an excessively heavy vehicle. Instead, the new design was intended to be hard to hit due to its high speed.

Entering service in 1963, the Leopard did gain increased armour protection in development, but retained its impressive mobility. It was armed with a British 105mm (4.1in) gun, capable of firing a range of ammunition and disabling any tank of the era. Widely exported, the Leopard 1 was upgraded through a series of models.

LEOPARD 2

When Leopard entered service, its likely opponents were Soviet-made tanks armed with 120mm (4.7in) and 125mm (4.9in) guns, and carrying heavy protection. Development of a tank to follow Leopard 1 began almost as soon as its design was finalized. Participation in the US-German 'MBT70' project did not go well, with Germany withdrawing

SPECIFICATIONS (LEOPARD 2)

Dimensions: Length: 9.97m (32ft 8.5in), Height: 2.64m (8ft 8in), Width: 3.74m (12ft 3in)

Weight: 53.3 tonnes (58.76 tons)

Engine/powerplant: MTU MB 873 Ka501 12-cylinder diesel

Speed: 72km/h (44.7mph)

Armament: Main gun: 120mm (4.7in) smoothbore L/44 (Model 2A1-4) or L/55 (Model 2A5-6) gun, Co-axial: 7.62mm (0.3in) machine gun

Crew: 4

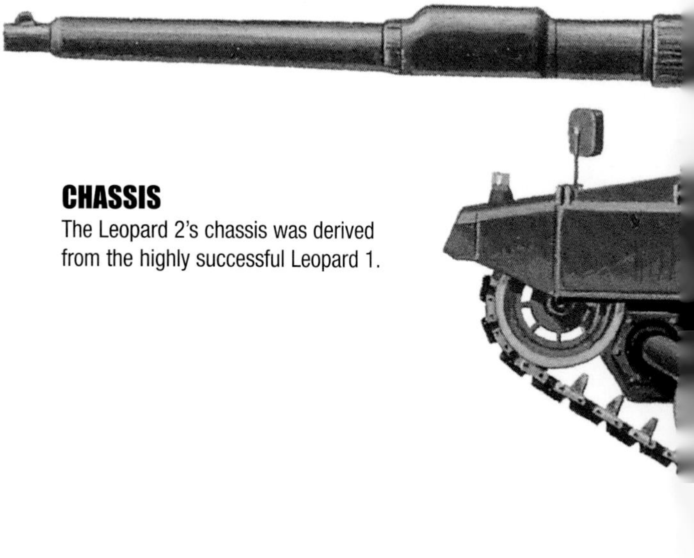

CHASSIS
The Leopard 2's chassis was derived from the highly successful Leopard 1.

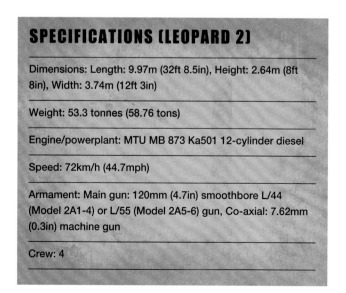

A Leopard 2 during training in Germany. Even in an age of electronic sensors, basic camouflage measures are still useful.

TURRET GUN
The Leopard 2's turret was designed from the outset to mount a powerful 120mm (4.7in) gun.

TURRET BUSTLE
The distinctive turret bustle contains ready ammunition in blow-out compartments, reducing explosion risk.

A Leopard 2 wearing three-tone northern-Europe camouflage enters water at speed. The Leopard 2 can ford water 1.2m (4ft) deep with no preparation.

in 1969 and the US later cancelling the project altogether. Instead, a new design based on the successful Leopard was implemented.

Leopard 2 was built on the proven Leopard chassis, but was constructed around a new 120mm (4.7in) smoothbore gun. Later models (Leopard 2A5 and onward) used a longer barrel to increase muzzle velocity. Internal features were designed to give maximum protection to crew and critical components, with composite armour offering improved protection over previous generations of main battle tanks.

Like its predecessor, Leopard 2 was widely exported and now arms several forces in Europe and worldwide. In German hands it saw service in Kosovo, while Danish and Canadian Leopard 2s have been deployed in Afghanistan. Although it has never been tested in action against an armoured force, the Leopard 2 has demonstrated an impressive set of capabilities.

FUTURE DEVELOPMENTS

The current 2A6 model is armed with a long 120mm (4.7in) gun and has received upgrades to its mine protection. In the modern environment, improvised explosive devices are one of the main threats to a tank, and mobility is no defence in this case. Although the Leopard family was designed to fight a major war against massed armour, it is currently more likely to be deployed in low-intensity conflicts or peacekeeping roles. A specialist 'PSO' (Peace Support Operations) variant has been developed that features a shorter gun barrel, a bulldozer blade for clearing obstacles and reconfigured armour designed to deal with threats from angles likely to be encountered in urban operations. It seems likely that tanks will increasingly have to survive in the urban environment, and the Leopard's capabilities in this area will thus continue to develop.

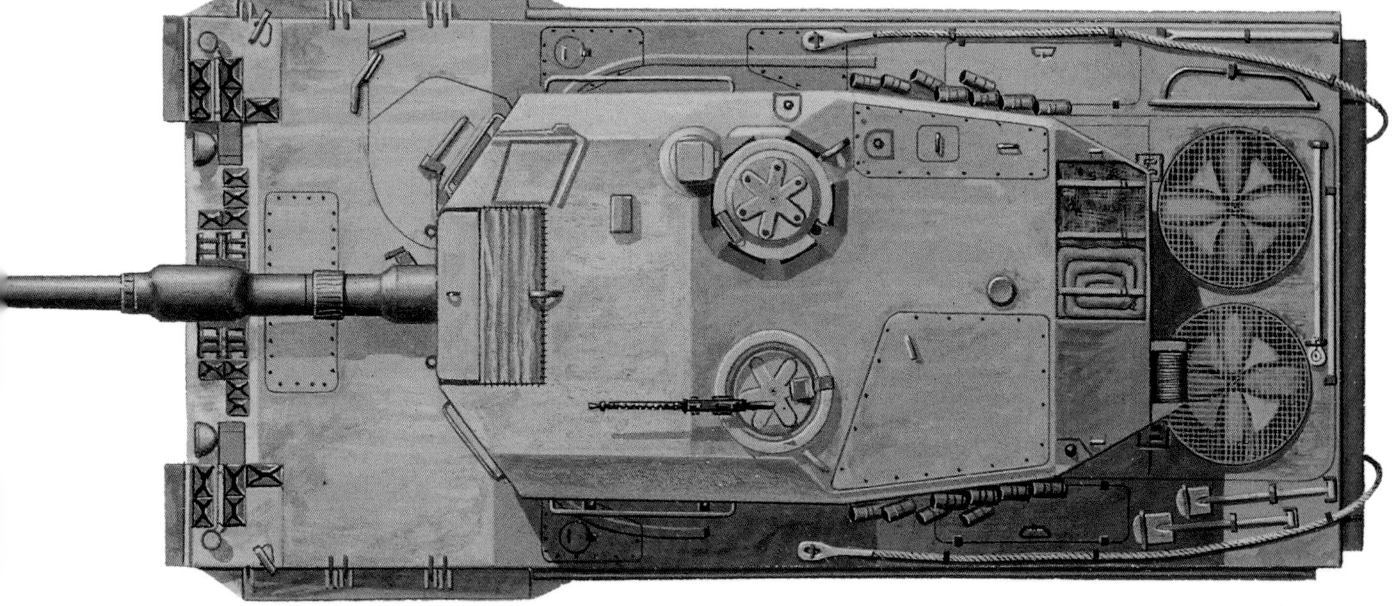

MACHINE GUNS
The Leopard includes two light machine guns, the co-axial and the external auxiliary mounted on the turret ring.

ENGINE DECK
Far less of the engine deck is visible from above on the Leopard 2 compared with most other main battle tanks.

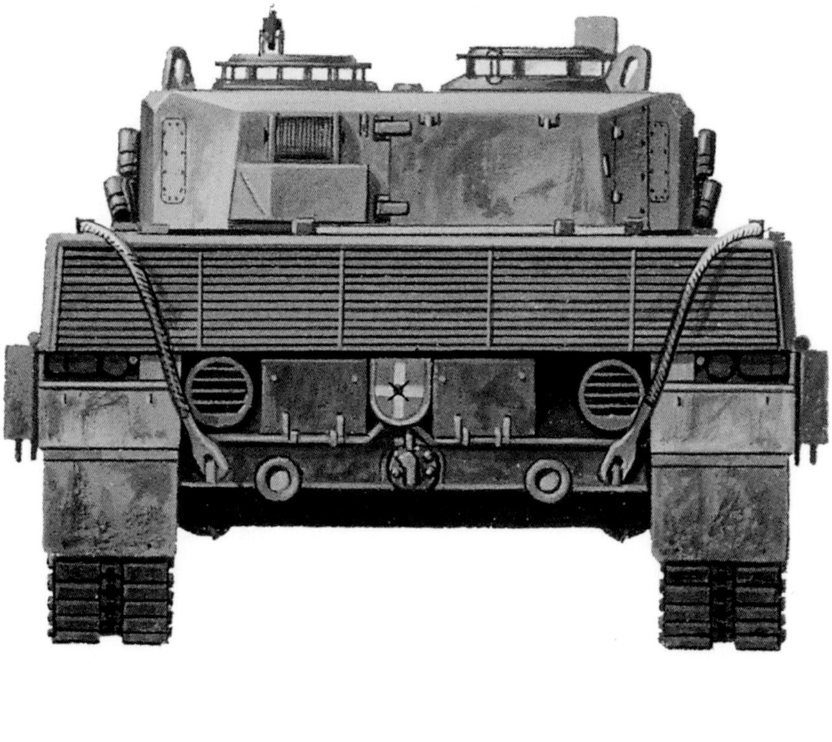

COOLING GRILLE
Early in production, the rear cooling grille was given increased protection. Resilience against mines was later enhanced with additional belly armour.

Mark V Heavy Tank

By the time the Mark V heavy tank emerged in 1918, the tank had matured into a proven weapon system. Reliability and radius of action, while both limited, were vastly improved over preceding designs. Its ability to be driven by one man was another critical improvement.

LOZENGE TANKS

British tanks of World War I were designed to help infantry break a trench line. Deep-penetrating exploitation was the work of the cavalry, if it was thought of at all. Thus the early tanks were 'lozenge' designs, with all-round tracks designed to cope with trench-crossing and heavily cratered ground. Mounting armament in sponsons on the sides was inefficient compared to a turret, since it required a tank to carry multiple guns, crew and armour to protect them in order to have all-round firepower. However, it did allow a tank to fire in several directions at once.

SIDE ARMOUR

Although slab-sided and easy to hit, the Mark V was armoured against small-arms fire.

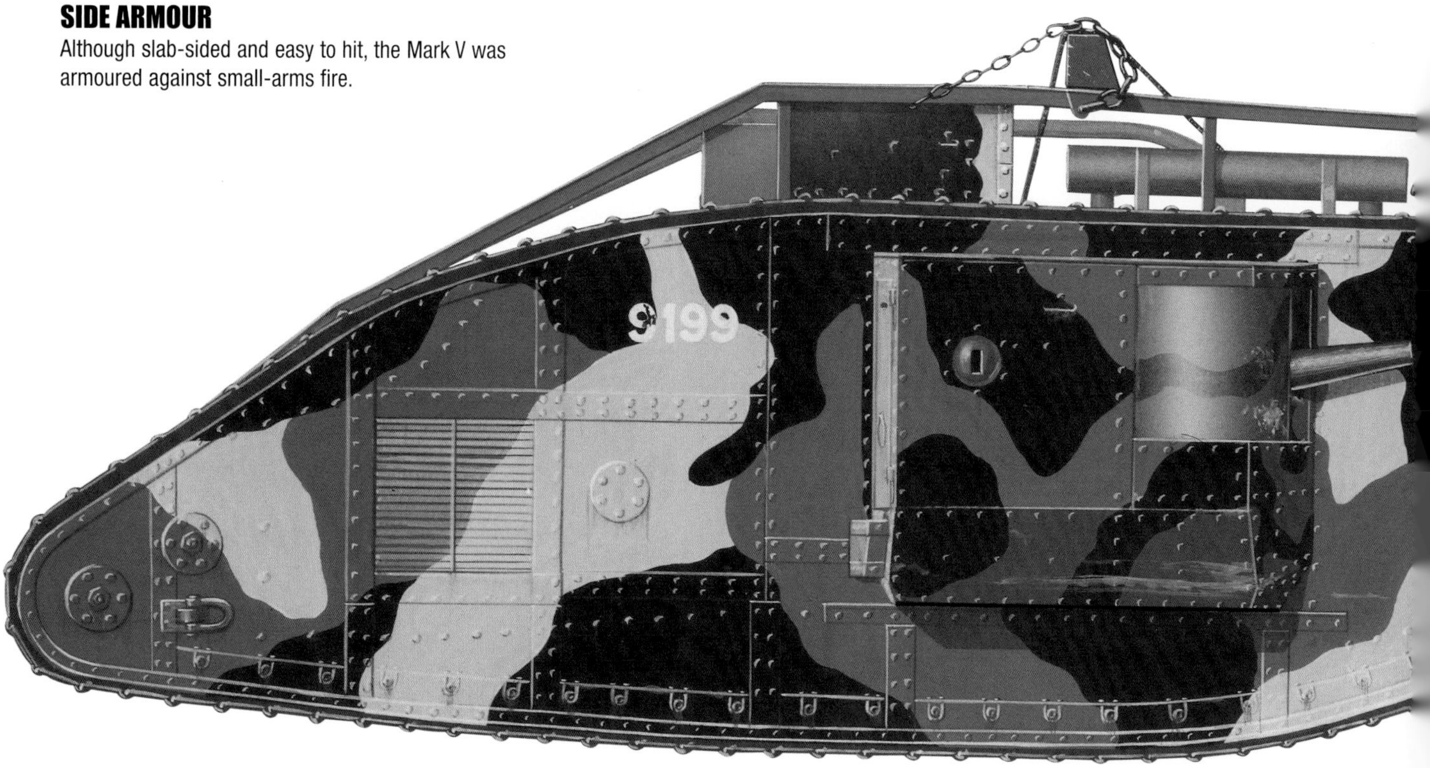

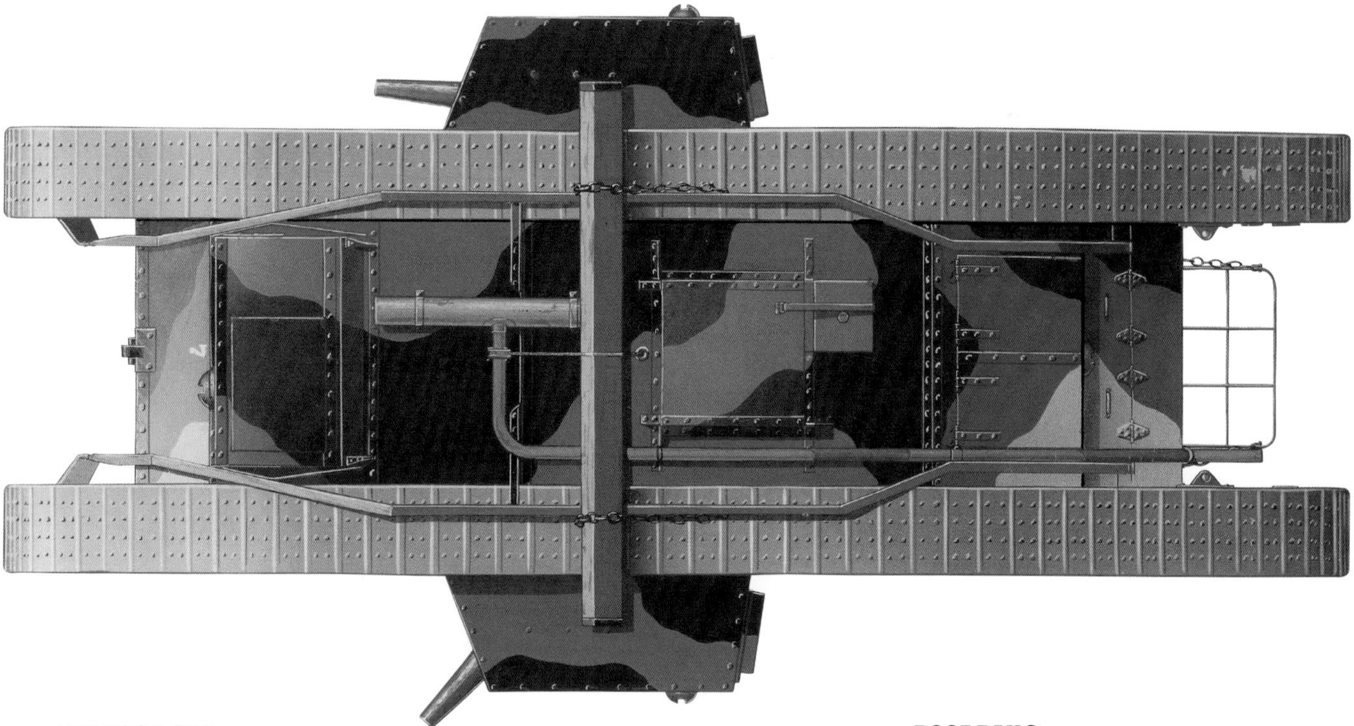

SPONSON GUN

The Mark V included two sponson-mounted 6-pdr (57mm) guns that could fire very effective high-explosive shells at enemy infantry.

ROOF RAILS

Rails along the roof carried an unditching beam, to be deployed if the tank became stuck.

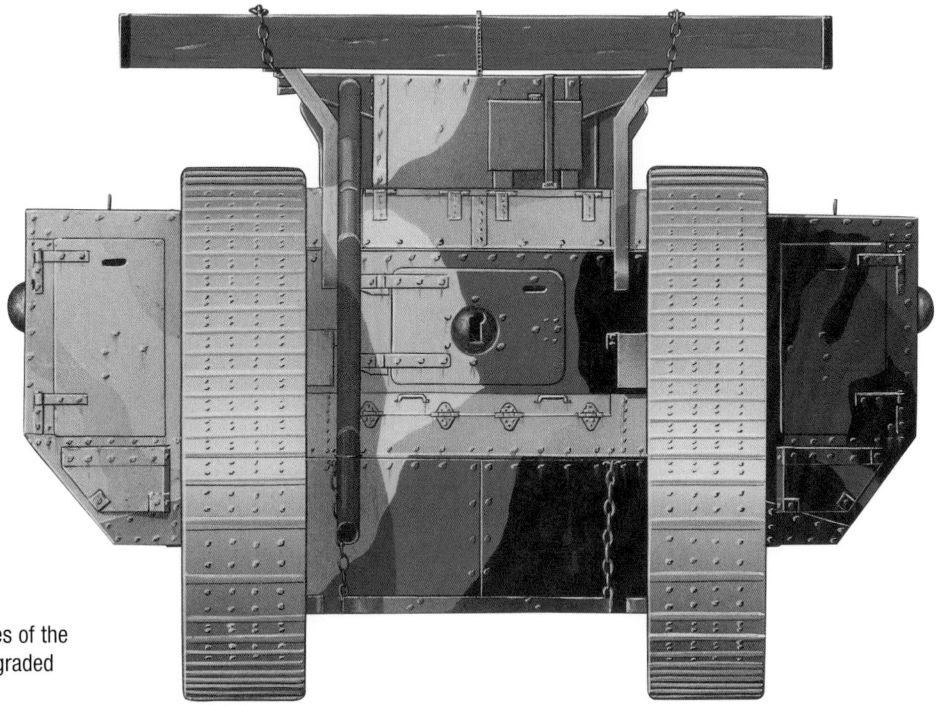

DRIVE TRAIN

The Mark V retained many features of the preceding Mark IV, but had an upgraded transmission and drive train.

The front 'horns' of the lozenge tanks limited the field of fire of their frontal machine gun and could restrict vision of the battlefield.

Tail wheels for steering were abandoned after the Mark I, and while the Mark II saw only minor improvements the Mark III received thicker armour. These vehicles demonstrated that tanks could be effective, but it was not until the appearance of the Mark IV that the concept really came into its own. German 'K' bullets, hurriedly issued in response to the appearance of the tank on the battlefield, were unable to penetrate the Mark IV, and at the Battle of Cambrai in November 1917 the Mark IV tank demonstrated what a massed force could do.

THE MARK V HEAVY TANK

The main problem with Mark IV tanks was the complexity of driving them, which required a well-coordinated crew in an environment unsuited to detailed commands and communication. The Mark V needed only a single driver and this, coupled with better visibility and ventilation, increased efficiency. The new tank was also better armoured than its predecessor. A lengthened Mark V* was designed to cope with the wide trenches of the Hindenburg Line. Further developments of the Mark V were implemented, but the war ended before the standard model could be supplanted.

At the time the Mark V entered service, it was becoming apparent that some day tanks might have to fight other tanks. The A7V was just starting to make its appearance,

SPECIFICATIONS (MARK V HEAVY TANK (MALE))

Dimensions: Length: 8.03m (26ft 4in), Height: 2.49m (8ft 2in), Width: 3.91m (12ft 10in)

Weight: 26.3 tonnes (29 tons)

Engine/powerplant: Ricardo 6-cylinder petrol engine

Speed: 7.4km/h (4.6mph)

Armament: 2 x sponson-mounted 6-pdr (57mm) guns, 4 x 7.7mm (0.3in) Hotchkiss machine guns (one each side, front and back)

Crew: 8

Mark V Heavy Tank 9186 saw action during the Russian Civil War, finally being captured by Red Army forces in November 1920 at Sevastopol. It now stands on a plinth in Lugansk, Ukraine.

A Mark V tank trundles through the mud of the Western Front. The Mark V was designed to meet the needs of warfare on the Western Front, and should be evaluated in that context.

and only in small numbers, but the German forces had begun to field captured Mark I and Mark IV tanks. The 'female' version of the Mark V, armed only with machine guns, could not harm another armoured vehicle. One solution was to include at least one 'male' tank (with 6-pdr/57mm guns as its main armament) in a tank platoon. 'Hermaphrodite' tanks, with a 6-pdr (57mm) gun in one sponson and a pair of machine guns in the other, were also constructed.

THE MARK V'S INFLUENCE

Initially the Mark V was available only in small numbers, and its contribution was minor compared to the larger forces of Mark IVs available. However, from July 1918 the Mark V played a major part in Allied operations, establishing itself as the best of the World War I era tanks.

A Male Mark V carried into action two guns capable of firing high-explosive shells or case shot for anti-personnel targets plus four machine guns. Its armament layout was inefficient but good enough for the task at hand. The idea of using space freed within the hull by more efficient machinery to transport up to 25 troops was considered, arguably making the Mark V the world's very first Infantry Fighting Vehicle, but the experiment was not a success. However, the Mark V made the most impact of any tank of its era and represented the best of the lozenge tanks.

BT-7

The Soviet BT series of fast, light tanks resulted in the best of all inter-war designs, the BT-7. Although lightly armoured, it was fast and mounted a more powerful gun than many larger tanks. The final model in the series, designated BT-IS, was the first Soviet tank to have sloped armour.

CHRISTIE COPY

In the 1920s, inventor and engineer J. Walter Christie developed a light tank in the hopes of selling it to the US Army. It was rejected, not least because the US military wanted heavily armoured infantry-support tanks and Christie's design was considered too lightly armoured. The Soviet Union was interested, however, and purchased a prototype Christie M1931. This was then copied outright to create the BT-1 light tank.

The BT-1 mounted two machine guns, and was quickly replaced by the BT-2, with a 37mm (1.4in) gun. This was the level of armament most nations were fitting to tanks in the 1930s, but the Soviet Union upgraded the BT-3 and BT-4 models to a 45mm (1.7in) gun. An improved version, with more armour and a more powerful engine, went into service in 1935 as the BT-5.

The BT-5 was lightly armoured and weighed 11.5 tonnes (12.7 tons). It could be penetrated by an anti-tank rifle and was very vulnerable to more powerful weapons, but its speed and mobility were considered to offer at least some protection. The Christie suspension system was adopted by several nations and proved very effective, although a feature that allowed the tracks to be removed so that the tank could run on its road wheels was dropped after the early models.

BT-7

The BT-7 model entered service in 1936, featuring improved armour and a greater fuel capacity made possible by an all-welded construction. An artillery variant with a heavier gun was developed, as well as a command tank. The BT-8 featured further improvements and mounted the same turret as the T-28 tank, but did not enter service in sufficient numbers to

MOBILE FIREPOWER

The BT-7 was the best of all inter-war light tanks, offering good firepower and mobility.

GUN PLATFORM

Although lightly armoured, the BT-7 was an effective gun platform that outperformed better-protected designs.

SPECIFICATIONS (BT-7)

Dimensions: Length: 5.66m (18ft 7in), Height: 2.41m (7ft 11in), Width: 2.43m (7ft 11.5in)

Weight: 12.6 tonnes (13.9 tons)

Engine/powerplant: M-15T V12 petrol engine

Speed: 72km/h (45mph)

Armament: Main gun: 45mm (1.7in) model 33 or model 37 gun, Co-axial: 7.62mm (0.3in) machine gun, 7.62mm (0.3in) machine gun (anti-aircraft mount), 7.62mm (0.3in) machine gun (ball mount at rear of turret)

Crew: 3

A BT-5 command tank takes part in manoeuvres. Command tanks could be distinguished by the horseshoe-shaped aerial around the turret.

DRIVE TRANSMISSION

Most drive and transmission components were retained from the previous BT-5 model.

A BT-7 is put through its paces on the training ground. The BT series was fast and extremely resilient in cross-country situations.

supplant the BT-7. The BT-IS was a prototype that was not put into production, but did demonstrate the concept of sloped armour.

IN ACTION

The BT-5 and BT-7 saw action in the Spanish Civil War (July 1936–April 1939), and later in the East against the Japanese. While there in 1939, BT series tanks took part in the world's first full-scale armoured counterattack at the Battle of Khalkhin Gol. This action demonstrated many of the principles of armoured warfare long before the German commanders credited with inventing 'Blitzkrieg' conceived of them.

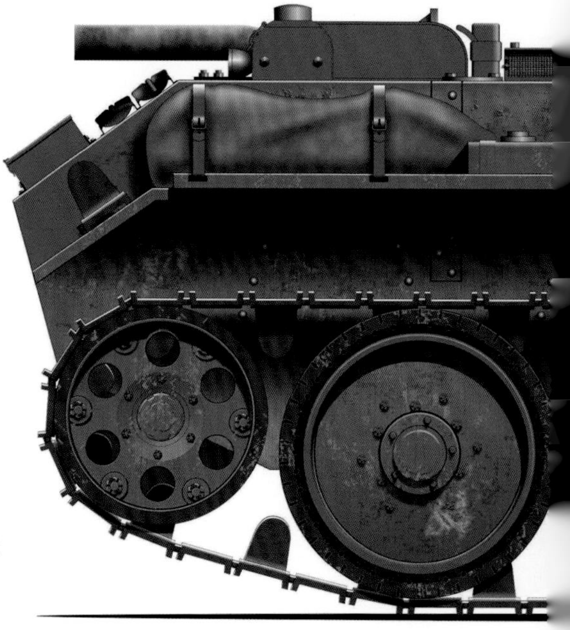

FAST TANK

'BT' (Bystrochodnij Tankov, which translates as 'fast tank') defined the design parameters as well as naming the tank.

The BT tanks proved extremely effective in this style of warfare, launching a fast-moving pincer attack without infantry support and routing the Japanese forces. BT tanks were very hard to hit on the move and could bring firepower to bear very quickly. The BT series was less successful in the Winter War against Finland (1939–1940), suffering heavy losses from close-quarters attacks with incendiary weapons.

The capabilities of the BT series impressed British officers who saw them demonstrated, and as a result the Christie suspension was adopted for use in many British tank designs.

BT-7 IN WORLD WAR II

By the outbreak of World War II, the BT-7 was outdated, although its 45mm (1.7in) gun was more powerful than many in service at that time. Of all the tank designs available at the time of the German invasion in 1941, the BT-7 was the most effective. Losses were very high, but only in part due to enemy action. At a time of desperate need, tank units were rushed from one crisis to another without time for maintenance or repairs; losses due to breakdowns accounted for large numbers of BT-7s. The design was supplanted by the altogether more effective T-34, but examples continued to serve right through the war.

LAYOUT

The BT-7 used a fairly conventional personnel layout; the driver sat in the hull with the commander and gunner in the turret.

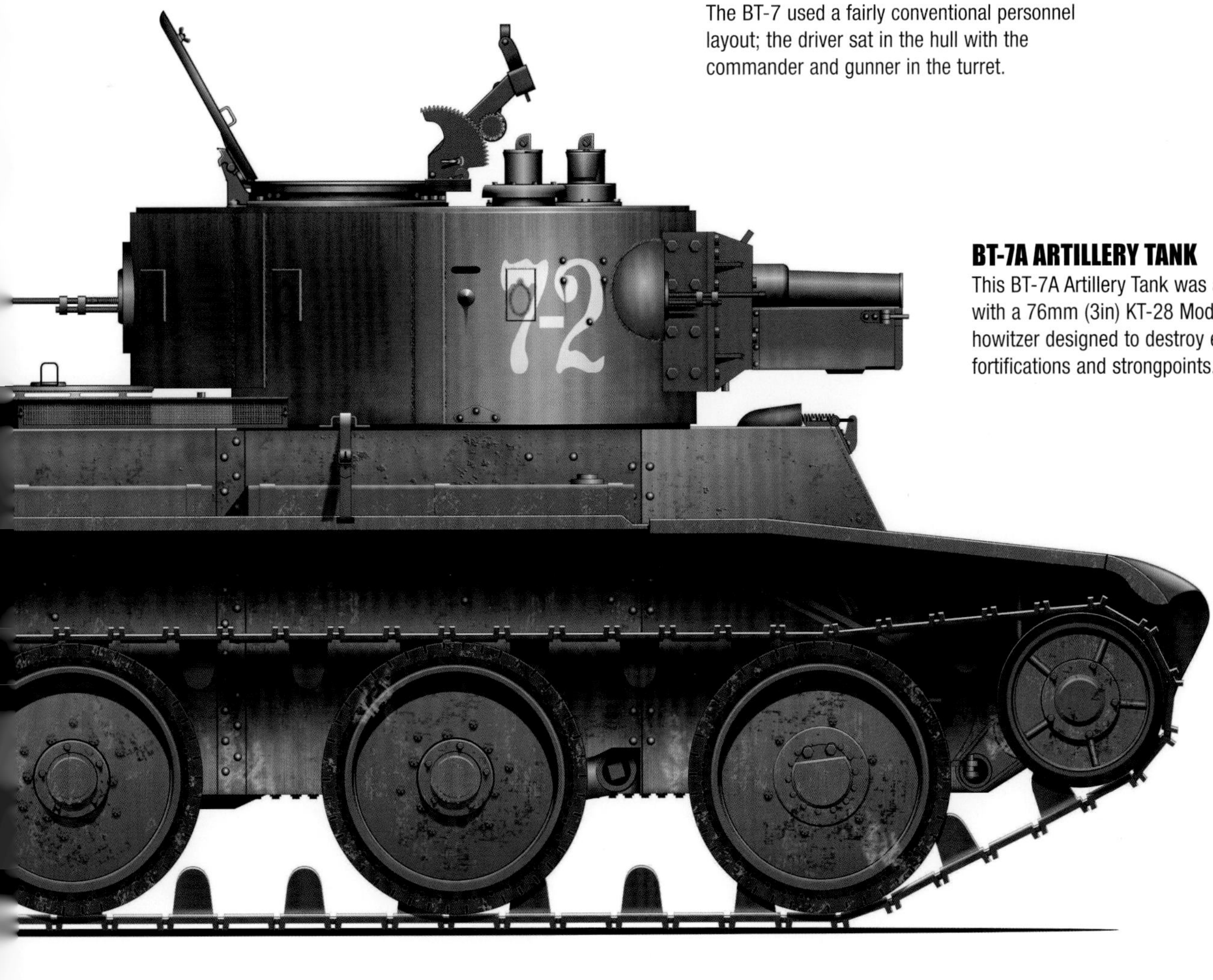

BT-7A ARTILLERY TANK

This BT-7A Artillery Tank was armed with a 76mm (3in) KT-28 Model 1932 howitzer designed to destroy enemy fortifications and strongpoints.

Challenger 2

The British Challenger 2 is comparable to the M1 Abrams and has a generally similar appearance. This is due to the use of composite Chobham armour that gives both tanks their distinctive slab-sized configuration. Although designed separately from the Abrams, the Challenger follows the same principles.

CHIEFTAIN AND CHALLENGER

Britain's first true main battle tank was the Chieftain, which entered service in 1963 and served through most of the Cold War. Its replacement was Challenger 1, which began its development as an upgraded Chieftain intended for export. The Challenger 1 served with distinction in the 1991 Gulf War, eliminating around 300 enemy tanks for no losses.

Challenger 2 was developed using the Challenger 1's hull and some of its components, but the version that entered service in 1998 was essentially a whole new tank. Like all armoured vehicles, Challenger 2 had to balance

MOBILITY
The Challenger 2 reflects the British preference for heavy protection over high mobility.

mobility against protection and firepower. Its designers chose to emphasize the latter two, providing a very high level of protection by using second-generation Chobham armour known as 'Dorchester'. Efforts were also made to reduce the tank's thermal signature.

CHALLENGER 2 IN SERVICE

The Challenger 2 first saw large-scale action during Operation Iraqi Freedom in 2003, where they proved vastly superior to the Iraqi tanks they encountered. After the initial armoured clashes, the Challenger 2 moved to a support and security role, with small numbers of tanks deployed to protect convoys or maintain a heavy armoured presence. Many of these tanks came under attack using infantry-launched weapons and improvised explosive devices.

SPECIFICATIONS (CHALLENGER 2)

Dimensions: Length: 8.33mm (27ft 4in), Height: 2.49m (8ft 2in), Width: 3.52m (11ft 6.5in)

Weight: 55.4 tonnes (61.1 tons)

Engine/powerplant: MTU 833 diesel engine

Speed: 60km/h (37.3mph)

Armament: Main gun: 120mm (4.7in) L30A1 rifled gun, Co-axial: 7.62mm (0.3in) L94A1 chain gun, 7.62mm (0.3in) L37A2 machine gun

Crew: 4

MAIN GUN

The L30 120mm (4.7in) main gun can be elevated to 20 degrees or depressed to –10 degrees.

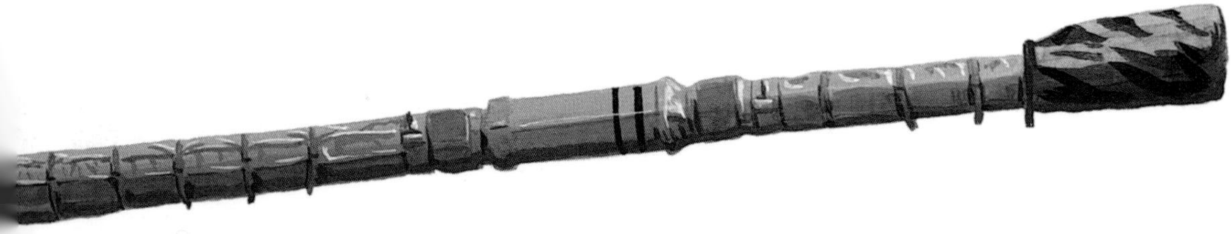

RIFLED BARREL

British tanks are unusual in using rifled guns rather than the smoothbores preferred in other tanks.

The Challenger 2 has six forward and two reverse gears and an advanced hydrogas suspension system capable of handling most terrain.

The blocky planes of composite armour give tanks using it a distinctive appearance. Protection can be enhanced with panels of reactive armour.

Protection against these threats, as against tank-fired projectiles, was found to be excellent. One Challenger 2 was hit by 14 RPGs and a MILAN anti-tank missile and required only slight repairs. Protection on the underside of the tank was improved, along with other armour upgrades, as a result of operational experience. Other additions include remotely controlled anti-personnel weapon mounts capable of carrying a general-purpose or heavy machine gun or a grenade launcher.

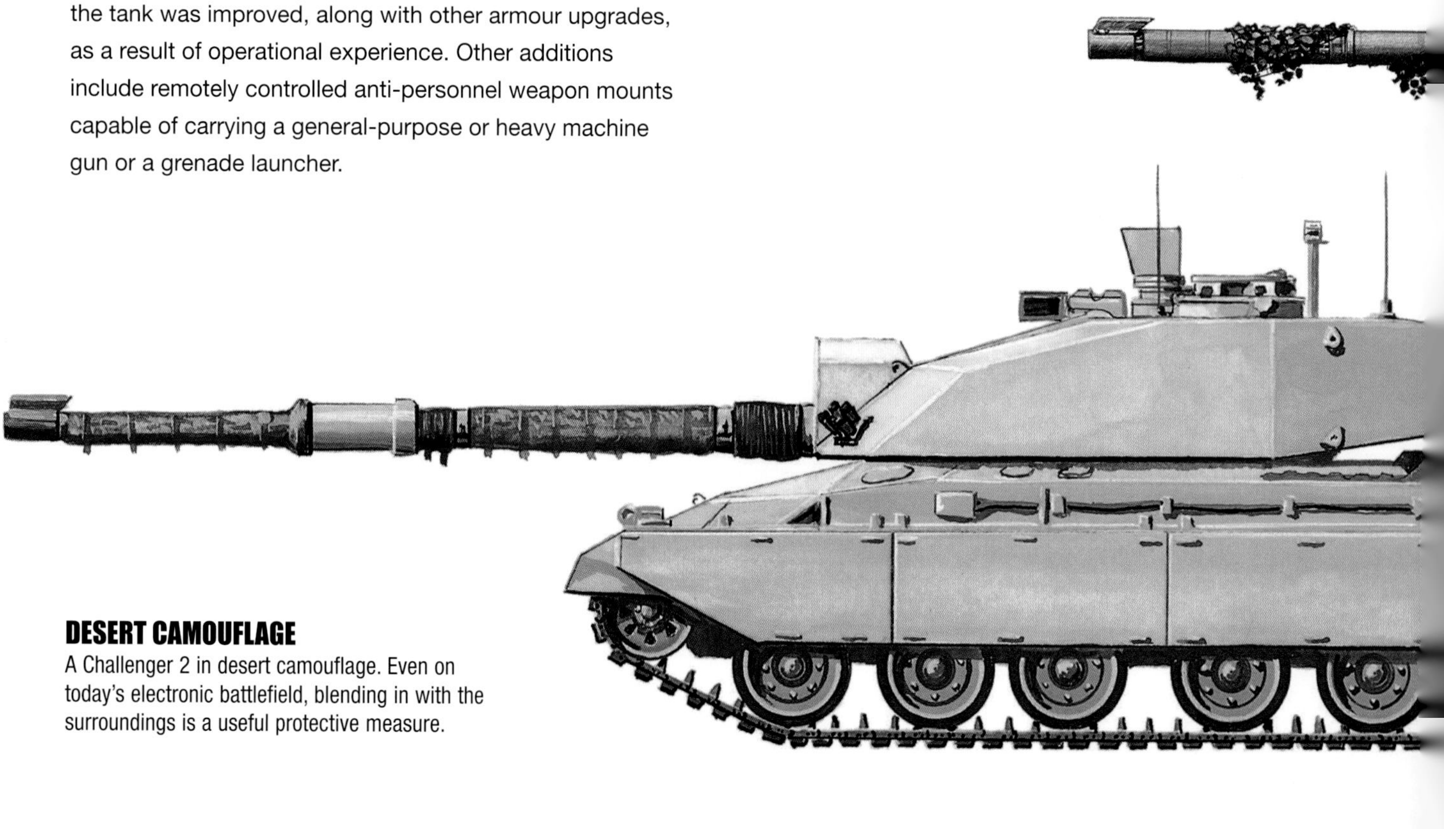

DESERT CAMOUFLAGE

A Challenger 2 in desert camouflage. Even on today's electronic battlefield, blending in with the surroundings is a useful protective measure.

FURTHER DEVELOPMENT

The Challenger 2 uses a rifled gun, whereas many other nations prefer smoothbores. Projectiles for smoothbore weapons tend to be single components, whereas the Challenger 2 uses separate projectiles and propellant. Although a smoothbore gun was trialled as early as 2006, its adoption remains questionable, as this would require redesign of the turret interior to accommodate the larger ammunition. Besides, the Challenger 2 does not use an autoloader, not least due to concerns about reliability. Having separate propellant and projectile reduces loader fatigue and allows the propellant to be stowed separately to the projectile.

British preference is for a high-explosive squash head round, which has good anti-armour performance but can also be used against more lightly protected targets. A smaller number of Armour-Piercing Fin-Stabilized Discarding-Sabot (APFSDS) rounds, which rely on kinetic energy rather than an explosive charge, are carried for engaging heavily armoured targets. Moving to a smoothbore gun would be accompanied by increased use of such kinetic energy penetrator rounds.

The Challenger 2 is the subject of a British project to reduce the costs involved in maintaining a powerful tank fleet, freeing funds for lighter vehicles better suited to low-intensity and asymmetric warfare. Along with a life extension project, these measures indicate that there is every intention of retaining the Challenger 2 in service for some time to come, although numbers have been reduced and some vehicles put into storage.

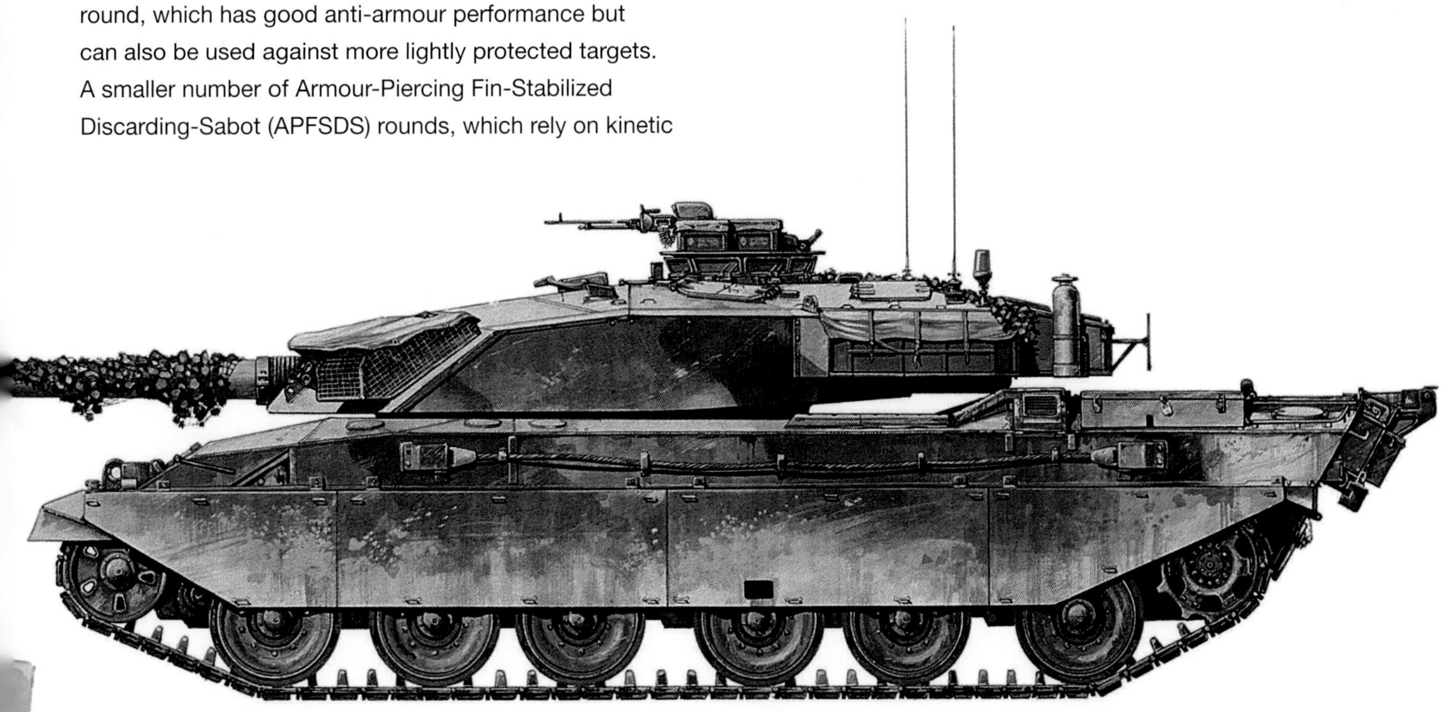

LOW PROFILE

The shape of the Challenger 2 reflects the needs of a defensive war in Europe, ideally firing from a concealed hull-down position.

Panzer IV

The PzKpfw IV was designed with infantry support in mind, with little anti-tank capability. In production throughout World War II, it grew into a highly effective all-round combat vehicle. Even in the closing months of the war, the Panzer IV could still hold its own on the battlefield.

EARLY MODELS

There may have been an element of 'World War I thinking' in the design of the Panzer IV. Armed with a short, low-velocity 75mm (2.9in) gun, the early models (Ausf A–E) were intended to assist infantry in making a breakthrough, with the lighter Panzer III undertaking exploitation and mobile operations. The basic design was sound, with good protection and adequate cross-country performance, and more importantly there was plenty of room for enhancement. Unlike the Panzer III, whose smaller turret ring made it impossible to carry a sufficiently large gun for later-war operations, the PzKpfw IV was able to mount a weapon that could threaten any tank of the era.

Early models did engage in anti-tank warfare, notably during the invasion of France in 1940. French heavy tanks proved impenetrable to the available anti-tank weapons, but could be put out of action by the large high-explosive shells of the Panzer IVs. This was not a very sophisticated or

SPACED ARMOUR
Extra metal plates were attached to the tank's turret to absorb the impact from anti-tank fire.

MAIN GUN
Armed with a long 75mm (2.9in) gun, later Panzer IV models remained effective throughout the war.

SIZE
A relatively large hull and turret facilitated both maintenance and upgrades.

A knocked-out wrecked Panzer IV Ausf D on the Eastern Front. Although it was tough, the Panzer IV was by no means invulnerable to early-war anti-tank weapons.

SPECIFICATIONS (PANZER IV AUSF F2)

Dimensions: Length: 6.63m (21ft 9in), Height: 2.68m (8ft 9.5in), Width: 2.88m (9ft 5.5in)

Weight: 19.9 tonnes (22 tons)

Engine/powerplant: Maybach HL120 TRIM V12 petrol engine

Speed: 40km/h (24.9mph)

Armament: Main gun: 75mm (2.9in) KwK40 L/43 gun, Co-axial: 7.92mm (0.3in) machine gun, Hull-mounted: 7.92mm (0.3in) machine gun (not fitted on Ausf B and C models)

Crew: 5

ENGINE

The Panzer IV used the same Maybach engine that propelled the much lighter Panzer III.

A Panzer IV Ausf F2 stands in a cornfield alongside other Panzer IVs at the Battle of Kursk. Many earlier 'short' Panzer IVs remained in service long after this variant arrived.

SHORT-BARRELLED MODEL

The Panzer IV Ausf F1 was the last version armed with the short-barrelled KwK 37 L/24 75mm (2.9in) gun.

effective counter to heavy tanks, but it sufficed for the time being. It was not until 1942 that the Ausf F model received a long 75mm (2.9in) gun capable of both infantry support and anti-tank combat.

DEFINITIVE VERSION

The Ausf A–E models represented gradual upgrades, largely to armour protection. This culminated in what became known as the Ausf F1. The F2 version received a remodelled turret mounting a long 75mm (2.9in) gun, and with modified ammunition stowage. This created a very potent all-round combat vehicle that was better than most Allied tanks of the era.

The subsequent Ausf G, H and J models were further upgraded, with the Ausf H receiving improved transmission as well as an armour upgrade. This was perhaps the definitive Panzer IV; certainly it was the variant produced in the greatest numbers. The J model received armoured 'skirts' in response to the proliferation of shaped-charge anti-tank weapons. By causing the warhead to detonate short of the tank's main armour, the skirts greatly reduced the effect of the weapon.

A Panzer IV Ausf F with the SS-Wiking *Division, Cherkassy pocket, 1944. The addition of* schurzen *(armoured skirts) to protect against shaped-charge weapons gives this model a very different appearance, making it look larger and more bulky.*

KEEPING PACE WITH CHANGE

The armoured combat environment changed radically during World War II, with tanks moving from a supporting role to leading the way, and facing an ever-increasing array of threats. Although by the war's end the Panzer IV was getting long in the tooth and had probably been developed as far as it could be, it managed to remain effective to the very end of the conflict, when many other vehicles were obsolescent as soon as they entered service.

The PzKpfw IV chassis was also used for a great variety of other armoured vehicles. The tank-destroyer variant, designated Jagdpanzer IV and armed with a very long 75mm (2.9in) gun, proved highly effective against Allied tanks. Similarly, the Sturmpanzer IV, or Brummbar, armed with a short 150mm (5.9in) howitzer, was valued for its reliability. Creating a family of vehicles based on a common chassis offered benefits in terms of spares availability and simplified logistics, as well as ensuring that new applications did not require extensive development to iron out problems already eliminated from the parent vehicle.

CAMOUFLAGE

This tank is painted with a combination of *dunkelgelb* (dark yellow) over the standard early-war base colour of *dunkelgrau* (dark grey). From 1943 onwards, all German armoured fighting vehicles were painted in *dunkelgelb*.

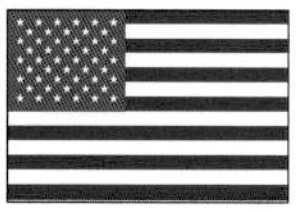

M4 Sherman

The M4 Sherman was by far the most numerous Allied tank of World War II. Almost 50,000 were built, with many variants and derivatives. Shermans remained in service after the war, with examples surviving into the 1990s.

STOPGAP MEASURES

In the early stages of World War II, the Allies fielded a variety of tank designs. Many were adequate at best, and few were up to the task of confronting the Axis Panzers. It was obvious that a general-purpose armoured combat vehicle, armed with a gun capable of penetrating heavy German tanks, was needed. The new tank would have to be produced quickly and in large numbers, and must also have

SHERMAN M4A3
During production of the M4A3 model, several improvements were made including a move to 'wet' ammunition stowage to reduce the risk of explosion.

ENGINE
Later M4A3s gained an improved engine, increasing maximum road speed by about 3km/h (1.8mph). Additional armour was fitted on some locations.

SPECIFICATIONS (M4 SHERMAN)

Dimensions:	Length: 5.88m (19ft 4in), Height: 2.74m (9ft), Width: 2.68m (8ft 10in)
Weight:	27.2 tonnes (30 tons)
Engine/powerplant:	Continental R-975 9-cylinder petrol engine (M4A1 variant)
Speed:	39km/h (24.2mph)
Armament:	Main gun: 75mm (2.9in) M2 L/32 or M3 L40; Co-axial: 2 x Browning M1919 7.62mm (0.3in) machine guns, Browning M2HB 12.7mm (0.5in) anti-aircraft machine gun
Crew:	5

good protection and mobility. This was a tall order, and US industry was not at that time geared up to mass-producing such a vehicle.

As an interim measure, the M3 Lee/Grant tank was introduced. The M3 carried a 37mm (1.4in) gun in its turret and a 75mm (2.9in) weapon in a hull sponson. Despite the limitations of this arrangement the M3 was successful, but it was always intended as a temporary measure. The M4, quickly named the Sherman, was derived from the M3 chassis but mounted its 75mm (2.9in) gun in a turret. Other components came from earlier designs, allowing the Sherman to be put into production in haste.

SECONDARY ARMAMENT

This M4A3 Sherman mounts a .50-calibre (12.7mm) machine gun for defence against enemy aircraft.

M4 SHERMAN

The M4 proved to be rugged and reliable, capable of operating for a long period with minimal maintenance. Its power-to-weight ratio was sufficiently good that it could climb slopes and cross obstacles that would stop a German tank. The Sherman could simply drive through most buildings, or into one to conceal itself among whatever remained standing.

This mobility, combined with numbers, enabled the M4 to outmanoeuvre many German tanks and attack them from the flanks. This was particularly important against heavy and well-protected vehicles such as the Panther, whose slow-traversing turret was a liability against agile Shermans at close range. Although the M4's performance was more modest than that of the best German tanks, it was capable of taking them on and winning. German commanders estimated that it took four Shermans to kill a Tiger – but the Allies had many more than four M4s per Tiger.

The M4's ability to clamber over rubble and drive right through a house was advantageous in urban engagements, as demonstrated by this tank during the Normandy Campaign in July 1944.

ENDLESS VARIANTS

The basic design of the M4 lent itself to all manner of improved versions and variants. Some were quite radical, such as the 'funnies' used to deal with obstacles during the Normandy landings. Tank destroyers, recovery vehicles and other specialist transportation used the M4 chassis, while the combat version was gradually improved.

The concept of the Sherman Firefly, which replaced the 75mm (2.9in) gun with a 17-pdr (76mm) one, was proposed in early 1943 but was rejected as new designs were in development. By the early months of the following year it was obvious that a tank with a gun capable of penetrating the heaviest German tanks was urgently needed.

Although less well protected than its chief foes, the Firefly was more agile and could reliably destroy even a Tiger. In some engagements, a single Firefly eliminated multiple heavy tanks, and such was the threat they posed that Fireflies were designated priority targets when Allied armour was spotted.

After the end of World War II, the Sherman served in Korea and was widely exported. Notable among its users was Israel, whose Shermans fought Arab-crewed T-34s. The Israeli 'Super Sherman', armed with a 105mm (4.1in) gun, served until the 1980s.

SHERMAN FIREFLY
The Sherman Firefly's 17-pdr (76mm) gun proved to be a highly effective tank-killer.

SPEED
Good speed and mobility allowed Shermans to outflank slower German tanks and attack their weaker sides.

A Sherman 'crab' with its turret rotated backwards while undertaking mine-clearance operations. The tank's offensive capabilities were not reduced by the mine flail.

CHASSIS

The Sherman's chassis proved an excellent basis for a wide range of specialist vehicles.

Panzer V Panther

The PzKpfw V Panther is arguably the most important tank design of all time, although it never realized its full potential. Its 75mm (2.9in) main gun outperformed the 88mm (3.4in) weapon of the Tiger, while its heavy sloped armour gave excellent survivability on the battlefields of its era.

SOVIET INFLUENCES

The arrival of the T-34 on the battlefield tipped the balance of armoured warfare firmly in favour of the Soviet Union. Outclassing the PzKpfw III and IV tanks of the German army, the T-34 was also fielded in great numbers. A new tank capable of defeating the T-34 was urgently needed.

Design studies were already underway in Germany, and although suggestions that the country should simply adopt the T-34 for its own service were rejected, many of its features were incorporated into what would become the Panther. Sloped armour was perhaps the most important of these, as it increased the effective thickness and protection of a given weight of metal.

The first production model, designated Ausf D, entered service in 1943, and 850 were produced before the improved Ausf A was fielded. This model tackled some of the Panther's reliability problems and featured improved armour protection. The Ausf A model was in production

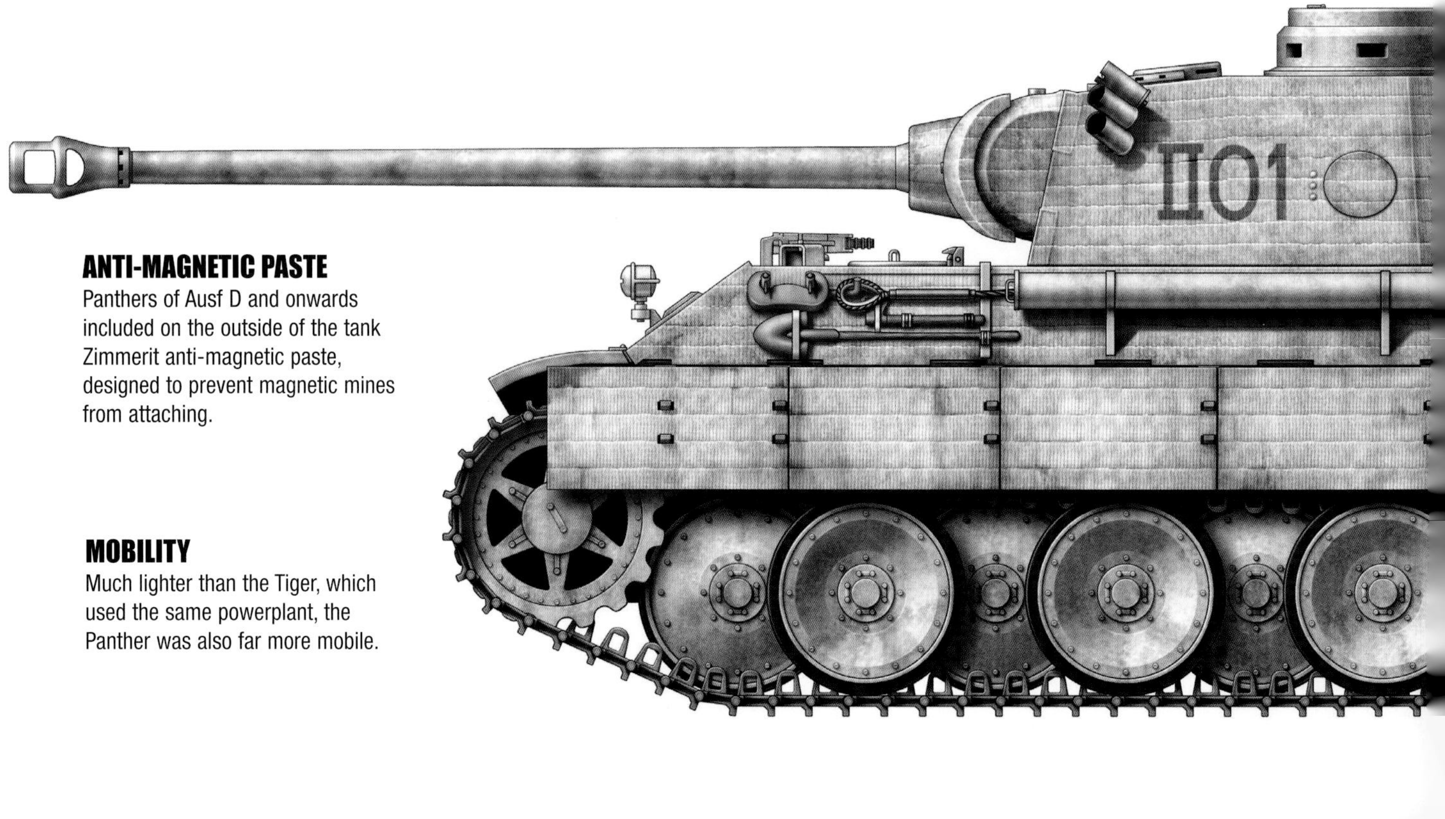

ANTI-MAGNETIC PASTE

Panthers of Ausf D and onwards included on the outside of the tank Zimmerit anti-magnetic paste, designed to prevent magnetic mines from attaching.

MOBILITY

Much lighter than the Tiger, which used the same powerplant, the Panther was also far more mobile.

SPECIFICATIONS (PANTHER AUSF G)

Dimensions: Length: 8.87m (29ft 1in), Height: 2.97m (9ft 9in), Width: 3.43m (11ft 3in)

Weight: 41.2 tonnes (45.5 tons)

Engine/powerplant: Maybach HL230 V-12

Speed: 46km/h (28.75mph)

Armament: Main gun: 75mm (2.9in) KwK42 l/70, Co-axial: 7.92mm (0.3in) machine gun, Hull-mounted: 7.92mm (0.3in) machine gun

Crew: 5

A Panther advances through the Ardennes Forest, December 1944. The Panther's well-sloped glacis plate offered few 'shot traps' and made frontal penetration by most available anti-tank weapons unlikely.

from August 1943 to May 1944 before being supplanted by the redesigned Ausf G model.

The Panther was in many ways the immediate precursor of modern main battle tanks. It mated a very potent 75mm (2.9in) gun to a highly mobile and well-protected chassis. Concerns that the PzKpfw VI Tiger, which was also being

SLOPED ARMOUR

The Panther's sloped armour made the most of the weight of metal it could carry. The Panther had up to 80mm (3.1in) of armour protection and sloped at 50 degrees to improve its effectiveness.

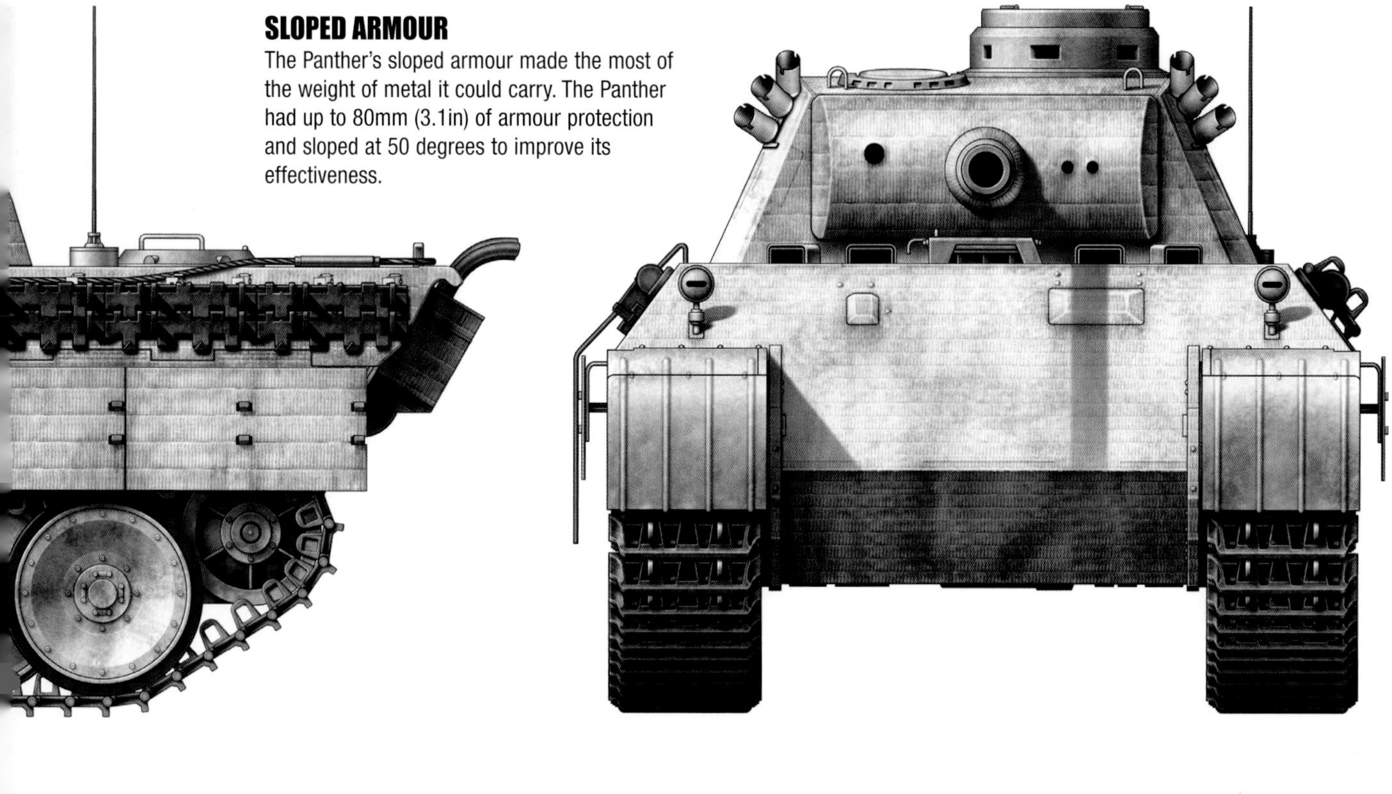

Panthers on the Eastern Front in 1944, with SS infantry wearing winter camouflage smocks hitching a ride. The Panther proved a match for all Soviet tanks except the IS-2, which outgunned the Panther and could penetrate its armour.

developed, was becoming cumbersomely heavy, with too much armour for its powerplant, caused the designers to aim for a much lower weight with the Panther while keeping the same engine.

THE FIRST MODERN TANK?

The original design was close to the modern main battle tank in concept; the MBT has been described as 'a heavy tank's gun on a medium tank chassis', with firepower exceeding protection. The Panther grew rather heavier in the design process, mainly due to Hitler's obsession with bigger and better weapons. Even with the additional armour, the Panther retained good mobility.

Although it was overshadowed by the Tiger's reputation, the Panther was, all in all, a far better tank. Faster and more mobile than the Tiger, a Panther actually had better frontal armour protection although its sides were more vulnerable. More importantly, the Panther could bring its impressive firepower to bear more quickly and in more places than a heavier tank, yet still outperformed most of its opponents.

TURRET
The three-man turret also included a commander's cupola and a bracket for an MG34 anti-aircraft machine gun.

SUMMER CAMOUFLAGE
A Panther Ausf A in summer camouflage. Note the interleaved road wheels, supported by a torsion bar suspension system.

The Panther's general appearance places it a generation ahead of early-war tanks. It has been credited with being the world's first 'modern' tank design.

DEPLOYED TOO SOON

The Panther never realized its true potential, largely due to the strategic situation in which it was employed. Various mechanical issues remained when the first Panthers were pushed into action at the Battle of Kursk in 1943, and a deteriorating strategic situation thereafter denied the Panther the chance to win great victories.

The Panther was well suited to mobile engagements and a highly aggressive strategy, and might have achieved more if the Axis armies had been able to resume the offensive – perhaps after a victory at Kursk. Its mobility was useful in the retreat-and-counterattack style of warfare adopted later in the war, but by then it was heavily outnumbered and often manned by inexperienced crews due to casualties among the veteran tankers of the early war.

Nevertheless, the Panther was a fearsome weapon that performed excellently in combat. It demonstrated the characteristics of a modern main battle tank, and exerted a profound influence on later designs.

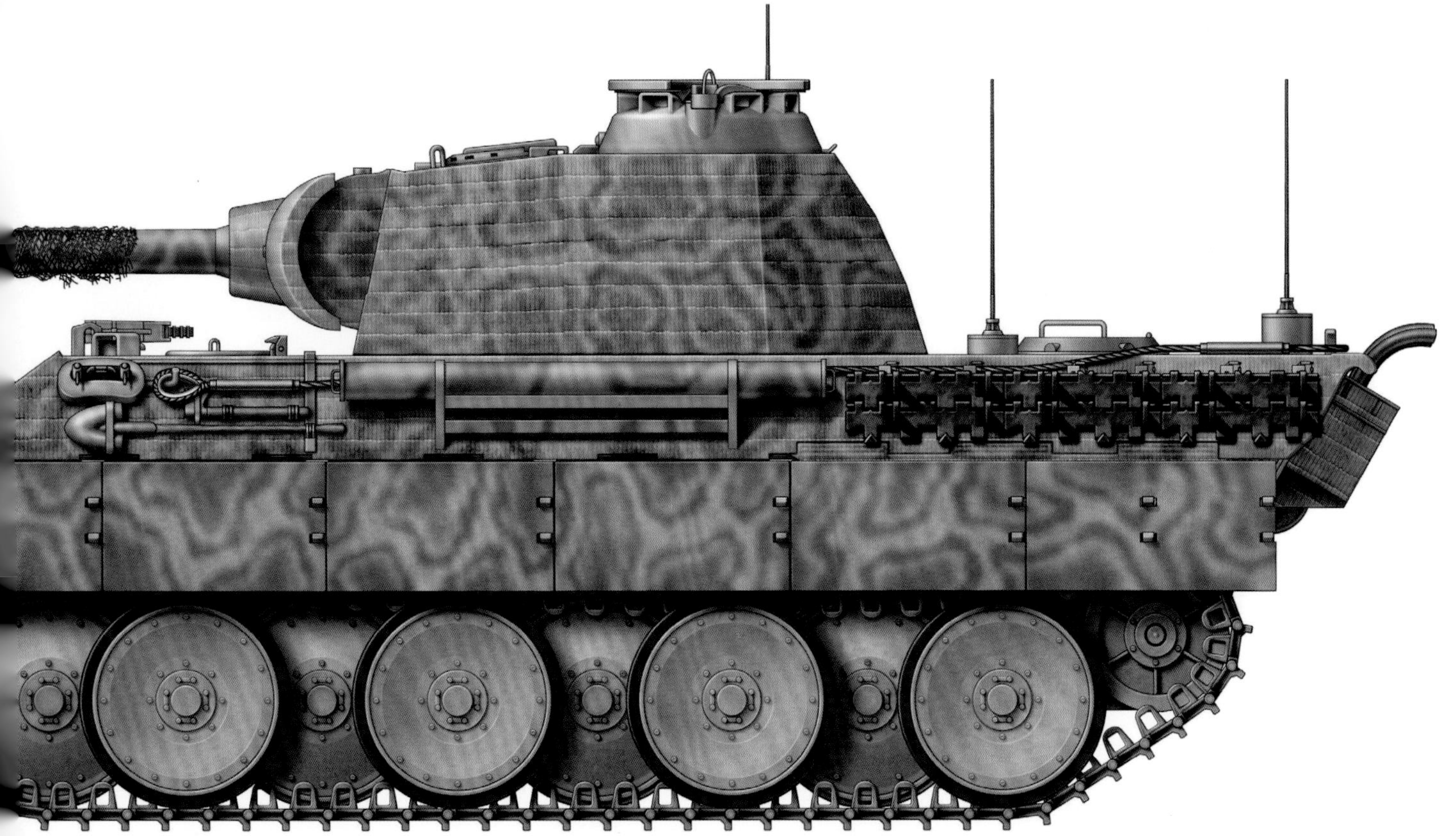

M1 Abrams

Until the M1 Abrams entered service in 1980, US tanks were essentially a progressive development from World War II designs incorporating new technology. The M1 represented a whole new generation of armoured combat vehicles, which may have been a factor in resetting its model number to M1.

A NEW TANK FOR THE LATE COLD WAR

The M1 Abrams had its origins in the MBT70 project, a joint US–German project to create a new tank with excellent mobility, protection and the ability to destroy the latest generation of Soviet tanks. The project was incredibly expensive and ultimately unsuccessful. However, it did create and demonstrate new technologies, some of which were incorporated into a new project that eventually became the M1.

The M1's distinctive slab-sided appearance is a result of using composite metal/ceramic armour, which is difficult to cast in curved shapes. Often known as Chobham armour (after the British tank research centre on Chobham Common, Surrey), the M1's protection performs better against both main anti-tank threats – shaped-charge warheads and kinetic penetrators – than traditional armour designs.

An M1A1 Abrams tank of the US Marine Corps during operations near Baghdad during Operation Iraqi Freedom. The tank's use of composite armour is obvious.

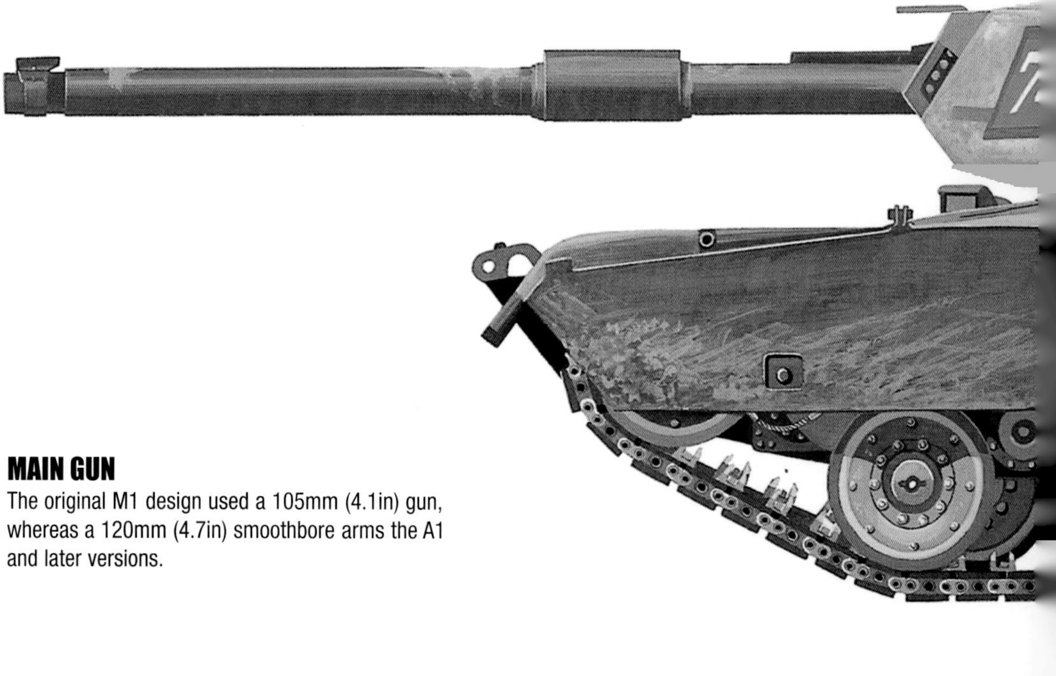

MAIN GUN

The original M1 design used a 105mm (4.1in) gun, whereas a 120mm (4.7in) smoothbore arms the A1 and later versions.

SPECIFICATIONS (M1A1)

Dimensions: Length: 9.77mm (32ft 3in), Height: 2.44m (8ft), Width: 3.66m (12ft)

Weight: 51.7 tonnes (57 tons)

Engine/powerplant: Textron Lycoming AGT 1500 gas turbine

Speed: 67km/h (42mph)

Armament: Main gun: 120mm (4.7in) L/44 M256, Co-axial: 7.62mm (0.3in) M240 machine gun, 12.7mm (0.5in) Browning M2HB machine gun

Crew: 4

The M1 was created in an era when the nightmare scenario of a massed Warsaw Pact armoured assault across Europe might become a reality. The Abrams was designed to match Soviet numbers with survivability and quality, initially fighting a defensive war before counterattacking. The ability to engage multiple targets in quick succession, and to kill a modern main battle tank at long range, was essential.

THE M1 IN SERVICE

Rather than the green plains of Europe, the tank saw its first major conflict in the deserts of Kuwait and Iraq. There, it performed brilliantly against the massed armour of the Iraqi army. The Iraqi tanks were of an earlier generation, including T-55s, T-62s and T-72s, and were largely unable to

ARMOUR
The Abrams' armour has proven highly resilient, even against its own 120mm (4.7in) kinetic penetrator rounds.

ENGINE
The multifuel turbine engine of the Abrams is very quiet compared to an equivalent diesel plant.

US Marine Corps M1s on exercise in Afghanistan. Although designed to kill other tanks, the M1 has proven highly useful in a fire support role, supporting infantry attacks in urban environments.

harm the M1. Indeed, only one account exists of an M1 put out of action by another tank in Iraq. The Abrams survived but needed repairs. Others have been disabled by various means, although the M1 is so robust that one vehicle was still able to drive and fight after an IED explosion lifted it off the ground.

Although conceived for massed tank battles, the Abrams has given good service in lower-intensity conflicts and has been exported to several nations including Australia, Egypt and Iraq. M1s in foreign hands have not always fared as well as US-operated tanks, with some M1s of the Iraqi army being destroyed by insurgents using advanced infantry-launched weapons and large explosive charges.

Questions have long been asked about the future of the tank, not least since asymmetric threats can be dealt with

A tank from the 2nd Infantry Division fire at a target from an M1A1 Abrams during exercises in Korea in 2012. Work continues on developing ever more potent tank-killing ammunition, suggesting that the days of tank-versus-tank battles are far from over.

using far cheaper vehicles. However, as long as foreign powers continue to field heavily armoured vehicles there will always be a need for tanks that can defeat them. Numbers may decline, but the main battle tank still has a future.

UPGRADES IN A CHANGING WORLD

As a result of increased operations in urban terrain, the TUSK (Tank Urban Survival Kit) was developed. This includes reactive armour panels to improve survivability when attacked at short range by infantry-launched anti-tank weapons such as RPGs. Remotely operated anti-personnel weapons allow the crew to defend their tank against infantry attack while remaining behind armour.

The M1A1 upgrade in 1985 was followed in 1992 by the M1A2. In the meantime, a number of smaller upgrade and modification programmes have been implemented in response to operational experience. The M1A3 version is currently in development, suggesting that the M1 family will remain the mainstay of US armoured forces for many years to come.

APPEARANCE

The M1 Abrams' external appearance has not changed much in the past three decades despite repeated upgrades to its internal systems.

COMPOSITE ARMOUR

The Abrams includes composite armour made up of components of steel, depleted uranium plating, synthetic fibres and ceramic.

T-34

The T-34 is the world's longest serving tank design. Almost 85,000 were built, seeing action from 1941 until the 1980s. Some examples are still in storage and could be put back into service if the need arose. Although outgunned by modern standards, in some regions the T-34 would still be a formidable piece of military hardware.

T-34/76

Soviet tank designs underwent a steady development before the outbreak of World War II. Some concepts proved unworkable or too prone to breakdowns, but vehicles like the excellent BT-5 taught the Soviets the principles of successful armoured warfare and the essentials of tank design. The T-34 combined sloped armour with a 76mm (3in) gun that was potent enough to kill any tank of the day. Its wide tracks provided good mobility in snow or mud – two conditions that were abundant in Russia. However, early T-34s suffered from serious technical issues. Accounts exist of tanks going into action with an entire spare transmission strapped to the engine deck.

One of the most important factors in the T-34's success was its simplicity. Relatively easy to build, T-34s could be produced rapidly and in huge numbers without construction bottlenecks caused by scarce components. They were also simple to operate, enabling the Soviet Union to field large forces quickly using conscripted crews. While German vehicles were on the whole better crewed and

T-34/76
The T-34/76 served the Red Army well during the early years of World War II, eventually being replaced by the upgunned T-34/85 in early 1944.

T-34/85s in Ukraine during the winter of 1944. The wide tracks coped well with muddy or snowy Russian terrain.

WINTER CAMOUFLAGE
A T-34/76 wearing winter camouflage. This was often created by using a thin whitewash over the green summer camouflage.

SUSPENSION
The T-34's suspension shows its derivation from the Christie design of the 1920s. Later Russian tanks moved to a torsion bar system.

The long barrel of the high-velocity 85mm (3.3in) ZIS-S53 gun enhanced the sleek, streamlined profile of the T-34/85.

technologically more sophisticated, the T-34 was good enough to do its job and was available in huge numbers.

The T-34 Model 1940 model was the result of a design and development process that began in 1937. It entered service in 1940, having benefited from lessons learned in combat against Japan in 1938–39. Initially, components were built in various locations, with final assembly taking place in Stalingrad. The German invasion of 1941 prompted a movement of tank production to less vulnerable locations, but the Stalingrad plant remained operational throughout the fighting for the city.

T-34/85

Improved versions of the T-34/76 appeared between 1940 and 1942, with an improved turret design that increased crew efficiency and the elimination of some reliability issues. Late-model T-34/76s addressed other problems such as a lack of all-round vision for the commander. However, the performance of the 76mm (3in) gun, entirely sufficient against the Panzer III and IV, was deemed inadequate to deal with the new generation of German tanks then emerging.

A new version of the T-34, designated T-34/85, was introduced in late 1943. This gun could penetrate the frontal armour of a Panther, and was housed in a turret designed for the abortive T-43 project. This larger turret allowed an

MAIN GUN
The original 76mm (3in) gun was replaced by an 85mm (3.3in) model later in the war.

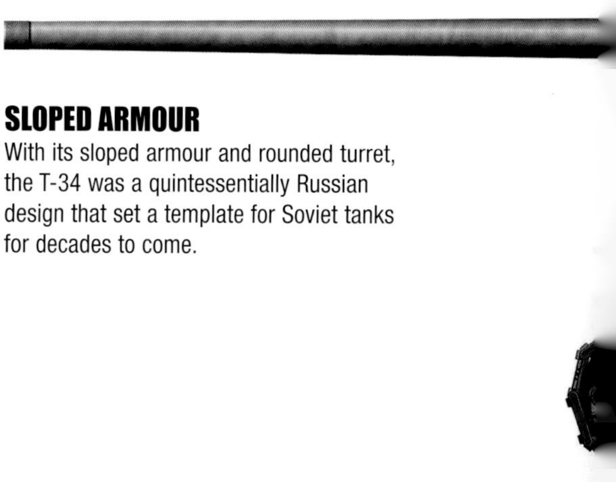

SLOPED ARMOUR
With its sloped armour and rounded turret, the T-34 was a quintessentially Russian design that set a template for Soviet tanks for decades to come.

extra crewmember to be carried, relieving the commander of responsibility for loading the main gun. The result was an overall more efficient vehicle as well as an increase in firepower. Although by no means invulnerable to the best German tanks, T-34/85s were available in sufficient numbers to overwhelm them.

COLD WAR SERVICE

The T-34/85 remained in production after the end of World War II, and was gradually replaced in Soviet service by the T-54 and T-55. T-34/85s were supplied in large numbers to Soviet satellite states and allies, and saw action in Korea and the Middle East.

Many of these tanks soldiered on for decades after production ended, often with local upgrades to electronics, optics and powerplant. Some examples remain in service or are held in reserve, and may yet re-emerge if the need arises. The simplicity of the design makes the T-34 eminently suitable for use by militias or technologically unsophisticated forces; in such an environment, an obsolete tank is still a very potent weapon.

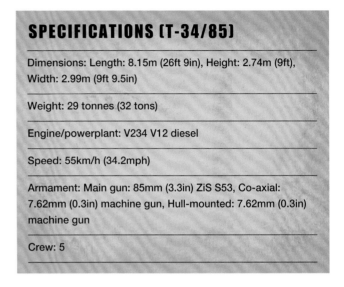

SPECIFICATIONS (T-34/85)

Dimensions: Length: 8.15m (26ft 9in), Height: 2.74m (9ft), Width: 2.99m (9ft 9.5in)

Weight: 29 tonnes (32 tons)

Engine/powerplant: V234 V12 diesel

Speed: 55km/h (34.2mph)

Armament: Main gun: 85mm (3.3in) ZiS S53, Co-axial: 7.62mm (0.3in) machine gun, Hull-mounted: 7.62mm (0.3in) machine gun

Crew: 5

TURRET

The turret of the later T-34/85 was made larger to accommodate three crew rather than two. This meant that the tank's commander no longer needed to act as gun loader for the main gun.

Index